T0356283

THE UNFORGIVING HOURS

THE UNFORGIVING HOURS

The Grit, Resilience, and Perseverance
at the Heart of Endurance Sports

SHANNON HOGAN

Published by:

 velopress®

an imprint of Ulysses Press
PO Box 3440
Berkeley, CA 94703
www.velopress.com

VeloPress is the leading publisher of books on sports for passionate and dedicated athletes around the world. Focused on cycling, triathlon, running, swimming, nutrition/diet, and more, VeloPress books help you achieve your goals and reach the top of your game.

ISBN: 978-1-64604-779-6
Library of Congress Control Number: 2024944972

Printed in Canada
10 9 8 7 6 5 4 3 2 1

Editor: Brian McLendon
Managing editor: Claire Chun
Copy editor: Christopher Bernard
Proofreader: Renee Rutledge
Production: Yesenia Garcia-Lopez, Winnie Liu
Front cover design: what!design @ whatweb.com
Artwork: front cover © Glenn Tachiyama

Dedicated to my parents, Jack and Pat,

who let me play all the sports.

CONTENTS

A SHORT INTRODUCTION ON GOING LONG

IT'S NOT AN URBAN LEGEND. THERE IS A GRASSROOTS TRAIL running event at the Lake Youngs Watershed near Seattle, Washington, with contests of various distances, called "The Pigtails Challenge." The races are held quasi-concurrently on the same course. Assembled during the long Memorial Day weekend in May, one of the events begins on Saturday morning at 6 a.m. on the looped course, summoning entrants to complete a whopping sixty-two miles, or one hundred kilometers of running, with 5,400 feet (1,646 meters) of elevation gain. Curiously, the 100-kilometer racers finish sheepishly and without much fanfare.

The centerpiece event that garners the weekend's real attention is the 200-mile (322-kilometer) running contest. The double-century race begins on Thursday at 6 a.m., two days before the 62-mile runners toe the line. There is also a 100-mile (161-kilometer) race. Lest the 100-mile runners begin to think too highly of themselves, historically their finisher's "trophy" was a belt buckle with a 100-mile logo and a button that read "I only did the half."

To put this wry commentary about ultra distances into context, the race was started by the Pacific Northwest's only runner—to date, male or female—to complete more than one hundred 100-mile (or longer) sanctioned races, pixie runner Van Phan. Often Van would run in The Pigtails Challenge while simultaneously serving as its race director and the personal cheerleader for each participant. She also worked more than full-time as a physician assistant and looked like your contagiously cheerful next-door neighbor. Never a member of a cross-country or track team, she was the quiet girl in pigtails who played badminton and tennis in school. Today, she still holds the course record for women in the 200-mile Pigtails race. To put a fine point on endurance humor, back in the day, if you ran The Pigtails Challenge 150-mile (241-kilometer) race, you received a 150-mile belt buckle and a dose of ultrarunning snappy repartee delivered by the doyenne of distance: Van Phan formally handed you a button with the race logo and three words: "The Middle Child."

Long-distance is not only growing longer on land. Another athlete who looks like your next-door neighbor (and might be that, if you're lucky enough to live in Colorado) is Sarah Thomas, a once-in-a-generation open-water swimmer and a veterinary recruiter by day. In September 2019, friends of Sarah began to watch a live GPS tracker sending real-time information about her location on Shakespeare Beach in Dover, England. It was 5:15 p.m. Mountain Daylight Time in Colorado on a Saturday evening when her tracker "dot" began to move east across the English Channel. When her friends woke the next day, Sarah was still swimming. That Sunday night when they fell asleep, Sarah was still swimming. And all day Monday, she was still swimming in that 64°F (17.78°C) water. When family and friends in the United States awoke on Tuesday morning (if they hadn't stayed up all night watching and cheering), they learned that Sarah swam 54 hours and 10 minutes nonstop and became the first person—male or female—to cross the English Channel four consecutive times. Tides and currents contributed to a distance of about 130 miles (209 kilometers) for the breast cancer survivor who finished sixteen rounds of chemotherapy and twenty-five rounds of radiation one year before her four-way crossing.

Going longer than long is synonymous with stretching one's imagination. In addition to complex planning, going long sometimes involves creating blueprints where none existed before. One such example comes from cycling. In the early days of the steep growth in mountain biking in the 1990s, a new format of 24-hour mountain bike races emerged: loop courses of about an hour—maybe ten or twelve miles (sixteen to just over nineteen kilometers)—with a campground area at the start/finish line full of music, beer, food, and shoulder-to-shoulder-style campfires, fostering a night of carefree festivity. Teams of four would see how many loops they could complete in twenty-four hours, passing a baton from the finishing rider to a timekeeper table volunteer to the next lap rider, Saturday to Sunday, noon to noon. There were races all around the United States, but in the early days, no one in cycling was having more fun than riders and spectators of the 24 Hours of Canaan in the Allegheny Mountains of Canaan Valley in West Virginia. To increase the level of difficulty, there might be costumes or self-inflicted tequila shots or hilarity provided by quad squads like Team Hugh Jass. Not only did the Hugh Jass lads ride the technical course on specific bikes with only one gear—called "fixie bikes"—they also raced with only one pair of shorts (*sans* underwear) among them. Yes, they transferred the relay baton and that one single pair of denim bib shorts for twenty-grueling-four hours. The shorts—also not an urban legend—throughout many years of team racing were unwashed since 1994. Spectators howled. It was this kind of environment, the juxtaposition of folly and creativity brought to endurance cycling, that prompted one cyclist to register himself for the race. He completed the four blank lines for team members with four variations of his name—John Robert Stamstad, age thirty, living in Ohio. Beside the echoing laughter and campfire camaraderie of 1996, every rider and spectator left Canaan that year in disbelief: it *was* possible to ride a bike, on narrow, rocky, rooty, muddy trails, for twenty-four hours straight. They returned to the big cities and the small hometowns with a staggering story: from noon to noon, a solo rider logged 156 miles (251 kilometers) on that ski hill. With their own eyes, they saw Stamstad fucking do it. Like Roger Bannister's mile in 3:59.4 and Diane Leather's 4:59.6 mile, both in 1954, once the barrier came down, others could suddenly complete the feat too. The floodgates of the solo 24-hour biking category burst open because of one set of blueprints in West Virginia made by a guy from Madison, Wisconsin, back in '96. A superbloom of solo 24-hour cycling—and then ultrarunning—categories and events would follow.

Long-distance sometimes describes the amount of mileage covered to get to the start line of an undertaking. This can be the logistics and training effort before a big hike like the John Muir Trail or time-intensive Appalachian Trail. It can look like finally qualifying for the Boston Marathon after many moons. It can also be as simple as a streak: like swimming every day for a year or running 3.1 miles (5 kilometers) at 6 a.m. every morning no matter the weather, the season, or life events. Zoom out on this commitment—great intestinal drive and patient dignity over countless hours keep a momentous dream or such streaks alive. Such imagination is a muscle.

When Rudyard Kipling wrote the poem "If—," circa 1895, in a gesture of fatherly advice to his one son, in the eighth and final stanza of the poem, Kipling counseled, "If you can fill the unforgiving minute / With sixty seconds' worth of distance run—/ Yours is the Earth and everything that's in it, / And— which is more—you'll be a Man, my son!" One can guess that Kipling would hardly believe the composure, the reputable and esteemed conduct, and the humility of athletes like Van Phan, Sarah Thomas, and John Stamstad in the twenty-first century, given their mastery of the unforgiving minute—in tests measured in hours. Sometimes days.

As more and more athletes fill grueling stretches in the elements, across sporting genres, there are two hard-and-fast rules in the hours of the unforgiving:

Mother Nature bats last.

And Father Time is undefeated.

Capturing our imagination, creating new blueprints, syncing with tides and weather of the untamed places, these athletes keep collaboration, courage, and good humor at the heart of these tests. Mileage in the wild is their buzz, no tequila necessary. The time in the outdoors is the feat's prize. These are the stories of regular people with real jobs who look like your next-door neighbor. They are not afraid to be beginners in a new event or to intrepidly take their beloved sport to a new distance, or to make fresh tracks with that distance at an unexplored chronological age. Sometimes these athletes fill the unforgiving hours with the carrot that is a crew team with cowbells and matching t-shirts up ahead. Sometimes they pass the hours using the stick of incoming rowdy weather chasing them. They bring a sense of wonder for the wild spaces above the tree line or in places with apex predators (or worse, malevolent insects) or in water that the hardiest swimmers call "invigorating." They regularly play three-dimensional chess in their heads: solving the puzzles of the task while managing the impatient mind. All the while, they are shoveling their own coal or chopping their own wood (so it warms not once, but twice), clicking off kilometers with intrinsic drive. They sink their only paid vacation days into the organizing of gear and precious people, the packing of bike boxes, and testing foul-weather layers before heading out into the unknown, with nary a guarantee. This kind of mileage in the open spaces cannot be fueled by anything extrinsic; such things fray and flatten in the first gust fronts before the hail in the hours of zero-dark-thirty.

Those who fill the unforgiving hours accept the two hard rules of Mother Nature and Father Time, but after that they make few, even no, concessions. These are hard-headed types. They are also gloriously original, wildly optimistic, and quietly industrious in the spirit of "If—." Unheralded, yes. But urban legend? No. Disciplined in the fashion of Rudyard Kipling's poem? Yes. Exemplars, tall and proportioned from the canon of the Greeks and Romans, chiseled as if from marble? No. The place where will—"Hold on!"—is even greater than skill? Yes. Store bought? No. Snot rockets? Definitely.

Legendary and poetic,
these athletes,
and their spittle-on-the-chin endurance?

As the day is long.

If you can keep your head when all about you
Are losing theirs and blaming it on you;
If you can trust yourself when all men doubt you,
But make allowance for their doubting too;
If you can wait and not be tired by waiting,
Or being lied about, don't deal in lies,
Or being hated, don't give way to hating,
And yet don't look too good, nor talk too wise:

If you can dream—and not make dreams your master;
If you can think—and not make thoughts your aim;
If you can meet with Triumph and Disaster
And treat those two impostors just the same;
If you can bear to hear the truth you've spoken
Twisted by knaves to make a trap for fools,
Or watch the things you gave your life to broken,
And stoop and build 'em up with worn-out tools:

If you can make one heap of all your winnings
And risk it on one turn of pitch-and-toss,
And lose, and start again at your beginnings
And never breathe a word about your loss;
If you can force your heart and nerve and sinew
To serve your turn long after they are gone,
And so hold on when there is nothing in you
Except the Will which says to them: "Hold on!"

If you can talk with crowds and keep your virtue,
Or walk with Kings—nor lose the common touch,
If neither foes nor loving friends can hurt you,
If all men count with you, but none too much;
If you can fill the unforgiving minute
With sixty seconds' worth of distance run,
Yours is the Earth and everything that's in it,
And—which is more—you'll be a Man, my son!

—Rudyard Kipling, "If—"

24 HOURS OF CANAAN | **9**
For Official Use Only

1996 TEAM ENTRY FORM

MUST BE ACCOMPANIED WITH RELEASE FORMS, COMPLETED AND SIGNED BY EACH TEAM MEMBER

TEAM NAME _Ritchey_

TEAM CLASS: _Pro_   AMOUNT PAID $ _432_

- FOUR-PERSON: Men's Pro, Men's Expert, Men's Sport, Women's Pro/Expert, Women's Sport, Masters (45-54), Vet (35-44), Junior (18 & under), Clydesdale (200+ lbs. each or 820+ lbs. total team weight)
- FIVE-PERSON: Open. Must have at least one woman and no more than one expert man. (No pros, male or female.)

Note: When filling out the section below, please list the class that each individual team member most recently raced in. For clarification of the rules, see the CLASSES section of Rules and Regulations for explanation, to avoid sandbagging.

Another note: Classes with less than four teams may be combined with another class.

SPONSORED BY: _Ritchey_

TOWN & STATE, COUNTRY: _Cinti, OH, USA_

		Class	Age				Clydsdales Wt.
1. TEAM CAPTAIN:	_John Stamstad_	Class _Pro_	Age _30_	M X F	Wt.
2. CO-CAPTAIN:	_J. Robert Stamstad_	Class _Pro_	Age _30_	M X F	Wt.
3. TEAMMATE #3:	_J. R. Stamstad_	Class _Pro_	Age _30_	M X F	Wt.
4. TEAMMATE #4:	_John Robert Stamstad_	Class _Pro_	Age _30_	M X F	Wt.
5. TEAMMATE #5:		Class	Age	M F	(Open)

MEN'S PRO TEAM ENTRY FEE: $108 PER RACER x 4 = $432
ALL OTHER FOUR-PERSON TEAM ENTRY FEE: $68 PER RACER x 4 = $272
FIVE-PERSON OPEN CLASS TEAM ENTRY FEE: $68 PER RACER x 5 = $340

MAKE CHECKS PAYABLE TO GRANNY GEAR PRODUCTIONS
MAIL TO: P.O. BOX 189, DAVIS, WV 26260;
UPS OR FEDEX TO: 24 FOURTH ST, DAVIS, WV 26260

All entries must be pre-paid, cash or check only. No faxed entries or release forms will be accepted. Entries will be limited to the first 360 teams. Once your team has been accepted, you have, in essence, purchased 4 or 5 spaces. If a team member drops-out you can fill that slot by registering a new teammate by sending in a new release form and notifying us who is being replaced by whom. Fees are NON-Refundable.

PLEASE ENTER OUR TEAM IN THE 1996 24 HOURS OF CANAAN MOUNTAINBIKE TEAM RELAY.

TEAM CAPTAIN'S SIGNATURE _John Stamstad_   DATE _4/30/96_

NUMBER OF TEAMMATES OWNING NITERIDER PRODUCTS & PLANNING ON USING NITERIDER SUPPORT:
CYCLOPS SYSTEM (6V)_____ AND/OR COMMUTER (12V)_____

Cyclist John Stamstad rewrote long-distance in the manner of a visionary and with the heart of a lion. On looped courses, he was known for graciously cheering on racers with earnestness, then lapping them. The 24 Hours of Canaan (rhymes with insane) 1996 was the first instance of one racer signing up for all four racer slots. *(race sign-up form courtesy of John Stamstad)*

CHAPTER ONE

THE FIVE FINEST SECONDS OF THE GREATEST GOLDEN HOUR

Gunhild Swanson

Cometh the hour, cometh the woman.

—*Female mitochondria*

ANDY JONES-WILKINS, A VETERAN JOURNALIST AND ELITE TRAIL runner, wrote, "Looking back on that Sunday morning, I can confidently say that I have never, ever seen something as extraordinary."

He continued, "And I probably will never see anything like it again."

Jones-Wilkins, an authority on long-distance running and an unofficial docent on the history of the sport in the United States, was describing the 2015 finish of a trail race in Northern California called the "Western States Endurance Run." Held every year since 1977, it is arguably the largest ultrarunning event in the world.

The Western States Endurance Run falls into the formerly niche sports category called "ultrarunning"; any foot race beyond 26.2 miles (42.2 kilometers) is called an "ultramarathon," and the participants are called "ultrarunners." Ultramarathons take place on running tracks and road courses but are most commonly held on trail routes of every variety. No longer a niche sport, ultrarunning participation increased 1,676% between 1996 and 2019. The world has always had ultrarunning, but the remarkable number of ultrarunners in the world has never been so high. From Andorra to Zambia, more than a hundred countries around the world host ultramarathon distance events.

The world's crown jewel of 100-milers, the Western States Endurance Run, puts on a Broadway-quality ultrarunning show every year. There are more than four official volunteers for every runner.[1] Ebullient crew teams, journalists, photographers, videographers, and excited spectators line the start area with dizzying cheering and clanging cowbells, as runners cross the starting line and begin their climb in the dark of oh-five-hundred. In a matter of moments, the spectating throng scatters in a frenzied hurry to reach the next accessible aid stations to see the runners again. It is a party—part righteous family reunion, part red-carpet running-celebrity watching, part G-20 summit of the world's best mountain runners.

---

1 A word about race directors, their teams, and the multitude of volunteers who provide the skeleton, large muscle groups, and the heart of long-distance events: From the necessary permits to course measurement and marking, safety protocols and first aid, equipment set-up and break-down, aid station stocking and working, registration and packet pickup, parking volunteers, timing and athlete check-in, course sweeping, and the "pack it out" core value standards that guide the cleanup after these events, the lifting is heavy and the work is seemingly unending. The longer the event, the more complex becomes the logistics and problem solving.

It is befitting that "the most unforgettable moment in ultrarunning," described by Jones-Wilkins, occurred on the beloved Western States' course. The instant classic moment involved Gunhild Swanson, a Spokane Valley, Washington, runner who had successfully navigated the 100-mile (161-kilometer) race in her previous two attempts. But 2015 would earn her a page in endurance sport history.

The earliest Western States run was first undertaken in the 1970s by a rider-turned-runner, on a funny, cocky lark, during the 100-mile Western States Trail Ride horse race. In the history of the Western States Trail Ride, the '74 escapade remains the only case of a rider—Gordy Ainsleigh—to have earned two finishes on horse (1971 and 1972) and one on foot (1974). The hot and dusty horse event, around since 1955, is part crazy dare, part wild west throwback. It has pushed the outer limits of what horse and rider can or should endure in the Sierra Nevada mountains. The ride is commonly referred to as "Tevis Cup" or "the Tevis Cup Ride," named for the trophy presented to the first finisher of this, the oldest endurance horse race. The course is a series of regrettable rocky steeps and dump-you-from-that-western-saddle descents.

The Tevis Cup race is built on the cornerstones of good horsemanship and good sportsmanship. This means that a completion certificate and the prize of a Tevis Cup silver belt buckle are earned only after the horse passes various vet checks along the route, a pulse test the first forty minutes after the race, a complete vet check the first hour after the race, and a final evaluation between 60 and 120 minutes after the race. Race officials are nothing if not thorough in checking for the metabolic stability and overall welfare of a steed in the "One-Hundred-Miles-in-One-Day" event. The routes of the modern Western States Endurance Run and the Western States Trail Ride horse race now differ somewhat from each other, so a comment often made by runners in the maw of the running course—that "You wouldn't treat a horse like this"—is a valid one. More than one runner has been heard to ask during the torment of the Endurance Run—in the manner of a shattered-legged horse—to be taken out back behind the barn. In the Sierra Nevada mountains, everybody knows what that means.

Hellfire treatment is an unofficial cornerstone of the hot canyons of the spinoff foot race, which runners informally call "States." The 18,000 feet (5,486 meters) of climbing and 23,000 feet (7,010 meters) of descent create a saw-toothed elevation profile for runners. Like the lower mandible of the meanest six-ton mastodon of the Pleistocene era that ever roamed between Lake Tahoe and Sacramento, the route is a series of troubles compounded by further woes. From the start line to Emigrant Pass, where the course joins the original Western States Trail, the path climbs 2,550 feet (777 meters). This is the first 4.5 miles (7 kilometers) of the race.

If the Western States Endurance Run owes its origin story to a horse race, Tevis Cup owes its origin story to the original endurance quest that first defined the Western States Trail—even before it had a name. This rough-hewn, slow-twitch muscle story shares a page with one of US history's most colorful and defining chapters: gold.

When gold was discovered in the Sierra foothills, a fever spread across the continent and abroad. Judges abandoned their benches, sailors their ships, doctors their patients. "Criminals slipped their fetters...and soldiers fled from their posts," wrote Hubert Howe Bancroft in 1888 about the feverish migration. About 80% of the original '49ers were Americans from the east, making the overland trek for their fortune. Would-be prospectors aimed to reach Sutter's Mill in Coloma, California—where, while a water-powered sawmill was being constructed, on January 24, 1848, gold nuggets turned up in the American River instead.

Following routes like the California Trail (originating in western Missouri) or the Central Overland Trail (part of the course of the 10-day Pony Express), treasure-seeking pioneers went endurance-style long toward the gold country, many through the Lake Tahoe area, a mighty fine place to resupply and rest the horses. From Tahoe, a traveler on the would-be gold corridor could hop on a trail made and used by the Washoe peoples from time immemorial. First designated as the "Auburn–Lake Tahoe Riding Trail" by lawman Bob Watson in the 1930s, it was later named the "Western States Trail" in 1956 by a horseman and businessman named Wendell Robie, one of the founders of the Tevis Cup event. As the crow flies, the finish lines of the Tevis Cup and Western States Endurance Run races in Auburn, California, are only twelve miles (nineteen kilometers) from Coloma, site of the first gold nuggets found at Sutter's Mill.

Tangentially, any long-distance athlete who has ever been awarded a belt buckle at the end of an endurance event can thank the Western States Endurance Run. The running race has featured buckles for its finishers since the official first race in 1977. Mine a little deeper, and the buckle fever that has captured long-distance athletes—from Badwater 135 to Leadville Trail 100 MTB to Ironman® Texas 140.6-mile (226.3-kilometer) Triathlon—can be traced to the origin point of the Tevis Cup ride. On this jagged course of denticle and mandible hinges the story of how silver belt buckles first crossed over to non-equine endurance finisher medals.

Western States 100 shines as the annual "Superbowl" of ultrarunning due to two major factors: it is the oldest annual 100-mile run in the world, and it features a unique limit to the number of runners who can participate.

Because of the location of the course through Granite Chief Wilderness, the US Forest Service limits the number of participants. It so happened that the year Congress passed the California Wilderness Act was 1984, so the race was "grandfathered" into legislation with the number of runners who ran Western States that year—369. In most years at States since then, 369 has been roughly the number of starters. The largest number of bibs on the course was in 2010, when there were 423 qualifiers at the start line.

By comparison, the annual 100-mile European event that has a similar Superbowl-quality in ultrarunning is the Ultra-Trail du Mont Blanc (UTMB), run in Chamonix, France. The European race has more than 2,500 starters.

Participants in Western States are mostly chosen by lottery. Among elites, one may earn an automatic entry by winning another qualifying ultramarathon or by finishing top ten in WSER the previous year. Otherwise, hopefuls earn "tickets" for the lottery and have a chance to win one of the precious 369 States race bibs by finishing as many qualifying 100-mile races as possible. This is where Gunhild's 2015 Western States began.

When Gunhild started trail running in 1987, the qualifying races for Western States Endurance Run were any race between 50 (80 kilometers) and 100 miles completed within the allowed time. The popularity of the Tahoe-to-Auburn event ultimately required the Western States Endurance Run board to increase the qualifying standard to designated races between 100 kilometers (62 miles) and 200 miles (322 kilometers). By 2014, when the notion of running the Western States Endurance Run 2015 struck Gunhild, a quiet widow from eastern Washington, she had run the grueling 100-mile distance at multiple tough courses, including Western States in 2002 and 2005. She also had run a speedy 2:56:38 road marathon at the 26.2-mile Seattle Marathon in 1982, so she was no stranger to race pressure and solid results. Once she embarked on her multistep road to Western States 2015, she discovered the only qualifying race left to sign up for in 2014 was the Javelina Jundred 100-mile run in Arizona over Halloween weekend. There were 511 starters and only 290 finishers. Gunhild was finisher 187. She completed the Sonoran Desert race led by the indelible ultrarunner and race director Jamil Coury in 27 hours, 25 minutes, and 17 seconds. This meant she qualified for the 2015 Western States race by finishing a 100-miler, but would the lottery be on her side?

The drama played out over weeks; first when her name was not drawn in the lottery. Then race directors considered, but ultimately denied, granting her special admittance. Ultimately, a race sponsor had an extra race bib (race sponsors are gifted a few), which was gifted to Gunhild five months before the race. One hundred and fifty days of training began. Gunhild went all in.

Gunhild toed the line at 5 a.m. on Saturday morning, June 27, 2015, in the ski village renamed Palisades Tahoe (formerly called "Squaw"), the site of the 1960 Winter Olympics. After getting up at 3 a.m., Gunhild ate toast with nut butter, a banana, and her typical two cups of coffee with cream to begin the morning. Though it was still dark outside, the start-line energy in the village crackled like a high-voltage transmission line in damp weather. The buzz in the village made Gunhild, usually cheerful anyway, giggly and nearly squirrelly with excitement. Following a booming group countdown of the clock suspended over the start line—*ten! nine! eight!...*—into the dark, racers took off at the crack of the gun. Gunhild marveled at the surreal line of headlamps that flew up the hill in front of her, stretching out like a serpentine. The trail climbed, curving left and right and continuously rising from 6,200 feet to 8,750 feet over Emigrant Pass and the natural contours of the Escarpment. She kept a steady pace to Lyon Ridge Aid Station (mile 10.3, checking in at 7:45 a.m.) and stayed steady in the section to Red Star Ridge Aid Station (mile 15.8, arriving at 9:20 a.m.). There were spots of collective power hiking by the racers, due to the relentless two-mile climb that followed, but the runners were then rewarded with a flowy single track down to Duncan Canyon Aid Station (mile 24.4, 11:25 a.m.) next. According to Gunhild's aid-station timeline chart she had made for herself, she was on target for her goal time-splits: going slow enough to finish 100.2 miles (161.3 kilometers) and fast enough to make all the time cutoffs along the course that were set in stone by the race officials. For example, the official cutoff time for the Duncan Canyon Aid Station is 12:00 noon, and thus, Gunhild was thirty-five minutes under the cutoff at that point. She averaged between thirty and forty-four minutes under each aid-station cutoff in the first three-fifths of the race. She crossed Duncan Creek, then climbed 4 miles (6.4 kilometers) to the Robinson Flat Aid Station (mile 30.3 at 1:20 p.m.), where the crowd support and cheering is not outdone by the fanbase of the professional leagues of the NFL, NHL, or MLB during any playoff season. While her hydration vest was being refilled, she saw a friend who sadly could not continue and was withdrawing from the event. Caught up in the dramatic moment when the man's prized racer band was cut from his wrist, signaling the end of his race, both runners watched tears fall from the other's face. No one tells you—one way or another—that going all in on your endurance dreams will require the facial tissues with the extra aloe. Gunhild consoled her friend, prioritizing racer over the race. That meant she left Robinson Flat behind schedule. Gunhild cruised the forested single track before Dusty Corners Aid Station (mile 38 at 2:38 p.m.), but the delay meant she was only twenty-two minutes ahead of the 3 p.m. cutoff. There was no time for blisters, cramping, or extended port-o-john breaks; these were the luxuries of the speedsters in front of her. Gunhild pushed to make up lost minutes on the way to Last Chance (43.3 miles at 4:46 p.m.), Devil's Thumb (47.8 miles at 6:29 p.m.), and El Dorado Creek (52.9 miles at 7:59 p.m.) aid stations without a blip. The daylight was waning, but she was more than halfway there.

At her next aid station, Michigan Bluff, she would pick up her pacer. A pacer is a runner to accompany a racer. Pacer rules vary from ultra to ultra; per the Western States Endurance Run guidelines, they may not carry water or mule supplies for the runner. Gunhild's first pacer was her son, Chris, an architect. This wasn't Chris's first rodeo, either. Chris had paced a friend at Western States before; more importantly, as a calm, gentle-spoken cross-country and track-and-field coach, Chris had the temperament of a world-class pacer: even-tempered, solutions oriented, capable as all hell.

Chris found his mom to be in great spirits as she cruised into Michigan Bluff's mile 55.7 at 9:05 p.m., full of stamina and ahead of her goal time-splits and forty minutes ahead of race cutoffs. Her athletic disposition was upbeat and positive, as Chris described it; categorizing her as a consistent runner and a "solid, stoic, German mom." On the trail, they talked the whole way, as two runners do. Passing time is part of the challenge of endurance events; talking passes the time. So they chatted about anything and everything—through Forest Hill (mile 62 at 10:59 p.m.), Dardanelles (mile 65.7), Peachstone (mile 70.7 at 1:25 a.m.) and Fords Bar (mile 73). The lower canyons had almost felt cool in the early hours; the course and the conditions had shown mercy on the mother-and-son pair. To explain how hot the course can become, any year in which the Saturday daytime temperature is 85°F (29°C) or less is considered a "cool year." For Gunhild in 2015, the high temp in Auburn was a manageable 91°F (33°C). Two years earlier in 2013, temps topped out at 102°F (39°C). The grizzled veterans of Western States Endurance Run still talk about 1995, deemed the "Fire and Ice" year. The first twenty miles of the course featured snow, but the official race thermometer hit 104°F (40°C), with sections of the trail reaching 107°F (42°C). Such an oppressive sizzling heat desiccated 46.6% of the field— many top in the sport—who did not finish the 1995 edition.

Gunhild cruised into Rucky Chucky Aid Station (mile 78 at 3:39 a.m.) a full one hour and twenty-one minutes ahead of the race cutoff for the checkpoint. It was here that Gunhild picked up her next pacer for the darkest hours of the night and into the predawn hours. It was Chris's son, her grandson, Turlan. The race organizers gave Gunhild special permission, following her request, to be accompanied by Turlan, a cross-country team runner. The high schooler with the whippet-like legs was only fifteen years old; pacers typically must be age eighteen. Chris hugged both athletes tight. He then held his breath as his son and his mother stepped into the waist-deep American River, holding onto a fixed rope. Once safely across the river, Chris watched their two forms run into the dark, shoulder to shoulder. Unfazed by the twenty-two miles (thirty-five kilometers) he had just run and the 3:45 a.m. hour, Chris jumped into a vehicle to leapfrog to the next aid station with crew access, Pointed Rocks (mile 94.3). Here he would wait.

The age range of the three generations together at Rucky Chucky captures the lifelong love of the sport that many runners in track houses, in running clubs, and at trailheads describe. And while Sundays are traditionally a multigenerational family day (multiple generations at the same function), this family's actions were intergenerational—where multiple generations are actually *interacting*. In this case, they were pulling hard together, none too superior, none too inexperienced, none to be addressed in a patronizing tone. At an intergenerational equilibrium point that Sunday morning (each would later describe their awe of the other two's contributions), the perfectly placed fulcrum underneath them, centering and balancing, was the beautiful sport of running in the woods.

As Turlan and Gunhild ran up the hill from the river, passing two men, Turlan waited a respectful distance before turning toward his racer conspiratorially and whispering, "They just got nana'd!"

Turlan was old enough to know the expression "You got chicked"—which is used to describe when a female passes or finishes in front of a capable male athlete, heard every so often in such sports as ultrarunning or road cycling. Turlan's version was updated and much more charming, and he made Gunhild laugh with his earnest sweetness. Depending on the runner, pacers may have duties like reminding their athlete to eat, or tracking the time, or keeping their runner steady as intense exercise-associated gastrointestinal distress leaves the competitor vomiting on a wholly undeserving whiteleaf manzanita shrub. But every runner loves a pacer who can make them laugh.

Turlan had just finished his freshman year of high school and was still young enough to be enthralled by the western foothills of the Sierra Nevada—the "saw" (*sierra*) of jagged mountains, full of "snowy" (*nevada*) peaked wonder. In his eyes, Placer County specialized in the patinated picturesque, still wild, still west. And there was also his delight in the gifts of the Coulter pine trees which dotted the foothills. The native conifer tree's seeds are tucked into spiky pinecones larger than an NFL football, and heavier—sometimes over 10 pounds in weight. Turlan was the perfect age: old enough to run in the mountains at 3:39 a.m. and young enough to be impressed by the wonder of the world's largest pinecones.

In a speech given at a meeting of the Sierra Club on November 23, 1895, by John Muir after his travels in the Sierra

Nevada, he said, "...few are altogether deaf to the preaching of pine trees. Their sermons on the mountains go to our hearts; and if people in general could be got into the woods, even for once, to hear the trees speak for themselves, all difficulties in the way of forest preservation would vanish."

Running in the dark among the pine trees, however, comes with its challenges. One hundred miles is a helluva long way for everything to go right, and a helluva long way for just one thing to go wrong, but such is the nature of ultras. At some point the grandmother-grandson team followed a pair of runners in the distance. Turlan and Gunhild eventually caught the pair, and collectively they asked, "Has anyone seen a trail marker?"

To be a trail runner, a proper trail runner, means one has gone off course at some time or other. The fastest Western States finish to date in 2019—14:09:28—was run by Jim Walmsley, who in 2016 was on record pace when he went off course. It torched his spirit, and he had to walk the final ten miles (sixteen kilometers) of the race (he still finished a remarkable 18:45:36—*that* gives an idea how much time he'd had on the field when he made that wrong turn).

In the same vicinity where Jim Walmsley got lost in 2016, Turlan looked at the other three tired faces on the dark trail and called an audible, "I'll go." He took off—running toward where they had all run from, scanning the trees left and right for any sign of yellow tape tied to a branch, signaling the correct route. He was wise to also be vigilant about the actual wild all around him. The race guidebook says, "Rattlesnakes, bears, mountain lions, and other potentially hazardous forms of wildlife live on the course and have surprised runners in the past. Keep alert and be careful where you place your feet and hands, especially at night."

It is no coincidence that Western States Endurance Run male and female top first place finishers receive a robust fifteen-inch-tall bronze sculpture on a walnut base, called the Western States Cougar Trophy each year. And the finisher's belt buckle, considered one of the most prized possessions in the endurance world—handmade in silver for finishers under 24 hours, handmade in bronze for finishers under 30 hours—features a distinct form. In the center of the hand-engraved buckle stands a slightly minacious mountain lion cresting a rocky outcrop of chunky basalt like the hunk called Needle Peak, just east of Lyon Ridge, the very first checkpoint of the race—a whole lifetime ago for Gunhild and her crew.

To Turlan, alone in deep dark, his progress to find the course felt as slow as molasses in winter. After three excruciating miles (five kilometers), Turlan came to the place where they had missed their turn, and relief washed away the sickening feeling of being lost in the dark. Having located the yellow tape race marker, Turlan then let loose, turning his legs over at his best 5K pace, racing back to the three off-course adults. With young legs and a 115-pound frame—maybe 120 pounds soaking wet in the American River—he felt his feet barely touch the trail. He was running to save his grandma's race. Pushing his pace, torso and head barely moving, his legs were fearless. It was valor without witness.

How much time they lost, they can't calculate precisely, but for Chris, who was expecting his two runners about an hour and a half earlier at the aid station, he described himself, using understatement, as "really, really concerned" about his missing mom and his lost kid. Night turned to dawn turned to cruel day.

Having run extra mileage and wasted time going off course, Gunhild knew she had burned through all the extra buffer time she had banked throughout the race since yesterday morning. Gunhild's watch confirmed she was now within minutes of the cutoff time at the next aid station. Miss the cutoff, and she would not be able to continue. Her wristband would be cut from her arm, and her race would be over. Sensing her despairing outlook, Turlan turned to Gunhild with the right amount of tough love. She needed to do two things, he said. One, stop the despairing thinking. And two, just follow him. He said he knew what they had to do, and he would get her there. She had no time to debate, or make excuses, or calculate their remaining cutoff minutes. She had time for one thing, and one thing only: to get to the Highway 49 Aid Station STAT.

Made for the moment, Gunhild and Turlan arrived at 9:08 a.m. Twelve minutes before the race cutoff.

Ann Trason, a marvel of a runner and absolute zenith of grit and perseverance on the Western States Endurance Run course, with fourteen wins from 1989 to 2003, coined an expression on the course, the trail that lay in front of Gunhild.

"You can be a whiner," Ann said. "Or you can be an ultrarunner," she continued. "But you can't be both."

On Sunday morning, the sun now firmly above the trees, Gunhild Swanson was on the eastern side of "No Hands Bridge" (known more officially as the Mountain Quarries Railroad Bridge), a

482-foot-long span constructed in 1912 over the north and middle forks of the American River.

A little about "No Hands Bridge": The area around it is described in state records as "some of the most spectacular and distinctive gorges and canyon lands found within the middle Sierra Nevada region." The longest concrete arch bridge in the world in 1912, it was constructed by a cement company to connect a quarry, filled with massive blocks of limestone in Cool, California, with a terminus alongside the Southern Pacific Railroad in Auburn. The distinctive closed spandrel design is solid between the three arch rings and the deck above, conveying substance and matching the dramatically striking gorge below. The quarry railroad operated the railroad bridge until 1940; subsequently, the metal rails and railroad trestles atop the deck were removed during World War II to contribute to the war effort. The official "present use" purpose of the bridge in official state records is "pedestrian, equestrian, hiking trail."

For those in the saddle, alighting one's steed and walking the horse across the span was standard procedure for the first forty years: You see, the bridge had no railings.

But Wendell Robie and his family were not typical horse people. Jeff Herten, a Tevis Cup rider and former Western States Trail Foundation president, described larger-than-life Robie as the kind of figure and horseman who spanned the time between the pioneers and the modern era. One day on a ride together with his niece, Ina Robinson, Wendell unflinchingly rode his horse without slowing across the high deck. Ina, the first female finisher of the Tevis Cup in 1956 in less than 24 hours, who was at least as fearless as Wendell, went one step further than her speedy uncle.

Ina, on a bridge deck without railings, 150 feet (46 meters) above the canyon floor, let go of her reins on the bridge, announcing "Look, mom, no hands," crossing the span with her arms raised above her cowgirl hat. The expression stuck.[2]

––––––––––

Gunhild was headed toward No Hands Bridge, downhill from Pointed Rocks Aid Station (mile 94.3) when a rousing voice shouted her name like a cheer. Tim Twietmeyer, a five-time winner of the race and the only person to have completed States an unthinkable twenty-five times, had descended the grade to lend some giddy-up encouragement to the remaining field. The five-time champion, and the only human in history to be presented a one-of-a-kind Western States Endurance Run belt buckle inscribed with "2,500 miles," Tim reassured Gunhild about how close the next checkpoint was ahead, telling her how great she was doing. For those unfamiliar with ultrarunning, this image captures the essence of the community, the uniqueness of mega endurance events and the humility they confer. Rare is the sport where the front-of-the-pack's respect for the back-of-the-pack is symmetrical to the inverse. The tandem pair demonstrated the courage at the heart of the No Hands name.

The National Park Service—which designated "No Hands Bridge" a property on the National Register of Historic Places in 2004—includes a description of the bridge in the registration

––––––––––

2 Thankfully, steel pipe railing was installed on the Mountain Quarries Railroad Bridge in 1984. Additionally, Ina Robinson lived her whole adult life in Auburn, passing away in 2018 at age ninety-one. Her bronze grave marker in Old Auburn Cemetery is inscribed "First woman to complete Tevis Cup ride / She named No Hands Bridge"; the bottom right-hand corner of the plaque shows, in relief, a saddled horse without a rider.

form paperwork that could easily describe Tim and Gunhild: "Plain in appearance, yet possess(ing) a gracefulness that is in perfect harmony with (their) rugged surrounding."

Gunhild, with Tim, Chris, Turlan, and a convoy of others alongside her, cleared the Robie Point Aid Station—named for Wendell—at mile 98.9 of the 100.2-mile (161.3-kilometer) race after having run for more than 29 hours and 43 minutes. When word traveled to the finish line at Auburn, California's Placer High School track, that Gunhild was through the last aid station, the exhausted crowd of runners, pacers, and crew began to buzz.

The race winner, Rob Krar from Flagstaff, Arizona, had passed the Robie Point Aid Station fifteen hours in front of Gunhild. He ran all out, missing Timothy Olson's course record[3] by just two minutes, but defending his 2014 title. He had also put together a perfect race in the previous year against another stacked field. On Sunday morning, Krar and his über-talented trail runner wife, Christina Bauer, walked toward the familiar aid station hand in hand to cheer on the final runners of the event. Rob described their clasped hands with heart: "It was less out of romance and

---

3 Timothy Olson became the first runner to break the 15-hour mark at States with his 2012 finish. His course record of 14:46:44 wasn't the only record that fell that day: Ellie Greenwood was the first female to post a time faster than the legendary Ann "You can be a whiner or you can be an ultrarunner" Trason, a record that had stood for eighteen years. Ellie's run in 2012 was the first time a female broke the 17-hour mark (16:47:19), and that record would stand for a remarkable eleven years, before the phenomenal 2023 race of the stellar Courtney Dauwalter. A special note about (or "aboat") the contributions of Canadian ultrarunners like Ellie: distance running has been especially blessed with athletes from the Great White North. The list, long enough to warrant a large book, includes the extraordinary Tom Longboat, from the Onondaga Nation, who broke the Boston Marathon course record in 1907 by more than five minutes, the perennial champion Al Howie, the four-time Boston Marathon winner Gérard Côté, adored B.C. ultrarunner and race director Gary Robbins, the mega-talented Jade Belzberg, the never-cracking Ihor Verys, the speedy and smiling Marianne Hogan, and Hamilton's golden son, Rob Krar.

more a practicality of supporting my broken and hobbling body."
Seated in a chair in flip-flops and a cowboy hat, Krar saw Gunhild
approaching and did some math: the woman in the green singlet
and black shorts would need to run at least a 9-minute mile on
legs that had been running since 5 a.m. the day before. Race rules
required Gunhild to finish in 29:59:59 for her effort to be official
and to be counted as a finisher.

"When Gunhild appeared in the distance, I looked at my
watch and was convinced the math would end in heartbreak
on or before the Placer High School track," the 2014 and 2015
champion said.

Rob Krar got to his feet.

Improbably, on the edge of town, the first finisher of the race,
ragged from his own effort and sporting flip-flops, ran *alongside*
Gunhild. "I don't know why I began running as she and her
crew passed, or even how my body allowed me to, but I did."
Krar pretended his legs weren't stiff and his feet not battered by
running the route in only 14:48:59, finishing forty-seven minutes
before sunset the previous day. Gunhild felt the lift from Krar.
The neighbors recognized the handsome thirty-eight-year-old
champion from his distinctive intense eyes and mountain man
beard.[4] Seeing the champion in civilian clothes alongside Gunhild
left spectators mesmerized, but Krar did not want to take away
from her race or the work of her support crew, and so he stayed
over to the side. Gunhild heard someone shout, "Run hard to

---

4 Back when the social media platform Twitter was fun and long before it became X,
Krar's facial hair was the kind of ultrarunner beard that had its own Twitter account.
It was the kind of wry parody account that would congratulate runners like superstar
clean-shaven Kilian Jornet with a tweet like "Congrats to @kilianj winning #HR100, in
spite of his disability of not having a beard."

the shade" to keep her cool while running every single tangent of the final stretch. She remembers someone shouting, "Pump your arms," in an attempt to increase her cadence as she ran through the houses of Marvin Way toward Finley Street. Krar, in his unassuming fashion, said to her quietly in a way that Gunhild appreciates, "Keep running." These words, like a benediction, were saved for the small rises in the final mile. Krar knew about these nearly imperceivable grade changes in the road. He had admittedly broken into a hike there all three years *he* had raced Western States. Gunhild had no such luxury.

Like Rob Krar, Tim Twietmeyer did the math based on pace and the placement of the minute hand of his watch. He knew how close Gunhild was to not finishing in time. He, like Rob, shifted toward the edge of the group around her, eventually letting the large caravan of runners go, and he fell off the back. Tim ditched the official course route and raced straight for the high school. There was no time to even text anyone at the finish. He was running like he had stolen something, using all the neighborhood shortcuts, and shaved a half mile off the course to the finish. His heart was in his throat: "Gunhild was going to finish at either 29:59:59," Tim explained, "—or at 30:00:01, and it was going to be the most agonizing finish in all of Western States 100 history."

Indeed, when Tim arrived at the finishing area at the Placer High School 400-meter rubberized oval, the oversized timing clock straddling the track continued to tick away indifferently, the way clocks do.

Tim had seen thousands of finishes from Robie Point to the track, as a runner, spectator, and member of the Western States Endurance Run board member. Many of those finishes around this time of the morning did not end well. Tim had seen an excruciating number of runners time out (fail to finish within the cutoff) on the track, where the assembly can quickly become a heart-rending cortège. Inexplicably, sometimes a runner's physiology or fatigue level means they can see the finish line and yet not take another upright step. "Runners must complete the entire course under their own power," read the rules. In long-distance efforts, it's not all Hollywood endings of swelling music and crescendos of victory; sometimes the mind is willing, but the body is not able. Every kind of malady can fell a runner in The Golden Hour—that precious sixty minutes before 29:59:59. But Tim, eternally positive, like Gunhild, loves The Hour: "You never know what people are going to be able to pull out of their soul at the finish," he says in a way that gives grown men goosebumps.

When Gunhild hit the track with 300 meters left, the clock read 29:59:10, and every man, woman, and child within a quarter mile radius seemed to scream "GOOOOOO!" in unison.

Chris remembers the wave of noise, an intense form of mechanical energy, willing his mom to have fleet feet.

Turlan remembers the heat in the final straightaway, where he and his dad pulled off to the outer edge of the track, to watch Gunhild grind toward the finishing truss.

Tim remembers every person on their feet, from inspired children to robust running royalty. He synthesized the moment: "The crowd was going bananalands."

Rob remembers how his eyes kept darting between Gunhild and the timing clock as she ran that last hundred grueling meters, while the roar and excitement of the crowd was deafening. Neither he nor any other first-place champion of the world's oldest 100-mile foot race had ever experienced such thunderous cheering.

Gunhild remembers thinking, "Oh, *now* I understand why running training plans—even for ultra distances—include speed work on a track."

With five seconds to spare and in fine upright running form, Gunhild Swanson broke the plane of the finish line. And more. It was her third Western States finisher's belt buckle prize. But in the 2015 effort, she became the oldest female finisher ever. It was five days before Gunhild's seventy-first birthday.

In ultrarunning races, rare is the bib that doesn't meet disaster of one ilk or another. Despite going off course, the grandmother-grandson team never lost hope. Gunhild found another gear she would have never known she had. The race champion Rob Krar joined her stride for stride in white flip-flops to the glee of the ultra family. He explains, "Truly, a SINGLE momentary break from her running stride would have changed history." Even his beard was impressed. "I'm still in awe of her perseverance," he avows with his notable sincerity. Every spectator was on their feet, willing Turlan's nana to cross the line before the 30-hour cutoff. Her grandson describes "seeing strangers hugging strangers in celebration" as the greatest experience of his whole life. The memory does not grow less important with time. In fact, it's more valuable than ever.

Bearing witness to an athlete beating the clock by five meager seconds, the crowd at ultrarunning's top event broke out into pandemonium. Everyone present knew their eyes had beheld an instant classic. But the story gets better: Tim Twietmeyer described how arguably the least-assuming person wearing a bib the day before at the start line at Palisades Tahoe had become the hero of "the most consequential finish in the fifty years of Western States Endurance Run." He also joked that it took restraint by the crowd who wanted to pick her up and carry her above their heads for a victory lap, "as if she was an Emperor." When the deafening cheering settled and strangers stopped high-fiving random strangers, the significance of the moment set in. No woman over age seventy had ever finished the race. This was gold country.

Like a faraway memory of a parable in which "the least is the greatest" and "the last shall someday be first," the music of the service at this nonsecular Church of the Long Run could have been provided by the troubadour, Bob Dylan, as celebrant: "The slow one now / Will later be fast / As the present now / Will later be past." Unscripted and unrehearsed, the sport's finest moment happened before the devout congregation on a Sunday morning at a sacred site of 100-mile racing. The flock, they *believed*.

And the times, they were a changin'. The finish caused a wave of people—particularly women—to smile with a knowing satisfaction. A fair number of folks at the storied Western States Endurance Run had doubts there would ever be a seventy-year-old woman who could conquer the epic course in under 30 hours. Instantly, the notion that the route was beyond the capacity of female septuagenarians was shown the door. Which is incredibly empowering to twenty- and forty- and sixty-year-olds. This includes the late bloomers. Those recovering from injury. Those who need the blueprints. And for all the women who take time off from sports due to pregnancy and childrearing, like the mother of four from eastern Washington.

Race officials told Gunhild later that the race entries for the 2016 Western States Endurance Race "blew up," and they credited this to the retired claims adjuster from Spokane Valley. Modest, nearly to a fault, Gunhild can barely believe how the finish of the greatest Golden Hour lives on after the forty-second running of the race. "It can be very discouraging to be a woman," she said without any complaint in her tone. But for one short time—for *five of the finest seconds ever*—"The best in the world were on their feet, jumping for joy," she describes. Spontaneous, improvisational joy created a large-scale, but completely intimate, time of euphoria for everyone there, as well as those watching the live-stream coverage at home, and ultimately, the ultra community, writ large. The 2015 race winner Krar poignantly speaks in superlatives about the effect it had on him: "Gunhild's finish remains one of the fondest memories of my entire athletic career."

The impact on the three generations—matriarch, son, grandson—at the heart of the work that created the euphoric moment is a deep intergenerational tissue between them, like the fascia that surrounds every bone, muscle, organ, and nerve in our anatomy. And for the athlete herself, a life's worth of an athlete's aches, the ubiquitous discouragement, and the rough sections of seven decades of human tumults and coil now weigh less than one minute of her lifetime.

By rewriting the history books on long-distance running's largest stage, Gunhild Swanson, wearing bib number 70, shortened the distance to the start line for the caravans of female athletes who dream of going long—*and* hands up above their well-worn cowgirl hats, playing the long game.

Rob Krar and Gunhild Swanson, Placer High School, Auburn, California, minutes after the final seconds of the Golden Hour of Western States Endurance Run, June 28, 2015. *(photo credit to iRunFar.com / Bryon Powell)*

CHAPTER TWO

RACING TO ALASKA WITHOUT A MOTOR

Kelly Danielson

> The snotgreen sea. The scrotumtightening sea.
> —*James Joyce,* Ulysses

THE LIST OF THINGS THAT CAN GO WRONG IN RACE TO ALASKA includes, but is not limited to, being mauled by a grizzly bear, t-boned by a two hundred thousand–ton freighter, or drowning in waves spawned by hurricane-force winds in the North Pacific.

The race is self-supported, which means no supply drops or arranged outside help is permitted. Racers are responsible for their own safety equipment, navigation, vessel repairs, and sufficient food and fresh water. The route begins in Port Townsend, Washington, at the southern point of the Strait of Juan de Fuca. It ends 750 miles (1,207 kilometers) north, through the Strait of Georgia, to Ketchikan, Alaska. Any boat can enter. You just may not bring a motor.

There aren't many other rules. Somewhere in the fine print, race organizers have a list of race contraband. In addition to motors, banned items include, but are not limited to, "guns, automatic knives, crossbows, tasers, blowguns, spiked wristbands, *manrikigusari* or *kusari*, brass knuckles, and *nunchaku* sticks." Also bear spray—for the aforementioned grizzly hazards—is not allowed. However, the race organizers do offer a link on the FAQ page: "How do I not get eaten by a bear?"

Curiously, Canadian authorities also do not allow racers to enjoy the possession of foreign-grown apples, imported avocados, or the dried leaves, flowers, stems, or seeds from the hemp plant, *Cannabis sativa*, during the race.

But guacamole abstinence is the least of the problems that await participants.

For example, day one of the 2022 race witnessed the mast of a thirty-two-foot trimaran snapped in half, a fourteen-foot trimaran capsized in the thirty-plus-knot winds and heavy seas, and two sailors were pitched out of their fourteen-foot C-Lark into the 52°F (11°C) water. To be clear, this was no pleasure boating or day sailing. This was during the first four hours of Race to Alaska.

Dubbed "the best worst idea" by race organizers, Race to Alaska (R2AK) captures the preparation, perspiration, pain, and piquant personality of the classic case study of athletes facing down the most grueling kind of hours. The undertaking centers around a test of endurance, but also includes deliberate planning, an underpinning of the comical, and the celebration of gifted teammates. Questionable ideas like R2AK are recognizable by the leap of faith required to accompany the absurdity of the venture.

Racers at R2AK in the past have included ocean rowers, kayakers, and First Nation racing canoers. The pull of the race is not unlike that of Everest, or the Grand Canyon's Rim to Rim to Rim, or the 1,000-mile (1,609-kilometer) Iditarod Trail Sled Dog Race. The distance is a puzzle to solve, the adventure is a defibrillator to the mundane, and the immersion in nature provides a thrill greater than civilization has ever made.

The pull of the natural world is proven in R2AK's race results: the quest has been finished in a rowboat, a kayak, and on a stand-up paddleboard (SUP).

In a place that the locals describe as raining twenty-six hours a day and ten days a week, sharing water with thirty different family groups of *Orcinus orca*, with their distinctive black color with white patches behind each eye and under the jaw and massive dorsal fins, no vessel appears seaworthy in the Inside Passage—and not only SUPs.

But in 2017, after liberal amounts of whiskey drinking, two female sailors concocted a strategy to buy a fixer-upper sailboat and crew it with Race to Alaska's first all-female sailing team.

This confluence of events provides some of the tell-tale signs of a sufferfest in the making. Whiskey-drinkin' Jeanne Goussev and Anna Stevens were experienced sailors and serious captains in the big-girl sailing community. They were not intimidated by the shit ton of work involved in finding and fixing up a vessel for a 750-mile feat. They were seasoned enough to provision it, practice with it, and find some "Hell, yes! What time?" gals to propel it. Planning, problem solving, and persistence were the "How."

Every such idea has its own "Why?" In this case, Jeanne Goussev and Anna Stevens wanted to make a point to the sport yacht racing world—a male-dominated affair—that a woman can hold any position on an elite sailboat, to include, but not be limited to, owner, skipper, engineer, helmsman, navigator, tactician, trimmer, bowman, pitman, mast man, and ballast. And that's why they found themselves a bicyclist.

On a rain-soaked island west of Seattle, Washington, at a slightly boozy Christmas party, open-water swimmer and triathlete Kelly Danielson was approached about this tomfoolery. Danielson, thirty-seven, originally from Georgia, had never raced a sailboat a single day in her life.

Without a motor, the 750-mile course of R2AK can only be fueled by wind or human power. Captain Jeanne Goussev found a used Melges 32 sailboat with an open transom—that is, its stern had no vertical back wall. This is the place where you'll often find the punny or cheeky name of the vessel and the home port painted on the back. The Melges 32-foot open-transom design allowed the women to mount two bicycles attached to propellers off the back of the boat. The group's purposeful preparation and wicked sense of humor convinced Kelly the triathlete that this was indeed the kind of absurd shenanigan for which she could not miss out.

A pediatric occupational therapist for two of Bainbridge Island's elementary schools, Kelly had the time off in the summer required for the commitment. Her family—a Seattle public schools assistant principal husband and twin nine-year-old daughters—supported the idea from the start. Her behind-the-scenes people helped her learn to tie sailing knots and to find a US Coast Guard–approved anti-exposure work suit made for the foulest of weather. Over that coverall, she would need to wear an additional ski parka–style waterproof outer shell, boots, a selection of hats, and sailing gloves. For a girls' trip. In mid-June.

———————————

Millions of years ago, massive glaciers formed a network of ancient fjords and inhospitable waterways along the west coast of North America in the 1,200-mile (1,931-kilometer) stretch commonly called the Inside Passage.[5] Part of Canadian internal waters, the thousand islands and webbed coves and bays in the hundred-mile-wide Passage are about as remote as any other place on the planet. Organizers of R2AK describe the scene: "There are squalls, killer whales, tidal currents that run upward of twenty miles an hour, and some of the most beautiful scenery on God's green earth." The gals of Team *Sail Like A Girl* (the name of their boat) would soon learn about nature's squalls and the nasty *bang! bang! bang!* chop of Queen Charlotte Sound. Not to be outdone by Mother Nature, the man-made water assault of wakes produced by colossal freighters and mega-gross-tonnage cruise ships would also test the sailors. The dizzying lift and sickening

———————————

5 The Inside Passage (or Inland Passage) describes the water route from Olympia, Washington, to the Alaskan Panhandle, on the eastern side of Vancouver Island and through a network of waterway passages among dramatic fjords, along unspoiled coves, and around every shaped islet and island formation on the way toward the forty-ninth state. Compared with the open ocean, the protection provided to those a-sea is matched by the exquisite beauty of the place.

fall of the sailboat in such wakes left team members hanging their heads over the gunwales of the boat, retching.[6]

To the queasy, the punishing hours between sunset and sunrise were the worst. With no visual clues to the brain about the movement of the water—while the inner ear was on a seesaw—the sea plague as old as seafaring itself bedeviled the crew. Ancient texts by Cicero, Ovid, and Seneca all include references to naupathia: seasickness. And coastal British Columbia waters have always been considered perilous by those in the know. The first survey ships of the Royal Navy in these waters, the *H.M.S. Plumper* and the *H.M.S. Hecate*, in the years 1857–1862, were 140 feet (43 meters) and 165 feet (50 meters) respectively, compared to the thirty-two feet (ten meters) of the monohull *Sail Like A Girl*. Early on, the short, steep rolling waves of the route forced Captain Jeanne to surf the waves, causing a longer route. As the conditions were not improving, the women had to put their heads down and head straight into what Captain G. H. Richards of the *Plumper* and *Hecate* called the "great violence" of these waters. The beating they took made one thing clear to Kelly Danielson: the sleek hull of a fiberglass and carbon fiber sailboat is indeed less than one inch thick.

---

6 Athletes of the unforgiving hours are known for their ability to "puke and rally" in more than one sense. It still makes Captain Jeanne laugh to recount the following story: During the first leg of the race, called the "Proving Ground" by R2AK officials, teams left Port Townsend headed toward Victoria, British Columbia. By ferry, this is a lovely ninety or ninety-five minute ride. For R2AK entrants it's considered a real puckerfest of grim conditions. Without a motor, the time cut-off to make the distance is a telling thirty-six hours. The wind and nasty currents made for a lumpy expedition, which left some of the women feeling wretched, heads hanging over the sides, barking at the sea. At one point, expert sailor Anna Stevens turned toward Captain Jeanne and asked in the messy winds, "Do I have any throw up on my face?" Except Anna wasn't talking about her own vomitus. Anna wasn't sick.

Seasickness would not be the only illness on the boat; tackling treacherous water on the edge of a continent with a tiny sailboat was like bringing a spiked wristband or a pair of nunchakus to a gunfight. And not a quick gunfight. Most finishers of Race to Alaska take at least two weeks to arrive at Ketchikan. For the last of the finishers, their time in an engineless craft lasts more than a month.

From the first stage it was clear, Team *Sail Like A Girl* came to play. Seasickness and weather be damned, these sailors were not about to spend a month at sea. After the "Proving Ground" (40 miles) the actual race to Alaska begins. The second stage (710 miles) of the two-stage race is named "To The Bitter End." It's when the race clock officially begins in an engineless mass start. Using charts unchanged from the work of the *Plumper* and *Hecate*, the women studied and strategized the fastest routes around islands and through straits—many places named for the men who served on those two nineteenth-century British survey ships: Pender Island, Gowlland Harbour, Browning Inlet, Bull Passage, Mount Moriarty. The women had barely tacked clear of Victoria Harbour on day two before they joked that they had to hurry up and finish. These women had too much stuff to do back home. The way women always do.

Their training showed in their racing. Three months of practice, they were a disciplined machine. What they lacked in motor horsepower they made up with pre-race dedication. They spent so much time together—the vibration undeniable—their menstrual cycles even synced up. They sailed tactically, laughed loudly, and the novice Kelly focused on her main task: to power their boat through the doldrums with her cyclist wattage. Lest their effort be romanticized today, the work included scarce creature comforts. In proper endurance event incongruity and hilarity, there were seven women on board, and there was no toilet.

The Melges 32-foot is a daytripper, which in sailing terms means it has no "head" on board. By way of explanation, a marine toilet is called such because since the days of old sailing ships—yes, before the motor—captains have sailed boats downwind, filling their sails with the wind at their back. In this most elementary catching of the wind, a sailor would most comfortably relieve his bladder at the front of a boat in a tailwind to avoid an unfortunate spray situation. The forward part, or bow, or "head," of the boat became the area where the first toilet facilities were installed on the old wooden ships. The term "head" stuck. A marine water closet is still called a "head" no matter where it's located on modern vessels. Except for this boat.

Kelly's teammates were equally last-frontier tough in their skipper, engineer, helmsman, navigator, tactician, trimmer, bowman, pitman, mast man, and ballast tasks. To passing thoughts like:

"I'm tired."

"It's too cold."

"I'm homesick."

"It's raining."

"I'm seasick."

"This sucks."

"It's foggy as all hell."

"I wish I had my crossbow."

"I can't believe we are all pooping in a bucket."

...all seven women shared the same response: "LET'S FUCKING GOOOOOO."

The arduous hours of endurance sports have unmentionable matters as motifs. To meet the low standards of a proper chunk of God-forsaken time where the misery is unforgiving, such athletic undertakings will have the imprimatur of public indecency, chafing, fuzzy teeth, blistering, brain funk, saddle sores, sunburn, snot rockets, and every kind of bodily function gone wrong. Cycling in high seas with sleep deprivation, Kelly met or exceeded each of these criteria. Her teammate Kate Hearsey, cofounder and CEO of Maiven Sailing and a competitive racer, described what Kelly brought to the long stretches of dehydration and sleep deprivation: "I loved having Kelly on board because she was so great about reminding people to be present—bringing them back from whatever funk their brain went into." Kate, a twenty-year veteran of sailing, clarifies her point, "I'm not very 'Rah-rah, go ladies! Pink things!' I love sailing with women because I think we're better at team work and communication."

A communicator who always pays close attention to tone and a thoughtful choice of words, Kelly may speak with the sweet pacing of her Southern roots, but she is no belle. A ruddy-cheeked adventurer, her hair is often gathered in a thick braid down her back like a tail of a chestnut horse with the flaxen gene. Intestinally tough and tupelo sweet, Kelly was disciplined enough to be assigned abbreviated sleep shifts and joyful enough to pull energy from the natural world the other nineteen hours of the day. Such unrelenting wear and tear—spelunking in the pain cave—often results in a metaphysical freefall and bottomed-out dark place. Rather than anything dramatic, such low-points cruelly creep up on athletes and take them to a low, where mood, circumstances, pain, insufficient sleep, exhausted glycogen stores, and waning blood sugar collide. The gut-punch sensation of The Dark Place announces that rock bottom has a pitch-black basement. For Kelly, the sailboat racing freshman, the low point of the diabolical distance and grinding hours arrived during day five of no privacy and no relief from the elements. With a deck only nine feet, ten inches wide, and a hull only thirty-one feet, ten inches long, the boat, all at once, closed in on her. The pathophysiology started with a tightness in her head and nose, advanced to her bronchioles, arresting the exchange of oxygen and carbon dioxide from the uncooperative alveolar ducts to desperate alveoli. Her lungs were suddenly no longer in compliance to distend, her chest no longer in agreement to rest. More than six feet (two meters) above the water line of the fiberglass composite hull, she gasped for air as if she were drowning. Captain Jeanne recognized the acute nervous system event or chemical low threatening her sailor. Embracing Kelly in a broad, swaddling hug, Captain Jeanne lowered her voice, guiding her rookie out of the elements and into one of the two tiny bunks below deck. While involuntary bronchoconstriction wracked the fatigued newbie, the captain wrapped her in blankets and spoke softly, in the low tone purrs of the minkes, gray whales, and humpbacks who live in the Inside Passage waters.

Sleep deprivation and a sudden sense of vulnerability fired synapses in Kelly's temporal lobe, causing her to become suddenly, devastatingly aware of the fact that there was no land in sight. Her brain stem—the survival brain—told her heart to start beating faster to help her get more oxygen. Her hippocampus—deep within the temporal lobe—which had been turning on and off, on and off, on and off, kept trying to construct the map of this route she had never traveled, delivered a terrifying mental image of immediate peril. She was stuck on a motorless boat in the birdless Pacific on the snotgreen sea. So far from the ocean floor. So far from her twin girls at home. It was like the on-land physical sensation of losing a toddler at the state fair or receiving a text that your child's school is on lockdown.

Throughout history, maritime illness has extended nautical miles beyond mere nausea. During the age of discovery, sailing ships brimmed with scurvy, venereal disease, polluted drinking water maladies like typhoid, and crowded living condition viruses like smallpox. In 1621, English Renaissance writer Robert Burton (1577–1640) described the fragility of sailors in his book, *The Anatomy of Melancholy*: "What is a ship but a prison?"

A century and a half later, Samuel Johnson, while touring the islands of Scotland in 1773 with his friend James Boswell, cheerfully said, "Being in a ship is like being in jail, with the chance of being drowned."

The term "under the weather" comes from instances of sailors coming undone in the nexus of body and mind and needing to go below deck—under the poor weather above. Sailors who become unwell at sea, often in low spirits, are thus described as "under the weather." Burton's book describes a kaleidoscopic range of melancholia "which goes and comes upon every small occasion of sorrow, need, sickness, trouble, fear, grief, passion or perturbation of the mind, any manner of care, discontent or thought, which causes anguish, dullness [sic], heaviness and vexation of spirit." With no land in sight, insufficient sleep, the disruption of diet and routines, and the delirium of exhaustion—with a shot glass of 200 proof landlubber claustrophobia—Kelly was nearly walloped by this version of The Dark Place. Endurance athletes who go long are often accustomed to a cage match with the demons.

The pain of debilitating hours of long-distance comes from boats too small, open-water too cold, running, cycling, and climbing vert too steep, and every kind of distance too far. Training for such undertakings requires the physical tolerance of the conditions, but also the only-earned-never-given *experience* for the mind to recognize the familiar low points—the inevitable sinkhole when the central governor of the mind announces QUIT, in all caps. Caloric deficits and sleep deprivation are to blame most of the time, and experienced unforgiving-mileage types have enough familiarity with the dark pit to recognize the inevitable depletion and the way the central governor will want to take over. An actionable plan for the lows during the hours is a part of the training for these mind and body blows that will not relent. Crew planning must account for the inevitable collapse.[7]

---

7 Crew planning is best done with a pre-event meeting where feed crews, running pacers, support swimmers in marathon swims, etc., discuss the mood collapse and physical bonk of the athlete. In long-distance events, especially those that go more than fifteen hours or through the night, an actionable plan for the creep and fog of The Dark Place is required. The good news is The Dark Place during particularly unforgiving spells is often quickly remedied by the sunbeams of sunrise or a favored candy bar, an old-fashioned nap or a few sips of heavenly nectar from a can of ice-cold Coca Cola.

Captain Jeanne recognized the malady in Kelly instantly, bundling her in blankets, holding her tight, assuring her that she was fine, that the feeling would pass. They were in a dangerous place full of legitimate threats that her brain could not make sense of after five days at sea. Assuring her that if she pedaled a boat through the Inside Passage to Alaska—and didn't feel the horrible way she did—well, sailor, that could only mean that *she was doin' it wrong.* Her suffering was proof she was doing it right.

Kelly recalls the incident with admiration for the team; she slept like a stone after her visit to The Dark Place. She slept longer than was allotted on the schedule. She slept during the other sailors' rack shifts. Captain Jeanne's experience was proof of the old adage that smooth seas do not make a skilled sailor. Calming yourself down takes practice. By practicing staying calm at sea—or on land, for that matter—new pathways are created in our brains. The more practice, the stronger those pathways become. With time, the response to stress and danger creates such a hearty brain pathway, that responses—like a seasoned captain's—are automatic.

But for first timers, the relentless battering of gusty wind, the sensation of chunky water, and the giant abyssal wretch of freaky-deep unending sea in a thin-hulled boat provide the lesson that pedaling a vessel to Alaska is one thing; it is another thing entirely to do so on a boat that is too small to live in. Such as, say, a puny watercraft without a bathroom. Both temporary and predictable, facing and overcoming these low points are the vexations that qualify a long-distance athletic beatdown as "unforgiving."

After some respite from the elements, a bit of distraction, a captain's soothing words in a hushed voice, a warm bunk, and some calories, Kelly's survival brain and emotional brain both settled down. "Jeanne had to tuck me in. And talk to me. Console me. The way women do," Danielson said. The way Danielson, before her first sailing race, had tucked in her twins every night for the last nine years. The way women do.

In a dramatic fashion, somewhere in the Hecate Strait, Team *Sail Like A Girl* realized they were out front of the field. Kate Hearsey described her reaction, "My racer brain kicked back into focus and all I cared about was getting to Ketchikan and getting there faster than anyone else. I wasn't thinking about the 'all-female team' part or the 'first-monohull-to-win-it' aspect or all the people around the world following the race."

She continued, "My focus was: the team, sail trim, and our position."

In spite of the odds and expectations, after six days, thirteen hours, and seventeen minutes, full sails delivered seven female sailors to Ketchikan harbor just after midnight, before any other vessel. Team *Sail Like A Girl* had become the first all-woman team to win Race to Alaska.

The fearsome seven celebrated their victory with a $10,000 award, as the trophy of R2AK is one hundred $100 bills stabbed onto a rough block of wood by a stake. By way of explanation, when R2AK was a horrible idea forming in the minds of the race directors, they asked the question, "What would happen if we stuck $10,000 to a tree in Ketchikan?"

Passing hours in unforgiving endurance events inspires R2AK sailor mouth, boredom doldrums, unmentionable maladies, unrelenting planning, and unfortunate functions of the body by outdoorspeople. Usually without physical prizes. A funny exception to this rule was the second-place team with whom Team *Sail Like A Girl* duked it out the last days of the race, trading the lead, back and forth. That second-place team received a set of steak knives for their effort. The wry "thanks for playing" is left, facetiously, unsaid. The third-place team received nothing at all. Such is the spirit of enduring the grueling hours. Because life is short. Only racing 750 miles to Alaska without a motor is long.

To contextualize R2AK, race creator Jake Beattie explains it perfectly: "Race to Alaska is a little about sailing and a lot about getting over yourself; it's about getting out there and doing something incredible. Every year someone wins, and the winner's story is usually dominated by how skillfully they executed, their tactics, their sail changes, and how well they endured all the little, 'Jesus, should I just quit?' moments that creep into your mind in the middle of the night gale, while your dry suit is leaking and you haven't slept in days. *Sail Like A Girl* was all of that, and they were a crew who arrived at the finish line at the height of #MeToo— and a nation cheered."

"They were the champions we deserved," Beattie said, "at the moment we needed them most."

Kate Hearsey tells the story and delivers goosebumps to anyone who has ever felt like a dark horse or an underdog: "We earned that win. Not because we're all women, but because we out-sailed everyone else."

As for the $10,000 prize, half went to pay for supplies and expenses, but the remaining $5,000 was donated to breast cancer research. No sailor saw a single dollar of prize money. Since ancient times, boats have been called "she" for the protection and benevolence associated with women. The 2018 R2AK race demonstrated from whence that tradition comes. And why it matters that female hands rang the victory bell on a Ketchikan dock in the middle of that June night. Because it was female hands that charted their course, and female hands that hoisted the 445-square-foot mainsail, and female hands that held the whole way.

The athletes of Team *Sail Like A Girl* from the top of the bow: Aimee Fulwell; next row, left to right, Morgana Buell and Allison Ekberg Dvaladze; next row Anna Stevens, in the middle, Captain Jeanne Goussev; front left Kate Hearsey and front right, Kelly Danielson. Not pictured, the super veteran sailor Haley Lhamon. *(photo courtesy of Sandy Lam)*

CHAPTER THREE

THE RIDICULOUSNESS OF ONE GEAR

Gordon Wadsworth

And then God said, "Let there be sexy people."
So he made single-speed cyclists.
—Unknown

On a Thursday night in November of 2018, the winner of countless premiere road races, triathlons, and mountain bike events, Lance Armstrong found himself a bit too shredded to speak.

It wasn't until Friday afternoon that the seven-time winner of the Tour de France summoned the words to describe the day before: "I'll make it real simple," he said. "Yesterday was not just the hardest day I have ever had on a bike. It was the hardest day by a factor of five or ten."

Armstrong had biked in an event from a beach on Costa Rica's central Pacific coast to Ciudad Colón, an unspoiled place, due west of the country's capital of San José. It took the powerhouse

Armstrong eight hours and thirty-one minutes to cover the distance. He came in at eighty-second place.

More than twelve thousand feet of vertical climbing was partially responsible for the long slog. But while racing in Le Tour, Armstrong had pounded the pedals of the biggest road climbs in Western Europe. He had dominated the Pyrenees, the Jura, the Alps, the Vosges, and the Massif Central ranges. Granted, Armstrong had been assisted by blood-boosting EPO, steroids, and transfusions of his own blood—but he was also an undeniable climbing master, obliterating the other rule breakers. His intimidation and lies led to a deserved fall from grace, but Armstrong crushed climbs of 12K days (a stage with 12,000 feet of elevation gain or 3,657 meters of climbing), clobbering all the other dopers in the pro field with aplomb.

So how was a ride on a random Thursday in November harder than all the other days of relentless mileage and blistering kilowatts in Armstrong's life? Harder than his wins on the twenty-one-switchback Alpe d'Huez, or the climb of Col du Tourmalet with a beast-of-a-man like Jan Ullrich attacking? How could a Central American course in and around the jungle of Carara National Park be harder than any other day by a multiple of five or ten?

The trail and weather that November 1 day—average conditions for the season and the locale—served the most dominant cyclist at the turn of the century its specialty: a rainforest version of a trouncing. The dense jungle of the wet side of Costa Rica produces trails that feature an unholy number of bobblehead descents to creeks and rivers with muddy kickers (steep inclines) on the other side. The climbing is legendary. Mud can be the knee-deep variety. The weight and adhesion of the clay soils of the route are second to none.

On Friday, Armstrong, still hearty and hale in his forties, described the cruel elements of the Thursday ride: "Oppressive, hot, humid, and exposed"—in the fashion of a man still too tired to conjugate verbs. Turned-you-inside-out fatigue, when acquired properly, can prevent an athlete from locating verbs and subjects to create whole sentences. It wasn't the first time the event—the three-day mountain bike stage race La Ruta de los Conquistadores—had reduced pros, elites, and Category 1 bike racers into the stunned and the nearly speechless.

There was no blame to be placed on Armstrong's equipment. He brought a Santa Cruz Highball from his home in Austin, Texas, to the event. The Highball is one of the best carbon bikes that money can buy, lightweight and made to fly. The premium drivetrain parts of the Highball included a lightweight cassette of gears to handle the gonzo climbs of the five mountain ranges of Costa Rica.

Regular bikes like your dad's old Schwinn or your sister's REI Co-op hybrid usually have gears that amount to a rear cassette the size of a bread plate. A custom bike like Lance's set up for nosebleed climbs will often have extra "granny gears" that make the back wheel cassette look more like a *dinner* plate. Still lightweight, these massive 12-speed cassettes allow mountain bikers to climb burly grades while not spinning out when descending at top speeds. Armstrong brought a dream build for a nightmare amount of suffering that day.

While words were hard to find for the wan Armstrong on Thursday, so too was color. The healthy blush was gone from his hands and his face; he was covered in crusted salt from his own effort. Lance Armstrong, skin and clothing tinted and textured white, hunched over a bike covered in peanut butter mud with a dinner plate of gears, serves as this chapter's prologue.

Because only with context can some relentless and thewy hours be properly enunciated and rendered.

Ask the gutsiest, toughest La Ruta veterans about their firsthand, eyewitness accounts of the most impressive feats and greatest riders of the last three decades. The grizzled La Ruta alumni shake their heads, eyes wide, and utter one word used in all of the international languages spoken at La Ruta: single-speed.

To pack a bike without gears for a three-day race with north of 29,000 feet (8,839 meters) of climbing takes real guts. But that's what Gordon Wadsworth did in 2015. Thereby hangs this tale.

He had only completed his first ultra 100-miler (161-kilometer) mountain bike race in his final year of college, 2010, on a dare. This is precisely how these things usually begin.

A photo from the first La Ruta was captioned on social media two decades after the inaugural ride:

"Cero clips,
cero suspensión,
cero frenos de disco,
100% huevos."

The faded picture, captured on film in an unintended homage to all the grainy moments before the crisp digital photos of cell phones, shows seven young men climbing with knobby tires and the straight handlebars of early mountain bikes. They were the pioneers of an event that would become a phenomenon in the world of adventure MTB racing. The sport looks different now: specific mountain biking shoes clip into cycling pedals; gone are the toe cages that strapped feet to the flat pedals. Modern mountain bike shoes are stiff-soled to transfer a cyclist's power to the pedals most efficiently, but with a bit of hiking tread for hike-a-bike sections that road riders, with their slick-bottomed shoes, do not face.

Cero suspensión refers to the front and rear suspension that many mountain bikes employ for riding enjoyment (read: comfort). With springs or pressurized air chambers, a front fork can provide 4 to 5 inches of travel in a typical mountain bike, cushioning the rider from potholes, rock gardens, and tree roots while improving their riding performance. On gnarly freeride and downhill bikes, forks can provide up to 8 inches of front travel. The high rates of speed and massive jumps associated with eight inches of front fork travel are affiliated with a full-face helmet, knee and elbow pads as well as shin guards. And nerve. Such gear would be a good idea at a majority of mountain bike rides in Costa Rica, but the humidity and climbing make extra layers and extra weight unthinkable.

Rear suspension describes a design with bump absorption integrated into the bike frame where one or two pivot points allow the rear wheel to cushion the cyclist's ride. Anyone who has ever hit a pothole or speed bump in the backseat of an older model car with blown shocks or broken coil springs can attest to the comfort and handling that accompany good suspension.

Bikes are no different. Rear suspension makes mountain bikes heavier, but it improves handling and decreases wear and tear to a bike's engine: its cyclist.

In the 1993 grainy photo from the first La Ruta, only one bike has a front fork with travel, and not a single bike features rear suspension.

The bikes in the photo all display the cable-actuated brakes that clinch the rim of the tires to slow and/or stop the bike—aptly called rim brakes. Today, most mountain bike racers favor *frenos de discos,* or disc brakes, for efficiency and performance. In an extraordinary nod to the superiority of these hydraulic disc brakes, even road cyclists have come 'round to the change. The professional peloton that Lance Armstrong dominated for seven years has largely moved onto *frenos de discos.* In January 2017, the first UCI road race was won on a bike with *frenos de discos* in Argentina at Vuelta a San Juan by the Belgian Tom Boonen. A curious moment, as the high-end designer teams synonymous with roadie purity and tradition—with their unspoken disdain for anything involving rocky, rooty, and dirty—hate change. Concessions to better technology are hard, especially when they come from your backwoods country cousins.

As for the *100% huevos* demonstrated in the picture, the Spanish word *huevos* technically means eggs...as in the Mexican breakfast dish *huevos rancheros*—fried eggs served with tortillas, pico de gallo or salsa, and often with rice, beans, and avocado. As informal language often does, the meaning of *huevos* in another context devolves rather quickly. A common double entendre in the Spanish-speaking world uses *huevos* to mean the testicles of men, which is then used to describe courage, nerve, or guts. (See also: *cojones.*)

While on the subject of this key contact point for male cyclists and the colorful slang used by men in ultra endurance saddles, the literal translation of the word "ball" in Spanish is *pelota*—the term used for the round object knocked about on a *fútbol* pitch or thrown around *beisbol* diamonds. *En pelotas* refers to being nude (*ahem*, "balls exposed"), or depending on context, can express someone being devoid of things other than clothes—like being short on expertise or defenses or caught unawares. Not short of a sense of humor, tangentially, Lance Armstrong named the café in his Austin, Texas, bike shop "Juan Pelota," having a self-deprecating laugh at his medical file. The testicular cancer treatment he endured in 1996 at age twenty-five included four rounds of chemotherapy, brain surgery, and a unilateral orchiectomy. The name "Juan" sounds like "one" and "Pelota" describes the post-cancer, *er*, equipment situation of the American who turned pro triathlete at age fifteen. Having a good sense of humor about this most private and sensitive subject confirms Armstrong has *huevos* ("*tiene huevos*") and has earned him respect from many folks in Colorado and Texas, where he has aimed—successfully—to be a relevant podcaster and a good neighbor.

Also tangentially, one source of the coffee beans sold at Juan Pelota are grown in the Tarrazú region of Costa Rica. The quality of the beans grown in the rich volcanic mountain soil of these shady, cool hillsides is so fine that in July 2018—the summer before Armstrong raced there—a new world-record price per pound was set by Costa Rican beans: $300 per pound. And the coffee is consistently good throughout Costa Rica: it is the only country in the world where it is illegal to grow any coffee plant that is inferior to the paragon 100% Arabica. Coincidentally, good quality coffee like Costa Rica's, ever a familiar lifeblood of cyclists, is often the liquid courage of the endurance lions and lionesses who go long.

Gordon Wadsworth started his Day One of La Ruta 2015 with such premium coffee, as well as made-from-scratch rice and beans (the sublime dish called *gallo pinto*), eggs, toast, mouthwatering plantains, and the whole color prism of fresh fruits. The abundant nutritious and delectable food that the Costa Rican land produces suggests this bounty is precisely what is necessary to fuel oneself to climb her mountains, cross her rivers, and cover her distances.

While digging into the country's typical breakfast of *gallo pinto*, Gordon Wadsworth's smile was spread cartoonishly ear-to-ear. The effect was heightened by his ginger-colored bushy mustache—which was clearly drawn on by a caricaturist at some state fair. His baby face, anime eyes, and strong Virginia accent made him resemble the neighbor kid your grandmother would bake a coffee cake for once a week, so charming and authentic was his company. He would call your gran "ma'am," then give her a nickname to make her howl, and shovel her driveway on snow days.

If "lift with your legs" is the mantra of snow shoveling, snow removal would have met its match with Gordon, whose lower appendages look like the distinct tree trunks of a long-track speed skater. The shocking thickness of his upper legs makes you look twice. Gordon Wadsworth's nickname amongst the cyclists who watch him rocket by, or with those who have had the misfortune to try to keep up with him on two wheels, is "Quadsworth," referring to the power of Wadsworth's quadriceps femoris, or "quads"; one of the body's most powerful muscle groups, they make up most of the human thigh.

There is an expression in Costa Rica—"*lava huevos*"—a coarse slang term about "washing balls," that equates to the English terms "brown-nosing" or "kissing up." Quadsworth's nickname is not ball-washing by others; it's said with athlete-to-athlete admiration for the fellow with the ferocious quads and the contagious positivity. Cyclists remind us that you inherit your height, but you earn your legs.

La Ruta, which started with a group of friends with a daring idea, would grow into a world-renowned cycling event, the first-ever mountain bike stage race: An entire day in the thick jungle rainforest. A second day launched over active volcanoes. A third day of a whitewater river and flat-out bike racing through sizzling banana plantations and across active railroad bridges. Three days to reach the eastern shore from the west coast, sandy beach-to-sandy beach, with more than 29,000 feet of climbing in between. Legs would be earned at La Ruta.

Quadsworth headed out after breakfast to the staging area of the race marked with an inflatable blue truss with a Shimano logo. The elegant dark sand of the central Pacific coast is unlike the start line of any other bike race. The beach was a postcard of clear water, elongated palm trees, and unspoiled tranquility. The pre-dawn sky eventually shook off the dark but held onto the humidity—80%—as cyclists entered the starting corral on Playa Herradura. The small U-shaped bay gave Herradura its name— herradura means "horseshoe"—and delivered its serene waters.

Out of sight of the cyclists, sunrise surfers formed quorums at the stellar beaches to the south—like Jacó and Hermosa, where the swell is legendary. Providing the best big-game sport-fishing in Costa Rica, with a high-end marina for fighting anglers, Playa Herradura was a fitting start to the day of numbing battles ahead, in saddles like fighting chairs.

In the front row of the race corral, the names of the elites and pros from Costa Rica and abroad were announced with gusto. Spectators sought photos of the famous (some) and the brave (all). The neutral start began to roll at 6:10 a.m., in the charming way things in Costa Rica always get done, just usually about ten minutes late.

Since its inaugural ride of eighteen Costa Ricans in 1993, the race organizer, Román Urbina has always gotten it done. This is despite the fact that La Ruta de los Conquistadores has hosted innumerable injuries, off-course riders, wildlife run-ins, volcanic detours, unsuitable bridge crossings, and at least one case of last rites. Outside of Central America, neither the Legal nor the Human Resources department of any organization would sign off on any part of the original La Ruta course. Román embodies the spirit of the hardcore Costa Rican sportsperson—a seriously unflinching assassin of a competitor, a gifted multisport athlete, as fit as a person can be, and a quality human. Serious when required, Román is also always quick with a laugh to lighten the mood. He doesn't stress about a ten-minute late start, but Román cared about the hundreds of athletes behind him. Román Urbina was inducted into the international Mountain Biking Hall of Fame in 2016 for the joy and adventure he has brought "to thousands of mountain bikers around the world" and his inspiration to other races, declared the Marin Museum of Bicycling. Sacrificing his urge to ride, most years Román selflessly leads La Ruta out front on a dirt bike.

Román leads the race leaders until the route hits the first section of the course where no ATV or dirt bike can go.

On the opening race day in 2015, Gordon "Quadsworth" Wadsworth stayed near the front of the pack as the neutral start left the sand of Herradura for a dirt road headed east. The ocean's gentle tailwind—*la brisa del mar*—was left behind. Good-natured shooting of the breeze in Spanish and English remained. The neutral start and police escort aimed to safely get the large group through the few streets between the great stretch of flat sand and the green thicket beyond, east of the pavement. The start illuminated the provenance of cycling—elegant, gentlemanly, proud of its etiquette. The unspoken agreement between competitors was distilled from this provenance: during the race, athletes would pass only when safe, cyclists would hold their lines, and there would absolutely be no whining.

The gentlemen and ladies would soon be turned into climbing beasts as the flat dusty road was swallowed by the jungle. The dirt of the double-track turned the color of terra-cotta under the dense canopy. In a matter of minutes, the grade doubled. Then tripled. The humidity seemed to form a wall.

With fresh legs, Gordon Wadsworth was able to keep the leaders in sight on the early climbs. But with the occasional flat or slight descent, the distance between the top ten or twelve guys and Wadsworth stretched cruelly apart, mile by mile. Guys with nine to eleven more gears than Wadsworth's single-speed Pivot bike flew past him. Hard gears make flats and descents a racetrack for geared bikes. Wadsworth's single gear (a super-easy 34X22 for this first and particularly vertical day) made this brutal thing harder.

How hard? *Mountain Bike Action* magazine did not mince words: "La Ruta de Los Conquistadores is the World's Toughest Race." And *The New York Times'* 2016 article about La Ruta was titled "Conquering River, Jungle and the World's Toughest Bike Race." Gordon chooses single-speed for its ability to make light of hard things by making them harder. Single-speed sings in its purity and its challenge, and thus, its beauty. *L'art pour l'art.* In Costa Rica: *Arte por el arte.* Tangentially, his sartorial cycling sprezzatura style is sharp. His stoke, high. A clever rider, on the bike he smiles with his eyes to avoid all the bugs that would land in his mouth at such speeds. He is a social secretary of the coolest events, the radiant ad hoc host at every trail, and magnanimous to all, the beginners to the pros and the midpackers in between.

Behind Gordon, amongst the midpackers, evidence of the difficulty of La Ruta would unfold in black and white, chapter and verse. An experienced rider from Colorado slipped in one of the many river crossings—this crossing about thigh high. He had stopped at a river somewhere in Carara National Park to relieve his bike of the dense mud—creamy, no stir—and down he went. The current took man and bike downriver faster than he could mount a plan. Whitewater pummeled him. The frothy turbulence in the water eventually tore the bike from him, along with his shoes, trip computer, cellphone, and all the contents of his three bike-jersey pockets. The jungle—with its unfamiliar danger and cacophony, especially overnight—was an inhospitable place to find yourself unaccounted for. For background, the word "*Carara*" in the original indigenous Huetar language of Costa Rica means "River of Lizards." Which is a euphemism for crocodiles.

In a national park named for sixteen-foot carnivores, the river had pushed the Colorado cyclist so far off course that race sweepers[8] never saw him. The first search party used scouts and locals on ATV four wheelers in the midnight hours, and the second search party left at 5 a.m. The third search party included professionals from the Red Cross and the Comisión Nacional de Emergencias (the National Emergency Commission, lead institution for disasters in the country). Urbina was up all night. Such is the way of La Ruta. Where hard core is a food group. The search for the missing racer continued.

Meanwhile, Gordon Wadsworth finished that first day of riding at the intended finish line in Atenas. He gave immediate credit to a Costa Rican named Alejandro, who rode with him in the first half—including through the walls of peanut butter mud and greasy descents—and credit to another Tico (the local term for a Costa Rican; the female version is "Tica") named Gabriel, who crushed the back half of the day with the American. Ale and Gabby, as Gordon called them affectionately, had an entire range of gears. Gordon fails to mention this when describing what

---

8 Race sweeping is a feature of long-distance events in running and cycling and an event like R2AK, that involves staying behind the last participant to make certain all athletes are off the course. In races with time cutoffs, sweepers will often escort those going too slow to the broom wagon (also sometimes called the sag wagon; although a sag wagon also sometimes rides alongside athletes providing support, whereas the broom wagon stays at the back of the convoy always). The broom wagon collects the slow or those who are done for the day and drives them to the finish. Race sweeping sometimes also includes the tasks of removing the course markings (such as staked signs or colored tape tied to trees) or any trash accidentally dropped by race participants, as "leave no trace" is a principle of these events. In this regard, organized long-distance gatherings often leave the wild places tidier than before the event thanks to race sweepers.

awesome mountain bikers they are, and how helpful they were. The trio were three of 351 finishers of Day One.

––––––––––

Day Two La Ruta has commenced from the country's capital, San José, every year except for a handful of editions around 2010, when the race was four days of racing, and beginning in 2023, when the race began to be run from east to west. The greater metropolitan area of San José thrums, the home of one third of the country's population and plenty of Latin American cosmopolitan panache. The night of Day One, Gordon would fall asleep on high-thread-count sheets in Escazu, a neighborhood called the "Beverly Hills of Costa Rica." The out-of-town racers had to ignore any introspection about the surreal whiplash between Day One spent in the jungle—and finishing the calendar date under an oversized rainfall showerhead in a marble and glass spa-inspired shower. Gordon elevated his legs with his heels atop an upholstered headboard, with a crisp-cased down pillow under his head. As a thunderstorm rolled in, with plenty of riders still on the course, a well-appointed hotel room was never more appreciated. Costa Rica can be as upscale as the most posh European capitals and wild to the point of potentially dragging you down a river, shoeless, to sleep on a forest floor with poison-arrow frogs. The threat of that last part, in all fairness, is reserved for cyclists who sign up for La Ruta.

Day Two breakfast in Gordon's hotel began service at 3:30 a.m. He entered the restaurant's dining room full of racers leaning over their plates piled with food. Yesterday's effort had left them all in a caloric deficit, for there is no way to consume enough food and water while riding at such intensity in such humidity. Day Two of the race demanded at least one extra trip to the buffet for a made-to-order omelet, extra *gallo pinto*, or a tall glass of guava or mango juice. And lots or hot coffee, given the hour, and given the route of Day Two.

The race start was at a large shopping center, with a massive parking lot capable of holding all the racers, volunteers, media, and the throng of fans from around San José who packed the mall parking lot. The fact that the sun had yet to rise did not impact the size of the crowds: one feature of Costa Rica is the tendency to rise early and get to work. In the countryside, on the farms, at the docks, at the ranches, and there in the middle of the capital, Costa Ricans are up early and getting after it. Its cyclists—and their fans—were no different.

Racers were met by volunteers who checked them in systematically. This housekeeping matter had been put into place after learning a hard lesson. Rare is the La Ruta lesson that does not qualify as a hard lesson.

It was in the late nineties when, at the Day Two start line, a competitor noticed that one of the international racers who had fared well the day before—a rare top-ten finish—was not lined up. Racers looked around and asked around, "Has anyone seen John?" until they felt compelled to approach Román Urbina. The race director quickly called the Hotel Don Fadrique to have a staff member check on the American rider.

"There is no response to my knocking on his door," the hotel housekeeper replied to the race director when she returned to the phone. Román, luckily, asked the housekeeper to enter the room with her key. If he was not in the room, he would not mind.

Ultimately, the rider did not mind that the housekeeper let herself into his room. He would have had to be conscious for that.

She found the cyclist in bed, unresponsive. She raced back to the phone to alert Román and to call 911.[9] Doctors would eventually report to Román what put a strapping young man in the local hospital.

When John had arrived for the race several days in advance, he had gone to the grocery store for supplies, like most athletes on an event-vacation trip. At the store, he bought several gallons of water so that he could combat the dehydrating flight from the US and to pre-hydrate before the sweat-fest that is La Ruta's Day One in the humid jungle.

To be cautious and to stock up, he bought bottled water. But not just any water—distilled water. This water is boiled into a vapor and then condensed back into water, purifying it to 99%. Distilled water, for example, is used in the sterilization of surgical equipment and medical tools. But there is a critical difference between purified water and distilled water. Purified water is free of contaminants but retains the minerals and sodium that human bodies benefit from. Especially those sweating profusely in a Central American jungle. On any given day, an average person drinking an average amount of water and doing an average amount of physical activity can drink distilled water without noticeable difference in their constitution, wellness, or blood work. But by pre-hydrating for a race with distilled water and filling water bottles and a hydration pack with distilled water, and racing Day

9 Costa Rica uses 9-1-1 as the telephone number for emergency services, like the United States, Canada, and Mexico. Other countries that use 9-1-1 include Ecuador, Peru, Paraguay, Uruguay, and the Philippines.

One all out with distilled water, is to destroy the mineral and salt balances of the human body.

Román was told the unconscious man in the hospital was suffering from acute hyponatremia—a condition that occurs when the level of sodium in the blood is too low. His sodium levels were so low, his brain had experienced rapid swelling, leaving him unconscious. If he had pre-hydrated with regular bottled water or just regular Costa Rican tap water—which is as safe and delicious as water can be—it's likely his sodium levels would not have left him in such a terrible state. How dire was the medical situation? Doctors and Urbina contacted the racer's family, who flew to Costa Rica to see him, as the prognosis was grim. He might never awake from the coma. A priest was called. He administered last rites.

Thankfully, the fine medical care available in Costa Rica shone that week, and the racer fully recovered. But ask any cyclist who has ridden La Ruta and they will confirm that Day One is just that put-you-in-a-fucking-coma hard.

And that's why Román Urbina is so careful about the check-in of racers each evening and morning of the race.

Endurance athletes often experience these day-of-days phenomena, the sense that you have been through an entire lifetime in a day. As Gordon Wadsworth found additional remnants of Carara mud in the fold of an ear or staining his nail beds on the way to breakfast on Day Two, he entered the hotel restaurant to a room full of racers who had clearly been through a lifetime's worth of experiences in one day. Ripped muscular legs, overused forearms, and jacked-up trapezius muscles peeked out beneath racers' kits. Digging into a plate piled with food so mouthwatering he couldn't stop smiling, he caught the eyes of racer after racer who offered him silent nods. They knew what they had been through to finish Day One—to hell and back, multiple times—*and they had gears*. A silent nod to the American with sideshow legs required no translation. Besides, there was no time for chatting. They filled their plates again, eating now for the harrowing later. And the funny thing about the Ticos and Ticas of La Ruta (and the majority of the international cyclists, too), no one spoke of the tribulations they had been through the day before. Gordon Wadsworth was a walking reminder: there is no sniveling at La Ruta. The more than 29,000 feet of climbing in three days with one lousy gear endured by the perpetually peppy Gordon shifted the metrics of suffering on a bike. And as in life, this shift in perspective muffled the fatigue and outright pain of the day Armstrong called harder than anything else by a factor of five or ten. As in life, someone else's unforgiving one-gear crucible is a helpful reminder: there is always someone having a worse day than you.

As for the sensation of experiencing a whole lifetime in a day, Gordon didn't know it during that breakfast of nods from his fellow conquistadors, but that curious compression of time awaited him on Day Two, a stage that would enervate every muscle fiber of the cyclist and the man. Years later, when asked about his toughest day ever on a bike, he would recall this day.

La Ruta derives its frightful grades of sickening climbs and hairball descents from volcanoes that tell the land's Genesis story. More than one traveler to the country has professed that on the eighth day, God built himself a playground, a place so beautiful and bountiful it was surely an annex of Eden. Peaks so regal, only the divine could be responsible for the design. The sea so inviting, only Heaven stood a chance to match it. And soil so rich, the earth bore the apotheosis of plant life, exploding in every kind of the specialty microclimates. This, in turn, supported fish and fauna, twelve climatic zones of creatures.

Like elegant ocelots (*manigordos* found in cloud forests), two species of comical sloths (*osos perezosos*—"lazy bears"— the national animal found along the coasts), five-foot-long Leatherback sea turtles (*tortuga laúd*, found on the Pacific and Caribbean coasts), basilisk lizards (the "Jesus Christ lizard" or *lagarto Jesucristo*—which "runs" on water), Crayola-colored scarlet macaws (*lapas*, found along the Pacific coast), and black-furred jaguars, with silky coats so dark their jaguar spots are barely visible in the rainforest. The people of this land, stewards of its biodiversity, in this playground of the divine, are protectors. And they have taken their role seriously, carving out thirty-two national parks, fifty-one wildlife refuges, thirteen forest reserves, and eight biological reserves for the creatures and plant-life of this natural Elysium.

On Day One of La Ruta, racers can confirm they are ten degrees from the equator—where valley temperatures average around 105°F (41°C). But Day Two usually served up thermal shock; a treacherous and hypothermic journey up and over one of Costa Rica's two highest volcanoes, that year somewhere in the territory of 100 kilometers (62 miles). The route has changed between

Volcan Irazú and Volcan Turrialba throughout the years, due to the genuine matter of actual volcanic eruptions. If climbing the 11,000-foot Turrialba or the 11,260-foot Irazú doesn't kill you, there is always the possibility some hot ash, toxic gas, and lava might. Mercy lava, the battered and bedraggled cyclists might call it.

Ask a La Ruta veteran: the brutal, relentless climbing of volcanoes in Day Two leave you plenty of time to consider the many ways you can meet your mortal end. Lava and deadly ash seem as good as any.

"Barring any sort of competition or mechanical or the need to support another rider, that was probably the toughest solo day ever," said Gordon about Day Two 2015. This coming from a guy who since that day has raced five days across Tanzania (Kilimanjaro 2 Natron Stage Race), the UNBOUND Gravel race in Kansas, six days in New Zealand (The Pioneer MTB Race), seven days in Brasil Ride, and the hardest trails of Virginia, the Carolinas, Georgia, and the entirety of BRAAAP-alachia.[10]

The black crushed lava rock and the last-minute course changes of 2015 created a once-in-a-lifetime ride, a detour harder than the original stage. There is no elevation profile graph for 2015's last-minute "day of days" course. "It was something like 16,000 feet (4,877 meters) of vert in 60 miles (97 kilometers). And just relentless," said Gordon. Just as he never strays from humility, he doesn't speak in hyperbole. He tends toward funny, low-country expressions and self-deprecation. Quick with warm words for others ("You are whistling fit!"), his conviviality

---

10 Braap is the MTB term for the sound of knobby tires on the trail and the noise made by dirt bikes; it's evolved to mean riding cleanly and aggressively through corners or through obstacles with flow. Braap suggests rad badassery.

in the saddle partnered with technical riding expertise, and his mechanical bike wrench know-how create a contrapuntal whole.

The hardest aspects of the day for Gordon Wadsworth— besides the chunky descents and sicko climbs and the wear and tear of Day One—was the cruel solitary toil. There is a phenomenon known across disciplines of endurance sports that can be described as "teammates for a day," or "battle buddies," or "foxhole family." It is that unscripted happenstance when you coincidentally share the same pace or cadence with a total stranger—like Ale or Gabby. Sometimes it is quiet, while you work together. Sometimes it's like a middle-school slumber party with too much caffeine, unlimited gummy bears, and the possibility of duet karaoke singing. Strangely, random sing-alongs by untrained vocalists are surprisingly common in endurance events. Perhaps this is because singing off-key is wholly easier on the ears—and less mortifying— than hearing your own strained, gasping breath at elevation.

In the course of La Ruta, Gordon fought to the edge of his endurance on Day Two through the gauntlet of social deprivation. Isolation is one of endurance players' worst enemies. What he lacks in gears, he tends to make up for in connection between "teammates for a day" and communion with Good Samaritans. It's also clear that Gordon likes people as much as he likes riding bikes. But it's one step further. Gordon doesn't mind exposing his vulnerability. At the heart of it is truthfulness. Which is something the wider sport—writ large, but mostly due to the former pro roadies—struggles with.[11] Being open to help, and

---

11 The previous eras of deceit and bold-faced lies in cycling (often without contrition) have kneecapped the infrastructure, and thus, the support of male and female Quadsworth-quality cyclists in American cycling. Amidst the scandals and boorish behavior, non-cycling corporations ditched cycling faster than a wet sandwich in a

transparent in the need for it, by looking for good company and soliciting this kind of neutral aid does not constitute weakness; it exudes positivity and a constant upward spiral of amiability. Not only do hard-core riders help other hard-core riders pass unforgivable stretches of time, but local hard-core riders—due to the cycling's transitive property—make for increased interaction with more volunteers, more race support, and more team support cars. If you ride with locals, you score intel, hydration, calories, and friendly faces in official or unofficial, neutral or not, vehicles. Which is key for a guy more than 2,000 miles from home and with only three jersey pockets across his lower back. Riding a single-speed bike without a hydration pack is the consummately pure ride. Gordon makes it look so effortless, so lightsome, it's easy to forget it must be knee-knocking scary at times.

Cyclists who know him say it's a party wherever Gordon Wadsworth is, and inevitably a bike race breaks out. The local people who met him through local racers (and marveled at his one-gear wizardry on Day One) were happy to pass him orange slices, a gel (a one-to-two ounce carbohydrate-rich energy aid), a sandwich. But on Day Two, Gordon spent more of the day alone and with fewer hand-ups. With insufficient calories and too few people and only a single gear on a re-routed climbing course, Day Two was a test of his seemingly perpetual jocundity.

---

musette bag. The downstream effects of arrogant lying and bullying shows up today in the dearth of small, local bike events, the disappearance of events on the American pro road calendar, a shortage of organized youth cycling, scarce junior/teen development, and a sad shortage of college teams. The harm of the deceit and doping are incalculable, on accounting ledgers and beyond. Thank goodness for the fresh slate associated with clean athletes and clean teams and the next generation of school-aged riders—which is the only way to reverse the tide of the perception of cycling as dirty kryptonite in the minds of corporate sponsors.

Three encounters on Day Two were material. The first, near a summit, riding over granular lava rock—like gunmetal-colored Grape-Nuts cereal—a local man standing alone, likely a farmer, offered Gordon a small clear baggie. He was surprised by the contents. It was honey, produced by diligent bees over a season, extracted by a modest apiarist. This liquid gold was perfectly strained and then gifted anonymously by a stranger. The trickle of drubbed cyclists grinding up the trail barely moved faster than *osos perezosos* in tights. Gordon describes the translucent nectar and that Good Samaritan alongside the slow-motion parade in the same earnest breath: "Boy, what a lifesaver."

On another remote section of wacko climbing, he recalls the roaring laughter he received when he asked the race support on a motorbike if the man happened to have a beer. Endurance racing is full of such "joking-not joking" banter. The surprise at the question and the surprise at the response doubled the laughter as the man produced a beer from his bag, and Gordon Wadsworth easily drank the electrolyte-rich *Imperial* up that dang hill. The laughter was as valuable as the calories. He was riding with a small 34X21 gear, but the grade that day hit 30% at times. Consuming one beer mid-ride was hardly the problem.

While Gordon is not much of a drinker—and he's never taken hard drugs or performance-enhancing drugs, and, yes, he has had to take his fair share of drug tests—in the early editions of European road races like the Tour de France, cyclists consumed beer *before, during,* and *after* the race. Sepia-colored photos from Le Tour's early days show greyhound-looking racers bellied-up at taverns and raiding cafés mid-ride for beer, wine, or champagne. Compared to the hydration offered from unsanitized wells in villages, a lager, an ale, or some wine was actually a safer bottle hand-up than the water at the time. But, like distilled water, everything in moderation.

The third instance of the kindness of strangers on Day Two occurred when the native Virginian emerged from a pine forest on the far side of the mountain range, and there stood a man offering a kind of sugar-cane juice Gordon Wadsworth had never seen before. Called *agua dulce*, this is the traditional farm worker's drink of Costa Rica. Easy to make and affordable, given the bountiful sugar-cane crops there, the drink is nothing more than boiled cane juice and water. It's the original energy drink or nature's noncarbonated soda. Gordon had never experienced the mighty boost of *agua dulce*. "That got me home!" he said, again not distinguishing the calories from the gift. A blood sugar boost from a thoughtful gift of a compassionate working man. The taste sensation was indiscernible from the overall Costa Rican spirit of amity in sport, benevolence toward those in trouble, and cordiality toward a stranger. When in the throes of endurance racing, these things are not distinct, the way the volcano summit is clearly distinguishable from the valley floor. The uplift from a few milligrams of salt sprinkled on a watermelon slice, or a perfectly ripe banana held out a car window from a bounced-around passenger, or school children in uniforms holding out a garden hose to passing cyclists—the goods and the goodness are inexorably intertwined.

Wadsworth finished Day Two turned inside out, but able to see the vague light at the end of the tunnel. His speed on the Day Two descents—when the climbing finally stopped, and the trail turned, eventually, to asphalt—his speed topped over 50 mph on his trip computer. He describes getting through the solitary hours as surrendering to the process and keeping steady on the throttle. Fifty miles per hour on unfamiliar terrain qualifies as a decent throttle on a mountain bike. He's too modest to say more. Román Urbina describes the impression Gordon Wadsworth had made on the tough Ticos and Ticas in climbing and descending: the guy is a legend, Román repeats, every time he is asked.

That afternoon the lost racer from Colorado was found in Carara National Park when he worked his way to a double-track trail. The relief was a massive lift for everyone associated with the event. He was in hospital being treated for dehydration and every kind of scrape and scratch, but he was in damn decent shape for a shoeless, near-drowned, broken-ribbed survivor of a night with the venomous pit viper snakes and poison dart frogs of Carara's jungle. Best of all, he was a good sport about it. Racing bikes is overwhelmingly more fun for the peloton when all the competitors are accounted for—and none of them is croc scat.

Day Three began with a merciful alarm. Gordon was able to sleep in until 4 a.m. and soon in the predawn was eating *gallo pinto*, one of his avowed new favorite things. His bags were packed and ready to go at 5 a.m. after devouring the bottomless cups of café and treating himself to a *pan dulce* here and there. Sure, food tastes better when you are that kind of ravenous, but also the food provided the most rudimentary critical needs of the aching and the exhausted—comfort and nourishment.

Day Three in 2015 began with the option to whitewater raft down the Pacuare River, eighteen miles of unspoiled class-three and class-four rapids, under waterfalls, bathed in warm sun and refreshing water. The rainforest on both sides of the river is first generation. Untouched. And some of the eight different groups of Indigenous people of Costa Rica live elusively within the rainforest there. Before bike racers crossed the country in three days, there were Spanish conquistadors in the sixteenth century who took twenty years to get from one coast to the other. But before the Spanish, there were distinct Indigenous tribes in this place, some who have lived on the land for at least ten thousand years. Before that, it took about fifty million years of eastern tectonic movement by the Caribbean Plate, subducting the Cocos Plate, to create an archipelago. It took an epoch for volcanic lava flow to eventually connect the islands, creating a solid mass of land bridge between North and South America. Time is relative. Even the longest hours of long-distance riding are less than the blink of an eye when compared to the pre-Columbian history of the Costa Rican isthmus. Riding a bike across an entire country. Rafting down a river in the actual wild. Working a lifetime as an oil painter. Nineteenth-century French Romantic painter Eugène Delacroix said, "We work not only to produce but to give value to time."

The bike racing on Day Three La Ruta—in astronomical time and La Ruta time—is a blink of an eye. Thirty-five or so flat, fast, and banana-plantation-hot miles from Siquirres to Playa Bonita in Limón. The massive handicap of gears on Days One and Two for Gordon shrinks during the flat, dusty Day Three hammerfest. But the all-out, redline flying at the front of the race used to be interrupted by a series of bridge crossings in the final push to the Caribbean coast. Though not your typical bridge crossings.

Racers had to disembark their bikes and, wearing funny shoes with slippery clips (of the "*cero clips*" variety), they had to cross spans that were too high, too wobbly, too long, and too exposed between steps for the average person. The bridges were not meant for cars, or bikes, or pedestrians in funny shoes. The bridges were only meant for the railroad. And yes, in the stretches of *sectores activos*, there is train traffic.

The first time Gordon Wadsworth got mid-way across his first railroad bridge, he was overcome by a totally sane reaction of wide-eyed shock verging on panic. The long steps between the chunky, unevenly spaced dilapidated ties allowed cyclists to see through to the murky river gorges below. The rickety trestles were wet under Gordon's feet, which were only inching along. He had to flat out ignore the sections of missing and rotted ties where the fall to the water below would have likely killed a man.

Rhythm is one of the keys to riding a single-speed bike on courses that most people are hike-a-biking (walking one's bike due to a steep grade or an uneven trail too hazardous or too challenging to ride). Gordon will do anything not to scrub speed. He leans or steers where other cyclists touch their brake levers.[12] He bunny hops obstacles and tucks on descents—anything to keep his bike moving forward, maintaining his speed. Despite the sickening height of the sketchy bridges of Day Three, Gordon pushed past the agonizing minutes of each span and just kept the rhythm of the local racer directly in front of him. Right foot. Left foot. Right foot, left foot. Right, left. Like the cadence of making ovals around

---

12 Watching Gordon ride a bike is to observe "flow state," that beautifully focused, seemingless effortless concentration and ease of being and doing. Flow state in endurance sports looks energized and ready for challenges, and is reached more and more frequently by athletes as skill levels continue to rise.

the cranks of the bike, Gordon just kept moving. There remains no way around unforgiving hours; one must go through them.

Seeing Costa Ricans celebrating the finish of the single speedster as he approached the soft white sand of Playa Bonita made Gordon's three-day odyssey worth it. He finished top ten that day amongst the pros...and the thirteenth racer *overall* for the three days.

With the one-of-a-kind detoured route, Wadsworth's 2015 finish was an end like no other for a race like no other by a single-speed athlete like none other. No racer received more cheers from the Ticos than Wadsworth—from both the crowd and, especially, his fellow riders. It says something about an athlete that his loudest cheerleaders are his closest competitors.

You just can't root against Wadsworth. It's like rooting against sunshine.

Gordon Wadsworth representing single-speed courage and fitness, coast-to-coast in Costa Rica in 2015 with his usual permagrin. *(photo courtesy of* The Tico Times*)*

CHAPTER FOUR

SWIM LIKE A GIRL

Lynne Cox

There are only about 13 days a year on which you stand a reasonable chance of getting across (the English Channel), due to the weaker tide; these occur at the end of each fortnight in July, August and September. Find a pilot—the chap who will watch and record you from Dover to France—and establish when he will take you and at what cost. You'll be looking at something like £1,250.

Grease, a blend of lanolin and Vaseline, is not compulsory but it helps to keep the cold out... for the first 30 minutes. And if you have a good layer of this on when you go through shoals of jellyfish, you won't be stung too badly. Cold is a major factor so start your open-water training early to acclimatize yourself. Eat what you like best and what likes you best while crossing, but don't eat it all in the first few hours, you'll just feel ill. You can have food thrown to you in a polythene bag, and tread water while you eat. You need a cast-iron stomach, because you will take regular mouthfuls of sea water, and this, combined with the diesel fumes from the boat and what you've eaten, has a dramatic effect on your gut. You will feel sick, and the pilot may lean over the boat and say, "Are you feeling all right?" and the answer is, "Of course not!" But when they say, "Do you want to get out?" the answer is, "No I don't." It will take you between 10 and 16 hours to cross. And remember, nothing great is easy.

—*Michael Read MBE, Channel swimmer*
The Independent, *February 6, 1999*

LYNNE COX WAS IN JUNIOR HIGH WHEN SHE ASKED HER PARENTS if she could attempt the most notable endurance swim in the world. When that opportunity arrived, less than ten months later, Lynne packed one suitcase for an open-ended trip. The Kodachrome colors of 1970s Southern California blurred by the Cox family's green Buick headed north from their home in Long Beach, California, to Los Angeles International Airport that June morning. In the front seat, Lynne's mother, Estelle, accompanied Lynne on the trip. The driver of the station wagon, father Albert, remained in California with Lynne's older brother, David, seventeen, and two younger sisters, Laura, thirteen, and Ruth, age ten. They were the kind of family in which siblings were eager to accompany each other on an exciting ride to the airport. And it was a time—1972—when such families could walk their two passengers all the way to the gate and jetway, all hugs and cheering. The itinerary had required Lynne to acquire her first passport. Testament to the exceptionality of the moment, Estelle's pocketbook held her first passport, too. Her daughter would envision, orchestrate, grow, and execute all the central elements of this trip, but both travelers would need to be patient, as the voyage would reveal itself slowly. Though sometimes not slowly at all.

Lynne arrived in England via the four-engine propulsion of the recently introduced jumbo jet. But she was intent on visiting France for the first time during this trip, too. No passport necessary. She was intent on arriving there by dint of her own latent fifteen-year-old power.

And it was not just the successful crossing of the English Channel that had captured swimmer Lynne's imagination and fueled her training determination. The girl with the focused eyes and dear smile had traveled to England to break the world record. She had just finished ninth grade.

The shortest distance between England and who-needs-a-passport? France is 20-to-21-ish miles, as the herring gull flies. The British Isles most closely approach continental Europe in the eastern bits of county Kent. Roughly 1,368 square miles of largely green space, some call the county "the garden of England." But it is Kent's 350 miles of coastline that has brought it the world's attention. Take, for instance, the first Roman invasion of England: Julius Caesar himself landed at Kent. Not once, but twice. In 55

BC, he brought two legions and five hundred cavalry; the second time, a year later, he arrived with five legions and two thousand cavalry in eight hundred ships. And the first major battle of the successful Roman invasion of the island in AD 43 took place in Kent, at the Battle of the Medway. Since that Iron Age conquest of England and Wales—Romans 1, Britons 0—the ports and military dockyard of Kent have been some of England's most important.

Following arrival at Heathrow, mother and daughter boarded a train from Victoria Station to Dover Priory, 68 miles and yet another world away. "I think my mother was a little nervous, but she tried not to show it. She was always positive that we would find our way, and that things would work out," Lynne said about the Maine native with the matte red lipstick and sleeves-rolled-up attitude befitting a Roman garrison.

Lynne had been advised to stay in Folkestone, Dover's neighboring town, by a former Channel swimmer, Dr. Fahmy Attallah, sixty-three. A gracious advisor to Lynne as fellow residents of Long Beach, Dr. Attallah had a mighty catalog of Channel knowledge because he had been denied a finish, time and again. In one swim attempt, his crew boat became lost. Once, he was forced from the water due to thunderstorms. Another time, he rolled onto his back for a pause and a member of his crew mistook his motion for swimmer distress. Reaching into the water, the observer grabbed the Egyptian champion, instantly disqualifying him. Dr. Attallah was denied the Channel seven times. Lynne knew the considerable number of gifted people in this Did Not Finish club. But for many there appears to be no cure for Channel fever. Folkestone, her advisor said, would give her respite from the Channel frenzy that could descend on this part of Kent in the summer. For example, the summer before, the Channel Swimming Association (the CSA, established in 1927; official governing body of Channel swims) registered ninety-four crossing attempts and eight successful swims.

Lynne's first assignment after arriving on June 25 was calling from a list of names provided by the CSA. Using the hotel's phone, she tried the first name on the list, but there was no answer. She set the rotary dial to a new task with the next name on the alphabetical list. Reg Brickell, Sr., happened to pick up the receiver, just home from the Channel where he had been fishing. Home from his full-time job, like his father before him.

The poised schoolgirl introduced herself in one steady breath, "Mr. Brickell, my name is Lynne Cox. I got your number from the Channel Swimming Association. I want to swim the English Channel, and I am hoping that you will be my pilot for the swim."

She answered Brickell's initial questions, explaining that she had swum between Catalina Island and Long Beach the year before. It was 21 miles as the Western gull flies, but due to currents, she had swum 27 miles (43 kilometers). She swam it as a part of a team, she explained, only going as fast as the slowest of her teammates. She assured Brickell she could have completed the Catalina Channel much faster than her posted 12 hour and 36-minute finish time. Lynne had her eye on the English Channel record. Not the women's record; *the overall record*. She explained that her pool coach of three years and recent open-water coach was Don Gambril. Brickell asked if Gambril had made the journey to England with Lynne? No, sir, he's one of the US Olympic Team coaches, and he's preparing for the Games in August in Munich, was her reply. "My mother came with me to help me on the swim," she said confidently. Sometimes, crew can be an ace up an athlete's sleeve.

Brickell must have liked Lynne's straightforward and comprehensive answers to his questions, as he invited Lynne and Estelle over for tea at his home on Folkestone Harbour that afternoon. There, he interviewed Lynne at length, probing for experience and motivation, and taking note of the healthy parent-child dynamic between the two Americans in his sitting room. Captains had been approached by all types of swimming sorts and unusual personalities since the merchant marine captain Matthew Webb's first successful crossing from Dover in 1875. Swimmers younger than Lynne had completed an English Channel swim before—like Leonore Modell, fourteen, in September 1964 (France to England, 15:27) and Jon Erikson, fourteen, in August 1969 (France to England, 11:22). These waters—like U-17 (under-17) tennis training camps, junior golf tournaments, elite ice-skating rinks, and gymnastics sidelines— had seen pushy parents before. The glaring difference between kids' land sports and the Channel involved water in the mid-to- upper 50s°F (10s°C). In water below 60°F (15.5°C), exhaustion or unconsciousness can befall a healthy adult in one to two hours. In water under 60°F (15.5°C), experts warn that due to hypothermia, an adult human body has an expected time of survival between one and six hours. Brickell was wise to proceed cautiously with the sunny Californian: the churlish currents combined with the cold water of the Channel were no child's play.

As luck would have it, Lynne had blindly happened onto the most talented EC boat captain of the era, and Brickell would be eventually inducted into the International Marathon Swimming Hall of Fame for his excellence as an escort pilot. Time would prove that the captain and swimmer were equals in both will and skill. But in the last week of June 1972, perhaps the matter of most significance was that captain and swimmer knew instant rapport. Their organized minds synchronized from the word go. More than just fond of each other immediately, captain and swimmer radiated on the same wavelength; the way world-class crew mates do.

Next, Lynne needed to secure an observer. Brickell recommended Mickey Morford, who, in keeping with the British hospitality theme, invited Lynne and Estelle to his home in Folkestone the following day. The Association official was charmed by the young American, and he charmed the mother-daughter team in equal measure. With a big hug upon the end of their visit, Morford said, "I'm sure you're going to do this, love. From the moment I saw you, I knew; you are strong and able to break the record." Morford was on board. Swimmer, captain, and observer had their eyes fixed on Cap Gris-Nez, with Lynne's average speed of two and a half miles an hour as their silent battle cry. They were going for the record.

But first, they needed to wait. Waiting for a decent tide and a window of reasonable weather can be a fool's errand for a swimmer in those seas. At the very least, Lynne had a fortnight of unforgiving time to pass; the first possible tides were two weeks away.

To keep the fitness she had fought for in the run-up to her trip to Great Britain, Lynne trained every day as she waited for the green light from Brickell. Back in California, to prepare for her attempt, Lynne had regularly swum parallel to Long Beach, Estelle walking the beach with her. Estelle had driven Lynne to midnight swims with her Catalina Channel teammates, kids in the inky sea, petite five-foot-three Estelle on the pier with a thermos of coffee for the darkest hours of the night. Estelle drove Lynne from Los Alamitos down the Pacific Coast Highway where she could swim outside the breakwater at spots like Seal Beach and further south at Huntington Beach, or swim *from* one to the other, for a nine-mile (fourteen-kilometer) training route.

Estelle, an artist, grew up in Waterville, Maine, where she learned *how to* swim, but she wasn't marathon-swimming serious about the sport like her dedicated daughter. And dedicated was an understatement. Lynne had a traditional swim team fitness base, borne of years in chlorine, perfecting her technique and creating staggering strength in her young body. But sometimes pool swimming plays favorites, rewarding arm span, feet size, or fast twitch-muscle composition rather unfairly. Open water minimized those advantages, celebrating mental strength and physical grit. Lynne's mental and physical open-water gifts allowed her to duel cruel white caps and churning chop, and to power through currents unsafe for most people. A faint figure at pool swim meets, *the kid could move salt water*. Her powerful stroke made it look like an unfair fight.

Standing on the rounded rocks and pebbles seaside at Dover Harbor, Lynne's bright face and soft pixie voice belied the fighter within. The water hosted a rotation of swimmers in the summer months—locals and foreigners, first timers and veterans, male and female, the fresh faced and the sage—in the safety of the harbor, protected by the cliffs above. The famous Cliffs of Dover were brighter, higher, and more magnificent than Lynne had expected. Unknown to most of the swimmers standing in the water about waist-high—congregating the way open-water swimmers do— the place held secrets.

The wall of white of the Dover cliffs gained its shocking color from chalk composition from fossils formed on the ocean floor some seventy to ninety million years before. In the chalk of the cliffs rest all kinds of matter, from the micro to the mighty. When the British Isles were still submerged under water, some seventy million years ago, scientists can confirm that the remains of microscopic single-celled algae fell to the sea floor like planktonic detritus. When fossilized over the millennia, the microorganisms turned into soft sedimentary carbonate rock. In non-science terms, the Earth's crust then raised the former seabed overhead, like a weight-room military press at a tectonic gym. Called "marine snow," this layer of dead plankton and algae compressed into solid—but porous—rock that now stands roughly 350 feet (106 meters) *above* the water's edge.

The concealed macro matters hidden in the cliffs north of the harbor are tunnels, deep and dark, and five large chambers dug into the porous rock. Unbeknownst to Lynne and the other swimmers, above them to the north of Dover Castle (and her tunnels), rested two fifteen- to twenty-square-foot spaces carved into the chalk and filled with concrete, forming a large just-past-vertical bowl. With amplifiers and the rudimentary acoustic equipment of the First World War, the sound mirrors were the beginning phase of the first early warning system in the world. The sound mirrors could hear enemy aircraft incoming at a modest distance, providing a helpful ten to twelve minutes of warning for the English military in Kent, from 1915 until the introduction of radar in 1935.

In 1940, amid the fighting of the Second World War, Winston Churchill toured the critical Dover shoreline, where, on a clear day, Churchill could see France with his own eyes. A student of history, the prime minister knew of Caesar's and Emperor Claudius's successful invasions on those beaches in 55 BC and AD 43, respectively. British, Belgian, and French troops were in full retreat across the Channel. He was reeling from the drubbing the British endured in battles around Calais and Dunkirk. The majority of western Europe had fallen without much resistance in a matter of weeks in the spring. Since taking office on May 10, he had seen the near total collapse of western Europe. By June 1940, Churchill knew the Cliffs of Dover were the first line of defense against the encroaching enemy. The Wehrmacht, which had rolled over France, was just twenty-ish miles away.

Churchill sent for the British Army's Royal Engineers from the 172nd Tunnelling Company—nicknamed "The Moles."

Behind the swimmers and Lynne, in the cliffs to the north of Dover Castle, were a labyrinth of hand-held-tool–built tunnels, connecting gun batteries to rooms, a hospital, a generator, bunk rooms, washrooms, and toilets in a bomb-resistant sanctuary called the Fan Bay Deep Shelter. The six-chamber hidden subterranean defense held roughly 185 men within about 3,500 square feet (325 square meters) at an average depth of about seventy feet (21 meters) below ground. The battery defended the English shore and attacked enemy supply lines—which had been moving freely—in the Channel waters. A caption of a drawing of the space in the archives of the Imperial War Museum in London reads, "Vaulted tunnels reinforced with corrugated iron. Bunkbeds line the corridors and equipment; uniforms and blankets are scattered around. Some officers are resting in their beds." The drawing held in storage in Duxforth near Cambridge depicts a battery that was hidden from the public. The shelter was rediscovered in 2012, restored, and opened to the public in the non-winter months for the first time on July 20, 2015. The hard-hat-headlamp tour testifies to the unseen work of servicemen and women in Dover who successfully shut down enemy shipping in the Channel during the rest of the war and defended England from their imperialistic enemies in Nazi-occupied France.

Days of swim training below the Cliffs became weeks, as Lynne waited for her turn to take a crack at the crossing. She and her mother would take the bus from Folkestone to Dover, where swimmers dotted the harbor. She met other hopeful swimmers: the Australian Des Renford,[13] a Kiwi named Sandy Blewett, several English swimmers, a team from Egypt, and four fellow Americans—Stella Taylor, Tom Hetzel, and brothers Dick and Bill

---

13 The exceptional Des Renford had nineteen successful Channel swims in nineteen attempts between 1970 and 1980. While his photograph graces the small English Channel swimming section of the Dover Museum, a homegrown memorial to him can be found near the picture window of the iconic pub, The White Horse. Not far from the harbor, on St. James Street, the walls of Dover's oldest pub are covered in the handwritten names of swimmers who have swum the channel—noting the date, time elapsed, country, and any special notes. Next to an inscription for Des, his son, Michael "Murph" Renford's 01/08/07 swim of 12 hours and 10 minutes is memorialized. A third generation Renford, Christian, swam the distance in 12 hours, 7 minutes on 08/28/24. Any trip to Kent should include a visit to The White Horse to read the thousands of inscriptions and inspirational messages. In a building that dates to 1365, the food, drink, and amiability of this informal hub of endurance swimming is unmatched.

Crowell. As happens in the swimming holes, the beaches and the dipping ponds of England—and around the world—the swimmers shared an intense and exuberant camaraderie. Relieved of life on land with its meddlesome jobs and chores, the swimmers felt the rush of event adrenalin and the glow of inarguably charmed long summer days.

Once bitten by the cold-water bug, swimmers—marathon swimmers especially—are easily addicted. Some cannot stop obsessing about the natural world below the water's surface. A place of sea stars and hilariously sideways shuffling crabs and seals who like to playfully boop a swimmer's feet—in a clear gesture of "Tag! You're it!" Some swimmers become obsessed with the cold water for what it does to their body. A large percentage of cold-water swimmers—since time immemorial—have sworn by cold-water immersion as a physical reset. Cold water creates a stress response in humans, releasing adrenalin, noradrenalin (also called norepinephrine), and cortisol into the body. This batch of stimulating hormones heightens awareness, raises one's heart rate, and increases blood sugar. Scientists surmise that when adrenalin and noradrenalin are secreted in this stress response, feel-good endorphins are released as neurotransmitters. And cortisol, in a secondary effect, kindly reduces inflammation in arthritic joints, areas around compressed nerves, and even parts of the brain. The synaptic vesicles of a cold-water swimmer take in a sublime cocktail of dopamine and serotonin. But it's not the athlete's typical endorphin high reported on land. Cold water has a multiplier effect on satisfied athletes, leaving them with

And Sarah Thomas's four-way swim of 54 hours and 10 minutes September 15–17, 2019 is in a special spot on the ceiling behind the bar. Her inscription is the only time "E -> F->E -> F -> E" has been written in The White Horse.

the feel-good buzz of top-shelf liquor. Cold-water immersion also clears the sinus, invigorates the mind, and turns one's skin aglow. Some doctors believe it supercharges the immune system. Anecdotally, many swimmers describe cold water—not pool water or warm open water—as a magic elixir for mood and mental health wellness.

Many say that open water swim gathering—in-real-life community—is its own reward. Beyond being accepted exactly as they are, mostly undressed, the swimmers gathering as a group was significant because, like runners and cyclists, swimmers can go farther, faster, in a pack. Also, while together, if hypothermia strikes one podmate, other swimmers will see the change in that swimmer's form and stroke count per minute. This is meaningful because sneaky hypothermia tricks swimmers into thinking they are fine, even when the whole world can glaringly see they are not. In other words, training in open water with a pod is a first line of defense from the cold for a swimmer—like the Fan Bay Deep Shelter hidden in the Cliffs of Dover.

Gathering in Dover Harbor daily, the summer of '72 swim club found strength in numbers. They reconnoitered for weeks, in the manner of the British Army's Special Air Service. Steeled by other exceptional swimmers, the daily communion was a lift. Paradoxically, the convivial assembly was the opposite of what lay ahead: the companionless unforgiving hours at the cold core of an English Channel crossing.

Lynne reported to her father in California by telephone that the water temperature was about 58°F (14°C) in the harbor. It was there that she first met her fellow fifteen-year-old swimmer, Dick Crowell. He said, "I don't remember who made the first contact, but I do remember from the very beginning Lynne being incredibly warm, generous, and outgoing. Acclimating to the English Channel and waiting for the right tides, we swam there together for a few hours twice a day—morning and afternoon— and became friends fast, as did my parents and Estelle."

While the English Channel hopefuls swam, the Crowells asked Estelle to join them at their hotel overlooking the harbor. Following their swims, the kids would join the adults. Lynne adored the hot tea, delicious English cheeses and crackers and digestive biscuits—and the warm hospitality of the Crowell family. They knew their way around Dover and English Channel crossing protocol because the previous summer Dick had swum 36 miles (74 kilometers) in 18 hours—before the Cap Gris-Nez currents cruelly pushed him back toward England, denying him landfall. Dick and his parents proclaimed that Lynne had the very best boat captain available in Reg Brickell, Senior. Lynne recalls the Crowells offering Estelle her first glass of sherry. On the tasteful second floor crescent-shaped corner balcony of the nineteenth-century White Cliffs Hotel[14] above the harbor, Estelle accepted, raising her glass. It would be a summer of firsts.

---

14 The stylish hotel retains its charm, and the Crowells' splendid corner room facing Swimmer's Beach remains perfectly perched facing the harbor; it is now called Best Western Premier Dover Marina Hotel and Spa. As for Captain Matthew Webb's first crossing of the English Channel completed on August 25, 1875, it began not from Swimmer's Beach, but from Admiralty Pier to the south of the beach. Lynne's swim began south of Admiralty Pier at pebbled Shakespeare Beach. Of note, the various piers, docks, breakwaters, and lighthouses surrounding the harbor over the years were constructed because this water could be so treacherous for mariners, fishermen, and the seafaring.

Twenty-four days after arriving in England, Lynne's observer, Mickey Morford, came rushing into her hotel on Wednesday, July 19, announcing they finally had a window. If Lynne could get to the beach by 11 p.m. that night, the conditions were favorable. Her swim would begin at midnight.

Lynne prepared her bag and food for the boat: she was responsible for beverages and meals for her mother, Morford, her captain Brickell Senior, and his deckhand Reg Brickell Junior. Also, Lynne and Estelle filled separate thermoses with hot water and warm apple juice prepared in the hotel's kitchen; this was while the rest of Kent was preparing to go to sleep for the night.

Lynne and Estelle followed Morford's direction to take a taxi from the hotel in Folkestone to Shakespeare Beach in Dover where captain, deckhand, and observer would meet mother and daughter. The gentlemen on the launch had the task of transferring wet-to-her-calves, never-a-snivel Estelle into a rowboat set for the 45-foot *Helen Anne Marie 137*. By 10:30 p.m., itching to go, Lynne and Estelle caught a classic black English taxicab to the beach named for The Bard. Shakespeare was known to have visited that very stretch of harbor and the cliffs above. The playwright even referenced the spot in *King Lear*, setting one of the play's scenes on the dramatic cliffs.

In the motif of the tragic, Estelle asked the cab driver to drop them off at Shakespeare Beach, and the cabbie's surprise was evident as he asked: Was the youngster in his cab a Channel swimmer?

Lynne recalls the way her mother proudly answered the local man, confirming in her solid Down-East accent her daughter's bona fides and this most imminent undertaking.

But then came his response: "Well, you don't look like a Channel swimmer to me," he said. It proceeded to get worse: "You're too fat to be one," he announced.

Lynne saw polite and reserved Estelle straighten her spine, like a lioness imperceptibly moving between the man and her cub. It wasn't only his driving that was on the left side of the road; there was nothing right about this exchange, minutes before the swim.

Was her mother angry? No, Estelle was the most uncharacteristic type of enraged, Lynne described more than fifty years later.

Never one to lose her poise, Estelle left that black cab with her jaw drawn tight in New England self-restraint. Anyone who knows about women from Maine would have recognized the granite constitution. With the women and their bags clear of the vehicle, before driving away, the cabbie took it upon himself to have the last word, "Well, good luck to you anyway—but you certainly don't look like a Channel swimmer."

Lynne stoically absorbed the blow of a grown man punching below his weight. She did not lose an inch of her composure as she and Estelle started down the steps—at least a hundred she remembers—from the Cliffs to the tan and tawny pebbles of Shakespeare Beach. The residual anger made her even more driven. With purpose, the swimmer doffed her sweats and stood barefoot in her one-piece suit. Others would have broken out in a case of instant goosebumps, but the girl in the English fog pulled herself up to all five feet six inches of her most defiant height. Estelle donned gloves for the application of a layer of rather ghastly lanolin for insulation and chaffing deterrence for her daughter. Neither Cox teammate gave oxygen to the exchange with the cabbie. If only a simple coating of sheep's wool oil could enable a parent to insulate their child from the callous, the cruel, and the cowards of this unseeing world. Like the fox said in one of Lynne's favorite books at the time by Antoine de Saint-Exupéry, "It is only with the heart that one can see rightly. What is essential is invisible to the eye."

Just before midnight, deckhand Reg Junior rowed a small launch toward the beach under the waxing gibbous moon. Morford jumped from the dinghy into the shallow water, greeting the women with unbridled enthusiasm. All the gear, undaunted Estelle, and cheery Morford joined the rowing Reg Junior in the launch headed for the *Helen Anne Marie.*

Lynne stood alone on pebbled Shakespeare Beach, with one swim cap, in her one-piece suit, and with no ear plugs and only her one pair of goggles—English Channel rules allow no neoprene, no booties, no gloves. Lynne took extra care not to smear the lenses of her goggles with the gloppy lanolin that covered her tan skin. Alone, but for the fog.

Others might have been nervous, if not terrified by the darkness in front of her, but Lynne-the-swimmer felt untethered by water, free to unleash the energy of her coiled spring. She was determined to swim faster than had ever been recorded in the Channel. When the timepieces—two wristwatches and one stopwatch—were ready, Morford got the sign to start from the athlete. *Tap*, went the watches. And into the water she went.

The start made newspapers around North America and the U.K. The Associated Press sent out a piece with the dateline July 20, 1972: "DOVER, England (AP)—A pretty teen-age American girl plunged into the fog-enshrouded English Channel today in a bid to set a women's record for the swim from England to France. Blonde, 15-year-old Lynne Cox of Los Alamitos, Ca., set out from Dover in a dense fog but with a calm sea. An hour later, she was reported swimming strongly and making 'good progress.'"

The visual crown jewel of Kent's coast grew smaller and less white as Lynne swam into the fog off the starboard bow of the *Helen Anne Marie*, away from the boat's exhaust fumes. Despite the conditions of the Channel, the swimmer made "good progress" look easy.

The cruel currents that tossed both boat and swimmer around in the wee hours of July 20, 1972, come from the shallow nature of the passage. The Channel was borne of the immense warming at the end of the last ice age. The melt was so significant and of such a colossal scale that the former land bridge between Kent and Cap Gris-Nez flooded. And the flood never subsided. The relatively shallow Channel floor wreaks havoc on the water above, turning into a heavy load saltwater washing machine unit—set on extra cold. The effect means a swimmer can freestyle ten or fifteen or twenty hours to just offshore France, only to land in Belgium. Or to be pushed hard to the south suddenly, past the French coast entirely. Or to be caught up in a current and sent backwards toward England—like the young and valorous Dick Crowell the previous summer—where they will be forced to abandon their swim altogether.

Lynne fought her way toward the continent, pushing a shocking pace toward the cape shaped like a gray nose jutting out into the sea. Her conditioning and engine capacity during the swim can be expressed best by her feed schedule. This term describes the frequency in which she paused to have Estelle toss beverages and food to her in the water. Before the crossing, Lynne and Estelle planned for feeds on the hour.

Quite a few modern marathon swimmers feed, on average, every thirty or forty minutes; treading water while their crew throws a sport water bottle (tied with a rope) filled with a water-based endurance drink mix. Some take bites of recognizable food. Others suck down gel products for athletes (which had not been created during Lynne's first English Channel attempt). On the third Thursday of July '72, as water bottles were not ubiquitous then, Lynne took her feeds when her mother threw her a cleaned-out shampoo bottle. The first bottle thrown contained fresh water to rinse her salty mouth.

One's mouth is an unexpected point of weakness in endurance athletes. For those who cover distances on land, sweet drinks and easy-to-consume carbs like gels, gummy blocks, and bakery-like bars can quickly deaden taste buds and turn teeth fuzzy. This is not a matter of inconvenience or unpleasantness. Deep into long events, it is not uncommon to hear athletes wave off a feeding or skip an aid station food table due to the condition of their mouth. Sometimes in endurance sports, the stomach is able, but the mouth is not willing. In ocean swimming, the stakes are even higher. The tongue can swell, and the sensitive oral tissues and gums can be shredded by salt water. Athletic efforts have been abandoned for far less pain.[15] Lynne stayed on top of her mouth's condition and her fresh-water rinses before the important business of nutrition.

Estelle followed the first bottle toss to Lynne with a cleaned-out shampoo bottle of warm apple juice. The juice agreed with her gut and aided her blood sugar level. The glorious warmth, transferred from an insulated thermos, was a toasty infusion of energy in the darkest part of the night. The obsidian water never relented from pulling every ounce of heat from her body. There were a few bites of oatmeal cookies, too, but none of Lynne's breaks lasted more than thirty seconds. Marathon swimmers will marvel at the statistic: in total, Lynne took four feeds for the entire swim.

Lynne answered every time her captain told her she needed to sprint in her brawl with the heaving sea. To those unfamiliar with the wind-driven waves and belligerent currents of the Channel, the chop of the rough water can be so immense it dwarfs a swimmer. A crossing can look like an unfair and rather cheap fist fight. But in contrast, Lynne passed the taxing hours of the slugfest with the scores of Bach, Tchaikovsky, Vivaldi, Handel, Mozart, and Chopin in her mind—although she didn't care for practicing piano at all. She sang the songs of Simon and Garfunkel, Joan Baez, Judy Collins, and The Beach Boys in her head. To the question, "But how do you pass the hours?"— Robert Frost poems and Saint-Exupéry's *Wind, Sand and Stars* accompanied Lynne Cox across the Channel. And every time she

---

15 In current long-distance events, a modern marvel for the athlete's mouth is the underrated tiny-sized disposable toothbrush that does not require water or a sink. These minibrushes, saturated with mouthwash and toothpaste, defuzz teeth, scrape clean the weariest tongue and gums, and often have the unexpected effect of giving a massive minty "second wind" to the fatigued or drowsy long-distance athlete.

turned her head to the left to take a breath, her mom was there in her peripheral vision.

The girl who had finished the ninth grade the previous month swam no fewer than sixty strokes per minute as she crossed. She cleared the water line of France atop big, barnacle-covered rocks that shredded her numb feet and wobbly legs. But she cleared the water line after 9 hours and 57 minutes. The schoolgirl had broken not the women's record, but the overall world record that had stood for twelve years. A few seconds after becoming vertical on Gallic rocks, a voice rang out from the headland above and behind her that morning: "Vous avez nagée La Manche?"

With nary a hesitation, the honor student—who had elected to take French in junior high school—responded confidently: "Oui, j'ai nagée La Manche"—*Yes, I swam the Channel.*

Without fanfare, Lynne swam back to the boat, where the crew could not believe what they had witnessed. Tears fell to the deck from Mickey Morford's eyes. Estelle, instinctively swaddling her daughter in towels, wrapped her own body around Lynne. Residual worry and an upwelling of relief caused a flood from Estelle's eyes next. Father and son Brickell simply beamed. Lynne, all smiles too, tucked in next to the pilothouse of the *Helen Anne Marie*, where she proceeded to fall fast asleep on the deck. Word traveled to Dover before the fishing boat arrived back to her harbor. Lynne was met on the dock by a throng of newsmen. When a reporter asked about her effort, Lynne said, "I've always wanted to swim the Channel. It's the Mount Everest of swimming." Curiously, the summit of Everest, like the Cliffs of Dover, is also made of limestone, though the gray variety.

Out of earshot of Lynne, observer Morford said to the journalists, "For a girl her age to beat a man's record is almost beyond belief."

On Friday, *The Daily Mirror* in London ran the headline on page two, "Lynne Smashes the Channel Time." *The Evening Post* in Avon, ran the headline, "Lynne Beats Them All." *The Western Daily Press* in Bristol reported on page one that the fifteen-year-old "claimed a new Dover to France swimming record—for men and women—of nine hours 57 minutes."[16]

Lynne graciously made herself available to every news outlet and reporter waiting for the *Helen Anne Marie* on the dock. But the thing she most wanted to do was to call her dad and siblings back home. She was most eager to share the reporters' enthusiasm with her family, to share the adventure of covering the distance, to share the puzzle of tussling with the tides and the currents for nearly ten hours. Her family knew the work that she had put in. Lynne had trained harder than a swimmer eying a finish. It

---

16 Another spunky female swimmer, age nineteen, broke the world record like Lynne, crossing the Channel on August 27, 1926—a record not bested until 1964. The accomplishment by Gertrude "Trudy" Ederle "proved definitely that women were not 'the weaker sex.' It led to a huge upturn in young women learning to swim around the world, and also participating in sport—whether competitively or simply for fun," said Gavin Mortimer, author of *The Great Swim*.

Glenn Stout, author of *Young Woman and the Sea* (the 2009 book adapted into film by Disney), describes how the Channel crossing mattered: "The achievement utterly destroyed the argument that men had been making for centuries—that women were not only incapable of competing as athletes and that they were lesser than men, but that athletics was bad for them."

"Aunt Trudy's" scrapbooks, cared for by her wonderful niece Mary Ederle Ward, catalog the print coverage of the sports hero of the era, a young woman of purpose and positivity like Lynne. Similarly, "Ederle not only swam the English Channel," said Tim Dahlberg, Associated Press sports writer and author of *America's Girl*, "she shattered the record of the men who had done it before her." In a similar fashion, Lynne Cox "smashed the Channel time" in 1972.

was Lynne's family who supported her when she silently set her eyes on the world record. Al and Estelle Cox, hardworking and independent New Englanders-at-heart, did not make their kids subscribe to convergent thinking. Not all crew are supportive parents buttressing kids' dreams, but Estelle Cox proved how supportive parents can be some of the finest crew endurance athletes can find. The finish lines of the hardest endurance events in the world overflow with older parents bursting with pride, often in full waterworks, for their adult children crossing the line. It is not uncommon to see the strong and the victorious fall into the arms of their older parents in that most familiar, child-to-parent way. Some top endurance athletes, however seemingly omnipotent, when turned inside out by fatigue and pain, need their moms and dads, too.

Much to Lynne's surprise, at the end of the celebratory call, her father instructed her to be sure to head to Dover Harbor the next morning. Lynne balked; more swimming? Surely he was joking! Likely significant for her inner focus and drive, Lynne's parents had never once prompted her to swim. Never cajoled. Never enticed Lynne or her siblings with the swim-meet Fun Dip candy bait or swim-team ice cream or pre-practice Pixy Stix bribes of the modern era.

Dr. Albert Cox knew that a recovery swim would be a sound prescription for his daughter's overworked muscles full of lactic acid. He also hoped to keep her moving before and during her long flight home—to avoid a blood clot caused by the combination of exertion from sprinting, dehydration, and the transcontinental aircraft confinement of an economy seat.

Dr. Cox's assignment in the afterglow of that July 20, 1972, swim bears more weight and makes more sense now than then. Like many lessons learned from older mentors or parental figures, such lessons are often most fully appreciated after the chance to thank them has left our shore. Into her adulthood, Lynne cared for her parents with warm filial affection when first her father, and then Estelle became sick. They had given her the strength to stand alone on a beach beneath ancient cliffs in a midnight fog one summer; and thus, she had the strength to make sure they did not feel alone in their twilight years. There were multiple illnesses and ultimately palliative care at home. As an adult, Lynne lived in her childhood Los Alamitos home to help her parents navigate those shoals, those long hours. They had taught her well.

Since Dr. Cox's passing in 2006 and Estelle's passing in 2012, the many verses of the swimmer's exceptional life are followed by the familiar refrain, "How I wish my father and mother were here." Her formative experiences in the Catalina and English Channels imprinted on her a kind of cheerfulness and calm associated with their togetherness. Lynne became valiant in the seas because her parents were there in the background—positive and highly capable. As Dick Crowell said, "Lynne to me has always been the personification of quiet confidence. Always stable and of real substance. Even though Lynne has the mental toughness to accomplish great swims, Lynne also is a wonderfully warm and caring person." Lynne is quick to credit Al and Estelle after such comments.

The summer of '72's usual suspects of Dover Harbor met Lynne the next morning at the beach. The understated and stiff-upper-lipped broke out with raucous cheers for their wunderkind representative. The less-restrained non-Brits practically burst in rowdy joy when she appeared on the shore in her suit.[17] Among the swimmers who lauded their summer teammate and hailed the first successful solo swim of the season was the American Tom Hetzel. Between 1967 and 1977, Hetzel completed eight successful English Channel crossings, and he and Lynne were fast friends, in every sense. Sharp and curious, Hetzel asked the fifteen-year-old about all the elements of her swim, as a way to share in her excitement, as well as to allow her a healthy, warts-and-all debrief between knowing veterans. Lynne had categorized the Channel as the Mount Everest of swimming to outsiders, but she and Hetzel knew that many more people had climbed Everest than had solo'd the Channel. And of those swimmers, none had ever swum it faster than Lynne Cox.

Hetzel asked a litany of questions, and being thorough, Lynne included every detail—including the cab-ride story from Folkestone to Shakespeare Beach—in her recap for Hetzel before her cool-down swim. Of note, Hetzel, thirty-six, was from a working-class neighborhood in Queens, New York, known for its substantial Irish, German, and Italian immigrant populations. He had served in the US Navy and was a New York City cop. No nonsense was his business, and real deal was his middle name.

---

17   A reminder that 1972 was a time without the benefit of location updates and smartphone communication. Swimmers had only newspapers and scarce broadcast journalism to track other swimmers. Modern tracking devices, which use satellite networks to provide GPS tracking of athletes, common today, were still more than twenty-five years away from civilian use.

Live GPS tracking today is thrilling for fans, friends, and family, allowing spectators to follow athletes like the incomparable Chloë McCardel, who has swum the English Channel the most number of times of anyone male or female: forty-four crossings.

By the end of the week Lynne would be back in California while Hetzel waited for fair tides and decent weather to align. It was one month after Lynne's swim that he got the call from Reg Brickell, Senior, for his attempt window. Riding to Shakespeare Beach to meet his boat and pilot, Hetzel was surprised when the cab driver asked him if he knew the American schoolgirl with the new Channel record. Seeing his passenger begin to nod, the cabbie described in detail how he was the last person to see the girl before her great odyssey. His encouragement of her was so timely and well received, the cabbie tacitly suggested he deserved a degree of credit.

Hetzel, knowing how the actual conversation between this specific cab driver and the girl really transpired, revealed his knowledge of the genuine dialogue. In a New York minute, the cabbie's eyes divulged his fallacious account—and his face fell in sheepishness. In the vernacular of a New Yorker born in the Rockaways, Hetzel let the guy have it. It was abhorrent to call a schoolgirl fat, he chided. Only a chuffer would brag about his role in her swim, he rebuked. In the local parlance, the cabbie received a real bollocking from the New York cop for trying to take some credit for the girl's world record.

That day, August 20, Tom Hetzel told off a man for mocking a fellow swimmer, and then swam the English Channel in 13 hours, 45 minutes.

That same day, with Mickey Morford observing and Captain Bert Reed piloting the *Accord*, an American Army second lieutenant, Richard Davis Hart, twenty-six, bested Lynne's time between

Dover and Cap Gris-Nez by thirteen minutes. News of the loss of the world record caused Lynne's determination to grow exponentially. She swam double days parallel to the shore in Long Beach, California; her mother accompanying her in the morning, and her parents alternating afternoons—parents acting as crew to their marathon swimmer daughter. As in the classical music that filled the swimmer's mind on her undaunted journey, her parents' understated help was a kind of rich bassline to her training, allowing her to go all in on her dream in the summer of '73.

With the patience of a bus driver, Lynne finished the tenth grade and finally returned to Dover that following summer. Though her route was three miles (five kilometers) longer than the previous year—due to currents—she swam the Channel twenty-one minutes faster than the year before. Reg Brickell Senior, Reg Brickell Junior, and Mickey Morford stood on deck and alongside her the entire distance. But in Lynne's August 10, 1973, effort—just a continuation of her training—it was Estelle, who quietly provided the day in, day out continuity and love-is-a-verb crew captain support. The forty-six-year-old woman who crossed the Channel twice on the pollock- and cod-scented fishing boat deck would be described years later in understatement: she was remembered as "an avid supporter of her children's educational achievements and aquatic activities." Lynne would later go on to become the cold-water marathon swimmer of her generation, male or female. The Channel Swimming Association records, the newspaper headlines, and the eventual International Swimming Hall of Fame awards did not include Estelle's name, but she did not mind. Her sweet girl safely completed her swim that day. Lynne crossed in 9 hours and 36 minutes. No one in history had ever swum it faster. Estelle Cox's oldest daughter was sixteen years old. And she looked exactly the way a swimmer should.

Later, in record-breaking swims across the Strait of Magellan, Cook Strait, the Bering Strait, and in Antarctica, Lynne Cox never forgot how to swim, more than sixty strokes per minute, like that girl.

Lynne Cox crossing the English Channel with Estelle Cox and Reg Brickell Senior aboard the *Helen Anne Marie*, on August 10, 1973. Her 9 hours and 36 minute swim broke the world record. *(photo by Getty Images)*

CHAPTER FIVE

WILL RUN FOR POTATO CHIPS: THE BOSTON DOUBLE

Yuichiro Hidaka

It must be love. Nothing more. Nothing less.
—*"It Must Be Love," Madness, 1981*

A MAJOR EAST-WEST ARTERY IN THE HEART OF BOSTON'S BACK Bay, Boylston Street is many things, but it is rarely quiet. Like Central Park South in Manhattan or Kensington Road bordering Hyde Park in London, Boylston Street serves as the southern perimeter of Boston's Public Common, the fifty-acre public park established in 1634 in the middle of the city. Boylston passes the northern entrance of the 930,000-square-foot Boston Public Library; to the west, the northern doors of the John B. Hynes Veterans Memorial Convention Center receive and deposit visitors from and onto Boylston. In the currency of the locals, there are five Dunkin' Donuts locations on the street. But Boylston especially overflows with commotion in the countdown to the third Monday in April, on the occasion of the world's oldest annual marathon.

As Yuichiro Hidaka made his way west on Boylston toward the temporary finishing grandstands of his sixth Boston Marathon, from curb to curb and as far as he could see, the street was empty. Completely free of pedestrians, devoid of parked cars and the usual glut of double-parked delivery trucks. Even the trees of green Copley Square were without the usual dawn chorus of busybody house wrens and gossiping sparrows. It was Monday, April 16, 2018. In typical unforgiving endurance fashion, it was 3:45 a.m. And it was the most comfortable Yuichiro would be for a while.

Yuichiro, thirty-nine, wore an extra sweatshirt and pair of gloves that he would eventually discard, but his legs—from the top of his knee socks to the hem of his nylon shorts—were cruelly exposed. His skin was shrink-wrapped around boney knees and made taut by ropey quads and angular hamstrings. Hundreds of additional invisible muscles—tiny ones attached to each hair follicle—were involuntarily contracting in piloerection, otherwise known as goosebumps in English or "bird skin" in Japanese.[18] His sympathetic nerves were dispatching noradrenalin to each of the tiny muscles in a sorry attempt to generate heat. Given what lay ahead, if a bit of fear contributed to those goosebumps, no man would think less of him for it. As the start times for Boston are later than most road races, the majority of the 30,088 registered

---

18 Known as goosebumps, goose pimples, and goose flesh in English and bird skin (*torihada*) in Japanese, the phenomenon of piloerection is described in many of the world's languages in this similar avian fashion: *piel de gallina* in Spanish, *gåsehud* in Norwegian, *gänsehaut* in German, *chair de poule* in French, *pelle d'oca* in Italian, and other versions describing plucked hens, ducks, or chickens.

runners were likely still asleep. Any runners who were awake were probably watching The Weather Channel and panicking.

If anyone had been on Boylston, they would have seen Yuichiro stop an inch short of the seamless ten-foot deep, fifty-foot-long vinyl adhesive that straddled the empty street from edge to edge. They would have seen the Head Athletic Trainer of the University of the Southwest cue his watch and check his laces. His shoes were the same shade of cheerful blue as the capitalized block letters that read F-I-N-I-S-H on the vinyl surface in front of him. The adhesive's background color was the distinctive shade of April daffodils. If anyone else had been on Boylston Street, they likely would have left to seek protection from the twenty-five-mile-an-hour wind registering on anemometers across Back Bay. Despite everything, Yuichiro squared his shoulders to the line, leaned forward, and pushed the button on the right side of his watch, activating the timer. *Tap.*

Sunrise was two hours and two minutes away as Yuichiro started running alone into the light rain and fog of Boylston. After .35 of a mile, he took a right into the light rain and fog of Hereford Street and then a quick left into the light rain and fog of Commonwealth Avenue. He was twenty-six miles (forty-two kilometers) from the start line of the 122nd Boston Marathon.

Under his sweatshirt and over a hooded rainshirt was pinned Yuichiro's race bib, #5725, a low-number testament to his running chops. In his first four Boston Marathons, Yuichiro had covered the 26.2 miles (42.2 kilometers) from the town of Hopkinton to Boylston Street in exactly three hours or less. If there was ever a list of virtues marathon runners admire most, precise finishing consistency—like Yuichiro's—would likely earn a medal. How precise? Sixty seconds or less separated his four finishing times.

Also, marathoners revere finishing times like Yuichiro's 2:59 magic. In the category of "Shit Marathoners Say," road runners love to revel in stories of fighting for, say, a sub-3:15 (3:14:59) or a sub-2:30 (2:29:59)—by amateurs and elites, respectively. Likewise, marathoners heap merit on running each mile of their marathon at an even split—called a "mile split." Yuichiro's dedication to training had earned him a mastery of the 6:51 mile split required for back-to-back-to-back-to-back three-hour Boston finishes. This quest for precise pacing of every mile gives serious marathoners a distraction from (what non-runners consider) the relentless tyranny which is their hobby.

With only one exception, there was never a marathon more serious than the very first marathon. While the *length* of the original run by a Greek messenger-soldier from the battlefield at Marathon to Athens to relay the news of Greek victory over the Persian army is still debated amongst experts, the courier's fate was described by multiple secondary and tertiary sources over the five hundred years after the battle. As for the distance, from Marathon to the capital, the trail route along Mount Penteli to Athens is about 22 miles (35 kilometers). By way of a road, the northern route around Penteli is about 21.4 miles (34.4 kilometers), while the southern road is roughly 25.4 miles (41 kilometers). Whatever the route taken and distance run, Greek texts by such figures as Herodotus, Plutarch, and Lucian describe how the courier entered the capital assembly and announced some derivation of "We have won!" or "We were victorious!" or "We have conquered!"—after which the man proceeded to collapse and not recover. The various texts and accounts also had left the messenger's name unclear. That is, until a British poet got involved.

Credit goes to Robert Browning, in 1879, for creating a composite poem of those fateful events of 490 BC. High on halcyon days and hopped up on classical imagery, Browning wrote,

So, when Persia was dust, all cried, "To Acropolis!
Run, Pheidippides, one race more! the meed is thy due!
'Athens is saved, thank Pan,' go shout!" He flung down his shield,
Ran like fire once more: And the space 'twixt the Fennel-field
And Athens was stubble again, a field which a fire runs through,
Till in he broke: "Rejoice, we conquer!" Like wine through clay,
Joy in his blood bursting his heart, he died—the bliss!

And thus, long-distance running's most fateful urban legend was born of dreamy-eyed Hellenism in Victorian England. In fifteen eight-line stanzas, with no fifth-century BC primary sources, Browning assigned clear marathon credit to a messenger named Pheidippides and successfully hijacked the ancient story with romantic British flourish. Buzzing with poetic license, Browning's version of events became the shared story in the English language of the messenger with victory on his lips and bliss in his fleet feet—and with massive influence in modern distance running.

When the Olympic Games were revived in 1896 in Athens, organizers included a 25-mile-long race for a distance event with an exciting, authentic-ish "Rejoice! We Conquer!" theme for athletes and spectators. Of course, the 25-mile event was clearly never a part of the original discus-hurling, javelin-throwing classic contests of Ancient Greece. But Browning wasn't the last Brit to change long-distance running forever.

On a timeline, it is worthwhile to mention that the first Boston Marathon was held the next spring on April 19, 1897, after the Olympic Games revival in Athens. The marathon event had been so popular in Greece that the Boston Athletic Association decided to include it in their city equivalent of a version of elementary school "Field Day" for adults. Of note, the B.A.A. chose 24.5 miles (39 kilometers) as the length for the long-distance event, called "the American Marathon." Officials knew they wanted runners to finish on a track in Back Bay called Irvington Oval. The most convenient route happened to travel alongside the Boston and Albany Railroad tracks to the west-south-west. A mile counter tasked with measuring 24.5 miles landed at Pleasant Street in Ashland, Massachusetts. The starting line of the race would remain in Ashland, on Pleasant Street, for twenty-seven years.

Meanwhile, for the 1900 Olympics in Paris, marathon competitors ran a distance just over 25 miles. In the 1904 Games in St. Louis, Missouri, the distance amounted to 24.8 miles (40 kilometers). In fact, six different marathon lengths were run in the seven modern Games from 1896 to 1920. The peculiar length of 26.2 miles debuted, accidentally, at the 1908 Games in London. The story goes that the marathon distance was intended to be 25 miles from the grounds of Windsor Castle to the stadium built for the Olympic events, called White City Stadium, in West London. The course was extended at the beginning to start alongside the windows at the Royal Nursery (according to lore) per the request of Mary, Princess of Wales, for her children's viewing pleasure. In a similar fashion, on the far end, the distance was lengthened to have runners enter the stadium, run (oddly) clockwise, and finish directly in front of the Royal Box in the interest of the best view for Queen Alexandra, wife of Edward VII.

The International Association of Athletic Federations, which attests to the nursery window and viewing box sway on the length of the 1908 race and serves as the ratifying body for track-and-field sports as well as running, standardized that 26.2-mile length in May 1921. Officials at the B.A.A. lengthened their marathon course to 26.2 miles in 1924 to conform to this IAAF standard. And as arbitrary as that, from Browning to nursery windows to a wrong way lap toward the king and queen's viewing box, the 1908 course, which randomly happened to measure 26.2 miles, nonsensically became the standard.

And thus, Yuichiro Hidaka, who had mastered the 6:51 mile split for a nonsensical distance in four consecutive years, had graduated to a kind of DIY twist for this event with a higgledy-piggledy past. He doubled down on the nonsensical. He loved the event so much, Yuichiro trained to run the Boston Double.

Not much is known about The Double. It's rumored to be one part Fight Club, one part secret menu at Dunkin' Donuts. No one tracks the outbound marathon but the runner, and the B.A.A. does not indicate which marathon finishing times include an early morning 26.2-mile run before the official race. There are a handful of inconspicuous Boston Double runners each year, and their quiet about their feats says as much about America's Marathon as it says about their anonymous tenacity.

Yuichiro had plenty of examples of runners who have gone all in on Boston. Some of the fastest Boston Marathon runners of all time are from his home country of Japan, a nation about the size of California with an obsessed running culture. The men's foot race at Boston has been won by a Japanese athlete nine times. In Adharanand Finn's book, *The Way of the Runner*, the author describes the many running building blocks in Japanese society—from diet to school relay racing—that help make Japan the fastest marathon country worldwide behind Kenya and Ethiopia.

Anecdotally, as Yuichiro ran alone, peppered by a New England icy rain on the way to the start line of the race, the cultural principle of *gaman*—the Japanese version of Britain's stiff upper lip—steadied his nerve and girded his loins in the insufferable conditions. The term *gaman* translates into English as "enduring the seemingly unbearable with patience and dignity." *Gaman* describes the practice of calm endurance through suffering; the suffering that unforgiving distance endurance athletes face in choosing to seek out discomfort and adversity in their life. In this combination of adventure, work ethic, and divergent creativity, these endeavors are as much about the state of *gaman* that descends upon these adventurers as it is about the special physical places where they compete. *Gaman* is a practice of patience and dignity when you are nowhere close to the finish line, and you are puking over the gunwales, or are bleeding from chafing, or your nose won't stop forming snot bubbles. *Gaman* is grace and humility in the middle of unending, and wholly unnecessary, long-distance bludgeoning.

With the air temperatures in the low 30sF, Yuichiro's nose was indeed a leaky spigot; but in the tradition of *gaman*, he focused on honor. It was an exclusive privilege to have the prestigious Boston Marathon course to oneself. As a glassy lake free of all boat traffic is to the water skier, or as off-piste fresh tracks are to the snowboarder, to have the historic course to oneself was worth the mileage and the early hour. To the thousands of runners each year who strive to meet the qualifying standards of Boston, many without success, Yuichiro's sense of reverence for the privilege to be *on* the course—backward and forward—qualified him as a torchbearer. He was a defender of amateur excellence and an everyman exemplar for all the dreamers who ever set off on a quest for a bib at Boston.

To enter his inaugural Boston, Yuichiro submitted an application with proof of a race finish that met the qualifying B.A.A. standard—called a BQ, a Boston Qualifier. At the time, September 2012, Yuichiro was in the 18-to-34 age group, which meant he needed to submit a 3:00:00 finish OR BETTER from an approved race from the last twelve months. Next, all runners who beat their qualifying time by more than 20 minutes were admitted to the race. This meant a blistering time of 2:40:00 or better for men and a smokin' 3:10:00 or better for women 18-to-34 (with more forgiving qualifying times for older runners, mercifully). Next, since the race limit of thirty thousand runners had not been met, the B.A.A. admitted all applicants who submitted qualifying times of 10 minutes or better. Then the B.A.A. began the difficult work of adding rounds of the next-fastest times in all age categories: nine minutes faster, eight, seven, and so on, checking the totals against the race cap. But there's the rub: depending on that year's number of applicants and how fast that field happens to be, there are runners who earn a BQ time but don't get in the race. For example, in 2016, 4,562 applicants who finished up to two minutes and twenty-eight seconds faster than their qualifying time were denied acceptance. The 2018 race had a 3:23 "cutoff time," denying 5,062 runners a bib. Curiously, when Yuichiro rolled into the Athletes' Village in Hopkinton in the freezing rain, the faces of the athletes around him suggested an undeniable plot twist: it was clear there was no shortage of runners who would gladly swap places with those 5,062 marathoners then and there.

Long-distance athletes—like climbers, swimmers, cyclists, through-hikers, triathletes, skin- and cross-country skiers— often train with a schedule, a calendar of workouts, forcing themselves out the door daily; in a practical sense, this is so they may test equipment and their nerve in all kinds of God-forsaken conditions. Psychologically, a training plan that strips away fair-weather tendencies in an athlete leaves them temporarily miserable, but eventually much more confident and competent overall.

Yuichiro began his daily marathon training after graduating from college in Japan and during his time earning two more degrees at Wichita State University in Kansas, a place where people joke that classes can be canceled for snow and heat in the same month. Yuichiro had faced track workouts of sticky humidity during his three years as Assistant Athletic Trainer at Radford University in southwest Virginia. He had stared down big mileage weeks during the long Laramie winters as Assistant Athletic Trainer at the University of Wyoming. Around the world, on any given day, in every kind of Holy-Mother-of-God weather, you can find marathoners who refuse to miss out on their run. It's as if they enjoy it. Yuichiro had earned membership in that club.

When asked about his admirable running discipline, Yuichiro demurs, in the spirit of extreme endurance types and in the tradition of the fine runners of skill and will that Japan produces. Instead, Yuichiro deflects away from his effort and perseverance to the subject of potato chips. He half apologies for needing to train so hard at running to counter his continual searching for, trying of, and complete obsession with new and unusual flavors of potato chips. Pesto-flavored, pizza-flavored, ramen-flavored. Foie gras–flavored Torres from Spain, dill and chives–flavored OLWs from Sweden, olive oil–flavored Amicas from Italy. Krinkle-cut, ultra-thin, stix, wavy, wedges, popped, matchsticks, hand-cut, or stacked in a cylinder; to the uninitiated, the exotic flavors and styles appear limitless, but stalwart Yuichiro is undeterred. Potato chip appreciation by the connoisseur and collector, upon closer inspection, may not be that dissimilar from the bewitched infatuation some people develop for marathons. And most extreme endurance events are an elaboration on this nexus of quest and fun. In matters of multiple rotations on the Boston Marathon course and flavors of potato chips, to Yuichiro, more is simply more.

And more awaited Yuichiro's senses when he arrived at Athletes' Village staging area after running from the finish to the start line of the Boston Marathon. Puddles were iced at their perimeters. The fields of Hopkinton High School and Middle School had turned to tatami-colored mud soup. Large white tents were overflowing with humanity, and wholly overflowing with pre-race jitters. Every hardship seemed amplified. The worst? The lines for the porta potties seemed to never improve: it appeared that runners were waiting an unholy amount of time in the drenching rain because some people were using the blue plastic structures for shelter, not for the facilities. It says something about the weather when humans were opting to spend time in such a place.

The dread around the deteriorating weather, the stagnant lines to use a toilet, and the unrelenting demands of bladders and bowels pressing for evacuation services caused every kind of tension. The quietus experienced on the floor of the Assembly by Pheidippides was more dignified. At least Greece was dry and warm.

Yuichiro was in another level of trouble. Feeling fine in body and mind after his 26.2-mile run, the tax man eventually came 'round. See, finish a long run in the cold, and two things follow physiologically: After stopping, a warmed-up runner will be mauled by the discomfort of the cold temperature. The second blow is the way loose, warmed-up muscles will stiffen up—like the Tin Man in *The Wizard of Oz*—when one stops running. Yuichiro had to keep moving despite the soupy mud of the Village. Standing around was no option. He jogged to the start line as soon as the red bibs, Wave 1, were called.

The start line was no less a mess. Discarded clothing, cheap umbrellas, and plastic ponchos formed soggy piles everywhere. There were enough abandoned running shoes to stock a store.[19]

---

19 Among serious runners, special shoes are often saved for such "A" races, or runners bring new or new-ish shoes just for the big occasion. Recently, "supershoes" have captured the imagination of these runners. These lightweight, carbon-plated shoes made with lightweight, energy-returning foam are the current darlings of the performance running-shoe market. On average, shoes in this category cost about $250, which broadly is at least $100 more than the typical performance marathon shoe.

The runners in the first wave of a high-profile race like Boston can easily resemble excited thoroughbreds, snorting in the starting stalls, boldly bouncing at the line, chomping at the bit. At the start line of the 2018 race, the field more closely resembled a slightly stunned and visibly shivering cluster of Italian greyhounds. Eyes wide and unblinking, the runners looked as if they were waiting for the announcement the race would be canceled. That announcement never came. Yuichiro cued his watch and passed through the start line unceremoniously. He was packed between runners wearing trash bags and $250 neon shoes. Lined up in a tight row, the runners' heads were lowered in submission, perhaps in silent prayer. The less reverent were less taciturn; it so happens there are as many swear words as there are potato-chip flavors in the world. Ninety-four countries were represented in the soaked multitude, with all the best curses from around the world addressing the freezing rain.

On a clear day, the runner traffic at the world's major marathons can be overwhelming for runners accustomed to the space and freedom of movement synonymous with long-distance training. To the athlete who equates marathon running with—and prizes it for—quiet and solitude, an event like the 2022 TCS New York City Marathon, with its 53,627 finishers, can be a noisy, claustrophobia-inducing whammy that one cannot train for. In years past, each of the major intersections of Yuichiro's route—from Hopkinton to Boston—featured DJs and music bands and screaming spectators. Like their worship of, and affection for the

---

Frequently at important marathons, serious runners will wear older running shoes to the event and put on their "A" race shoes at the start line. The "travel" shoes are then donated or recycled. At the top races, it's wild to see piles of high-end shoes that look practically new abandoned around the start line, often cast off for supershoes.

Bruins, the Celtics, the Patriots, and the Sox, the good people of Boston love The Marathon. And sports love in Boston is not fair-weathered. On this, the coldest Marathon Monday in thirty years, Yuichiro marveled at the noisy die-hard fans along the route.

The spectators—screaming, singing, landing sharp tongued comments like a Simone Biles vault—set Boston apart from every other marathon host city. During the hot years—the B.A.A. lists eleven Mondays when the race temperatures were over 80 degrees—Boston fans are known for their Otter Pop ice-pop handouts, neighborhood kids with orange slices, and garden hoses stretched to the street to counter the steaming asphalt. There are legendary squads of friends and family who turn out for one racer at Boston; they are recognizable by matching oversized big-head cardboard cutouts along the route and their matching t-shirts that read such as, "She runs marathons. We run bartabs." The course is also full of generous neutral support, too. In 2014, along the way from the Athletes' Village to the start line of Yuichiro's second Boston, a homemade poster advertised BEER DONUTS CIGARETTES; the irrepressible locals extended Bud Lights, crullers, and Marlboros out onto the street. At the halfway mark of the race, the students of predominantly female Wellesley College offer runners legendary good-luck kisses. The young women carry signs that range from "Wicked Kissah" to "I Won't Tell Your Wife" to "Finally, Some Men Around Here." The weather in 2018 inspired a wave of drenching double-entendres: "Kiss Me, I'm So Wet."

The only group worthy of taller praise than the spectators on the soaked route were the 9,500 volunteers who stood in the cold, while the wind chill registered at 29°F (-2°C). The volunteers who handed Yuichiro water, Gatorade, and gels were his crew for the back half of his 52.4-mile (84.3-kilometer) odyssey, and the undertaking would not have been possible without them. As he wore a tank over his rainshirt with his name, "Yuichiro," many volunteers cheered for him personally, calling him by name. The psychological boost of hearing your name and "Good job, Yuichiro!" or "You've got this, Yuichiro!" was more valuable than any fancy racing shoe with a carbon plate and magic foam. The short connections made between athletes and cheering fans, saintly volunteers and fellow athletes suffering at the same pace fall into sociology's "weak tie" relationships. The sporting version of weak ties are short but profound exchanges that substantially buttress an athlete's mood and keep the fire burning. The power of a stranger with a kind word, a fellow runner flashing you a thumb's up for your pace, or a Wellesley co-ed kissing you while her friends gather to pat you on the back can create euphoric surges that defy 52 miles of wet feet and frozen fingers. Science confirms the direct effect on happiness and energy that is unique to weak tie exchanges; athletes have anecdotally always known this. Weak tie interactions reinforce how important relationships, however minute, are during unforgiving stretches. In Double Boston Marathon math, love of sport and love between humans— sometimes strangers—creates outcomes much greater than the sum of their parts.

As Yuichiro made his way through women blowing him kisses through Wellesley, toward the Newton Hills, en route to the cheering Boston College Eagles, the deck was being shuffled up ahead in the men's pro race. The 2017 Boston Marathon champion, Geoffrey Kirui, of Kenya, with his yellow bib—#1— pinned to a rain jacket, began to feel the cold on the backside of

Heartbreak Hill, in the freezing headwind of miles 23 and 24. The second-place man surged: his name was Yuki Kawauchi of Japan.

"I am freezing cold right now, but when I was running, these were the best conditions I could have possibly run in," said the thirty-one-year-old Yuki Kawauchi, a full-time administrative clerk at a high school in Saitama Prefecture, with his *gaman* worn on his sleeve. "It's the best crowd support I've ever had anywhere in the world. Thank you, Boston," Kawauchi said after the race. He averaged 5:11 minute mile splits in the heavy rain. It was Kawauchi's fourth marathon in 2018. And his fourth victory.[20]

Not everyone called Patriots Day 2018 "The greatest day of my life," as Kawauchi did during his tearful post-race interview. But there was no shortage of tears that Monday. The B.A.A. reported that 2,785 runners needed medical assistance from the 1,700 medical volunteers along the course. Home to twenty-five hospitals and more than thirty colleges, universities, and medical schools—and since Massachusetts Institute of Technology's original campus was located on Boylston Street—Boston is a center of science and medicine in America. A better-educated, better-trained, and more highly organized race medical staff does not exist. And they were put to the test.

---

20 For what it's worth, Kawauchi was not wearing supershoes, but a classic racing flat. Also worth mentioning here is the paragon marathon moment provided by the delightful Des Linden. Her historic win (2:39:55) on rain-soaked Boylston was the first time an American woman had won the race in thirty-three years. The drought was over, the hard way.

In interviews after the race, Linden described resisting the urge to drop out of the cold and windy race, then breaking down the painful effort bit-by-bit: Just show up for one more mile, she thought. Just show up for one more minute, continued the internal dialogue. Des Linden's motto, "Keep showing up," remains a long-distance maxim and an intestinal covenant for everyday life.

The most serious foot race in 2,500 years witnessed medical tents turned into trauma units at the 117th Boston Marathon. It was during the 1 o'clock hour on April 15, 2013, and first-timer Yuichiro had turned left from Hereford Street onto joyous Boylston, on his way to his inaugural Boston finish line and a solid 2:59:35 result. He was shepherded by race volunteers straight on Boylston toward his finisher's medal, food, and his gear bag with a change of clothes. Wanting to cheer on his fellow runners, Yuichiro walked on a less crowded Newbury Street—parallel to packed Boylston—back down to Hereford to cheer for other runners as he had been cheered for. As he took pictures and clapped for the runners, he was walking through the crowd up Boylston when he heard a loud sound in front of him, which he assumed was fireworks at the finish line. Fourteen seconds later, 210 yards from the first, the second of two homemade pressure-cooker bombs exploded directly behind Yuichiro on the sidewalk.

"People started screaming and running everywhere, and I did not know where to go," Yuichiro said, recalling the unspeakable violence that killed three spectators instantly.

Because waist-high barricades line the 656 yards of Boylston between Hereford and the finish, Yuichiro guessed that the middle of the street would be the safest place from a possible third bomb that his brain was alerting his nervous system to prepare for. He jumped the barricades and headed west on Boylston toward Hereford, away from the foul smoke and chaos. In the FBI's collection of photos of the minutes after the detonation of the second bomb, a photo captures Yuichiro running in the middle of Boylston Street as a young man in a white hat, worn backwards, walks on Boylston, making a right onto Fairfield Street. The young man was Dzhokhar Tsarnaev, the younger of the two brother terrorist bombers responsible for the three deaths and countless devastating injuries at 2:50 p.m. on Boylston Street.

The two pressure-cooker bombs killed Martin Richard, eight, Lingzi Lu, twenty-three and Krystle Campbell, twenty-nine, on Boylston Street.[21] The unspeakable harm of the instant mass casualty incident would have been exponentially worse had it not been for the quantity and quality of the medical care provided immediately on those two blocks. The first bombing patients arrived at the city's trauma centers within a remarkable fifteen minutes. Doctors and nurses ran with stretchers and wheelchairs down Boylston from the finish line medical tents to the injured, transporting them promptly to waiting ambulances that had been at the ready for runners. To explain the severity of the nightmare, the medical staff cared for fifteen spectators with seventeen lower-extremity traumatic amputations. As a testament to the excellence of the medical staff, those fifteen spectators were among the 281 victims under the care of the volunteer staff on Boylston who survived.

What happened next deserves equal headlines. The following year at the Boston Marathon, the crowd size doubled. An estimated one million spectators turned out in 2014 to support

---

21 The fourth victim of the terrorists in 2013 was Officer Sean A. Collier, a member of MIT Campus Police; a memorial for Officer Collier has been erected on Vassar Street on the MIT campus. A memorial for the other three victims is on the sidewalk of Boylston Street. The pillar inscription reads, "All we have lost is brightly lost." Inscribed into the base, in the stone of Boylston Street, reads the words, "Let us climb, now, the road to hope."

the runners, the volunteers, the B.A.A., the city of Boston, and peaceful sport writ large.

Dating back to 776 BC in the ancient Olympic Games, held in honor of Zeus every four years, a truce was called far and wide across territories and city states for the safety of participants and spectators to Olympia both traveling to *and* during the Games themselves. Following the Boston Marathon bombing, a recommitment to the ethos of sports armistice (*ekecheiria* in Greek; translated as "holding of hands") rang out from every continent. Domestically, the city and the Bay State shone. In remarks at an interfaith service three days after the bombing, before the perpetrators were known, President Barack Obama said, in understatement, "It should be pretty clear by now (that the bombers) picked the wrong city." Obama said to the Commonwealth of Massachusetts and to the world: "You will run again because that's what the people of Boston are made of. Your resolve is the greatest rebuke to whoever committed this heinous act." Resolve was not confined to the Bay State.

The number of applicants to the race ballooned: 2014 was the largest (and possibly most talented) field in the event's history. Athletes worldwide submitted faster BQs in greater numbers, seemingly as a referendum on peaceful sport and the strength and solidarity Boston put on display.

An example comes from Boylston Street: At the northeast corner of Dartmouth and Boylston streets stands a campanile 246 feet (75 meters) tall—the bell tower of Old South Church. The congregation of the community there first organized in 1669; parishioners once included Benjamin Franklin and Samuel Adams. Following the violence of 2013, two other

Old South Church parishioners, Diane Gaucher and Marilyn Jackson Adams, hatched a plan. The two fierce knitters aimed to present a scarf to the runners who attended Old South Church's "Blessing of the Marathon Athletes" service in 2014. The annual blessing service is held the day before the race at 9 a.m. and 11 a.m. Sunday morning. Identifying that the 2014 athletes would attend in defiance of fear, and that some might have experienced the 2013 ordeal in some fashion, Diane and Marilyn wanted to gather several hundred handknit scarves in the blue and yellow of the race. They asked knitters to create scarves so that "The Church of the Finish Line" might wrap the athletes in support and comfort. Reverend Dr. Nancy Taylor, who served as the first female senior minister of Old South Church from 2005 through 2022, best describes what happened next. "Diane and Marilyn's plan blossomed beyond their wildest imaginations. In the months leading up to the 2014 Boston Marathon, Old South Church received nearly 7,000 scarves."

"Scarves arrived from every state in the nation and ten foreign countries. The scarves were designed and knitted by people across the country and around the world who wanted to be a part of the healing," she continued. Interwoven in the stitches were the prayers of love and wishes for courage that two Old South Church members had dreamed of on Boylston. "Every scarf was different in size, shape and design," the elegant Reverend Taylor describes, "yet each bore the colors of the Boston Marathon."

Signs in town in 2014 read "Strength Lives Here" and "Victory Lives Here." But also, "Humanity Lives Here." The "best of the best" moniker now officially expanded past those with a bib on Patriots Day. As veteran runners can attest, the volunteers, organizers, and the good people of Boston on Marathon Monday have always been the paragon of sport.

Suffice it to say, a few wind gusts up to 45 mph, and some driving rains, were no match for the Boston Marathon faithful on the fifth anniversary of the bombing in 2018. In the end, there were 30,088 registered runners, 27,042 brave starters, and 25,907 mollywhopped finishers that day—the kind of numbers that suggest one should never bet against patience and dignity in amateur sport. And never underestimate the power of sacrifice from volunteers. And never sell short the outpouring of love by spectators at the world's oldest annual marathon.

Sometimes endurance quests are about recognizing the magic of a specific route, a random distance, a place filled with incredible people, and the act of committing to it on a cellular level, with all your humanity. Sometimes these quests reflect a hunt for the next great feat after a 2:59:59 finish. Sometimes the work is a defensive strategy, like fleet footwork in the ring with the heavyweight champ and undefeated Father Time. Sometimes, to paraphrase runner and writer Haruki Murakami, the work is to allow you "to beat yourself, the way you used to be." Sometimes the work is born of a rebuke: the perfect answer to commentary by an uneducated taxi driver. A rebuke to the sedentary boredom of working in cubicles and endless adulting. A rebuke to odious radical fundamentalism by the wretched against the innocent. Sometimes endurance quests are built on the cornerstone of sour cream and onion-flavored potato chips. Nothing more. Nothing less.

About the Double, longtime race director of the Patriots Day event, Dave McGillivray, said, "I am always in awe of the folks who have run Boston as a double. The Boston Marathon is

In the freezing, windswept rain of 2018, Yuichiro Hidaka runs down Boylston Street past the Engine 33/Ladder 15 firehouse for the second time on Monday, April 16, 2018. His handwritten singlet reads, "Double!" *(photo by MarathonFoto)*

a tough course as is, but running it from east to west is actually tougher." He knows this from experience. But he does not brag about the numerous times he has run the Double. He is also the champion of another variety of an unforgiving stretch of time, not from a metric of distance, but from a streak: Dave has run fifty-two consecutive Boston Marathons. His first was at the age of eighteen, and he has never missed a race since.[22]

"These runners," he says about the quiet cadre of Double Boston lionhearts, "they thrive on special challenges." And, like Dave, they don't feel the need to talk about it.

For his part, without fanfare, and without anyone's knowledge of his 4 a.m. marathon, Yuichiro crossed the 10x50-foot finish line for a second, official time on Patriots Day 2018. As quiet as Boylston at 3:45 a.m. in a soft rain, he jumped with joy at the 52.4 finish—to the thrill of photographers—stopped his watch and smiled with silent satisfaction.

Yuichiro Hidaka has completed the Boston Double four times, but it's the conditions of that day in '18 that he savors the most, during every satisfying day that has followed.

---

22 A footnote celebration about Boston streaks: Hats off to Mark Bauman who has run fifty-four consecutive Boston Marathons—every year since 1970. Bauman's fastest Boston time was 2 hours, 30 minutes and 32 seconds. Ben Beach also gets a stout high five for his fifty-four-year consecutive streak; he ran his first Boston as a freshman at Harvard. Beach would successfully finish seventeen of those races sub-2:40, with three smokin' 2:26 finishes on Boylston. Finally, fist bumps for Nantucket's finest, Dr. Tim Lepore who ran an incredible forty-eight straight Bostons. The man with the greatest number of Boston runs was the Olympian John "Johnny" Kelley (1930–2011), who won the race in 1935 and 1945. Kelley finished a remarkable fifty-eight times.

A footnote to this footnote: When these four athletes began their streaks, women were not allowed to participate in the Boston Marathon. Eight women started (and completed) the 1972 edition—the first year the event was opened to female athletes. In 2024, 10,928 women finished the 128th running of the Boston Marathon.

CHAPTER SIX

BIKING 'TIL YOUR NECK CAN NO LONGER SUPPORT YOUR HEAD

Seana Hogan

For an additional $4.95 we will provide a receipt
that matches what you told your spouse you paid.

—*Sign at a bike store register*

THE AVERAGE-SIZED HUMAN HEAD WEIGHS IN THE NEIGH-
borhood of eleven pounds. Most of the time, the seven vertebrae
and twenty muscles responsible for hoisting this weight are up to
the task. With correct posture, the human head doesn't seem to
weigh much at all.

When you ride your road bike from California to Maryland,
however, correct posture is the first casualty.

Called "cycling's hardest race" by *VeloNews*, the 3,000-
mile (4,848-kilometer) Race Across America (RAAM) starts
in Oceanside, California, and travels over the rugged Rockies,
across the Great Plains, around the Great Lakes region, up and

over the tough Appalachian highlands, to a finish in Annapolis, Maryland. There have been different finish locations and a variety of routes, but RAAM is an all-out, nonstop race across, on average, twelve states. The clock does not stop. The clock does not care. Top riders don't sleep for more than a couple hours a day, and sometimes not at all.

To compare RAAM to other ultra endurance events, it is said that *running* an ultra is an eating contest with some running thrown in. For the fastest racers in RAAM, Race Across America is a sleep-forgoing contest with some cycling comedy included for good measure.

So, what's the hurry? Unfortunately, the race clock is running from the moment a cyclist's skinny tire touches the start line. Three major time checkpoints await each cyclist: in Durango, Colorado; at the Mississippi River in West Alton, Missouri; and in Mount Airy, Maryland. Miss the time cutoff, and your race is kaput. Over. And just as the RAAM clock never stops, the more than 175,000 feet (53,340 meters) of climbing never seems to end.

Climb and ride your bike long enough, and even the human head can begin to weigh too much. Pedaling across the continent, stretched over a bike's top tube, torso parallel to the asphalt, eyes looking ahead—among other things, one's posterior neck muscles can be turned to overcooked pasta.

Occasionally, this has an unusual—and slightly farcical—result. Over time, in this aerodynamic cycling position, the vast length of RAAM has revealed to the world that sometimes the neck muscles just *fail*. After too much biking, a cyclist's head can be left flopping forward, chin rolling around haplessly on their chest.

For anyone who has ever spent time with a newborn baby, the similarities are obvious: newborns' necks are not strong enough to hold up their too-heavy head. Neonatal caregivers must cradle and support weak paraspinal muscles until neck and trunk muscles are up to the task. When these same muscles fail for adults in road cycling's toughest race, the onset is sudden and unforgettable. Tangentially, some (though not all) of the crying that occurs during RAAM mimics the inconsolable wailing of newborns.

The first example of this noodle-neck phenomenon in RAAM occurred on the outskirts of Harvard, Illinois, in 1983, during the second year of Race Across America.

For background, the first year's race was called "The Great American Bike Race," and its four racers set out to beat the existing transcontinental record of 10 days, 23 hours. Chased by groundbreakers John Marino, John Howard, and Michael Shermer, Lon "Marathon Lon" Haldeman beat his own coast-to-coast record in 1982, completing the route in 9 days, 20 hours, and 2 minutes. And ABC's *Wide World of Sports* won an Emmy for the coverage of the 2,968-mile (4,777-kilometer) race.

It was the ultracycling pioneer Michael Shermer who inexplicably lost the use of his neck muscles in the 1983 race. Flummoxed, he found himself crossing Indiana needing to dedicate one arm to holding his head up, lest it just roll around on his chest. So disturbing was his affliction and so dangerous were his steering and braking restrictions, the racer only got as far as Ohio before he had to drop out of the adventure.

In the unofficial Eponymous Sports Hall of Fame, innovator Dick Fosbury contributed his signature high-jump technique—the "Fosbury Flop"—to track and field. Boxing's Muhammed

Ali's center-ring jig became known as the "Ali Shuffle." In hockey, score a goal, land an assist, and get into a fight in the same game, and you have completed the "Gordie Howe Hat Trick." In basketball, an intentional foul committed against an opposing team's worst free-throw shooter is called "Hack-A-Shaq," from 52.7% free-throw shooter Shaquille O'Neal. In subsequent Race Across America events over the years, the event found itself with its own contribution to sport nomenclature: "Shermer's Neck."

In the subsequent decades of these broken bobblehead case studies, RAAM racers have constructed and worn every kind of homemade device to combat the effects of fatigue and gravity. Inventions have included chest plates with chin rests, PVC scaffolding around the torso, and improvised duct-tape-innertube-wire-hanger contraptions made on the fly. Even a vertical Pringle's potato-chip canister has been seen propping up a racer's chin during RAAM. With their unnatural pressure points and left-unsaid chafing, these contraptions can make an aerodynamic-conscious cyclist shudder; anyone with pain receptors from the waist up is quite likely to grimace at the sight. In photographs of athletes in Shermer's Neck contraptions on the RAAM course throughout the years—though the MacGyvered apparatuses are wildly DIY-different—the pictures all feature the same sullen mug and a five hundred-mile stare.

Michael Shermer, Ultra Cycling Hall of Fame inductee, professor, author of more than a dozen books, publisher of *Skeptic* magazine, former race director of RAAM and its cofounder, with a PhD in the History of Science, graciously laughs about the acute medical condition bearing his name: "A century from now it will be the only thing I'm remembered for," he evaluates good-naturedly.

The winningest American solo Race Across America athlete to date—male or female—is a senior firmware engineer at IBM in Silicon Valley. An ever-busy working parent of two sons, RAAM's champion has been employed full-time in firmware problem-solving and software engineering for International Business Machines Corporation for more than thirty-five years. Her name is Seana Hogan.

In her many transcontinental rides across America, blessedly, Seana has never had to be outfitted in a PVC-cage due to total failure of her neck muscles. And while she has never needed to bungee cord the back of her helmet to her bike saddle to keep her head upright, in the many rides since her inaugural 1992 race Seana has known a host of other RAAM afflictions. These included her feet turning deep violet from swelling. And respiratory distress and altitude sickness above 10,000 feet (3,048 meters). And electrolyte imbalances that finally made her quit one of the races in a Walmart parking lot in Conway, Arkansas. And once, after a successful RAAM finish, the sores on Seana's posterior were so bad she could not fly home to Valley Springs, California, as she was unable to sit for the flight. There is nothing in real life that can prepare you for riding your bike across America in less than thirteen days.

"RAAM is possibly the most insane competition a person could attempt," confirms Frank Strack, devout cyclist, editor and coauthor of the ace books *The Rules* and *The Hardmen*, and founder of the online cycling community called The Velominati. "Just you, yourself, and the worst companion you could imagine on such a journey: your mind. Your mind, when the body is in duress, becomes a needlessly chatty thing. All it does is try to tell you about all the warning lights your body is trying to send into the control room. *The legs seem to be on the fritz. The ol' neck is becoming a bit weary from holding your giant head up for hours on end. Maybe taking a break would be a good idea.* Your brain is responsible for letting all those useless messages through when all you're trying to do is get some good riding done."

In the 2019 edition of the race, Seana began riding from Oceanside as usual, her trusty Bianchi bike beneath her. The signature "Celeste" green—a more minty shade of Tiffany & Co.'s robin's egg blue—was instantly recognizable on her bar tape, her jersey sleeves, her helmet, and as a blur on her carbon Rolf wheelset. The first three California checkpoints of the race were ticked off in Borrego Springs (Time Station #1, mile 88), Brawley (#2, mile 145), and Blythe (#3, mile 235). The high temperature in Blythe that day was 110°F (43°C). The rider with the thick long brown ponytail kept racking up the mileage through Arizona checkpoints Parker (#4, mile 286) and Salome (#5, mile 342). Seana's first sleep was in Congress, Arizona, at mile 395 of the race.

In 2017, the race in which she developed altitude sickness, Seana rode without sleep to Pagosa Springs, Colorado. A 983-mile (1,582-kilometer) ride.

"Success is always doing your best. And learning from your mistakes to make your best better," Seana said. So, in her next two races, having learned from the mistake of riding 983 straight miles without stopping, she altered the plan and grabbed two to three hours of sleep around Congress, Arizona, in the heat of the furnace called June in the Sonoran Desert. The ability to learn from one's mistakes—and to cheerfully keep moving—is found on a list of gifts that are clearly bestowed by the divine. Like the ability to fall asleep anywhere. Another handy gift of Seana's while participating in RAAM.

After Congress, Arizona, the whiplash was real when it got seriously cold that night in the largest contiguous ponderosa pine forest in North America (Flagstaff, Arizona, Time Station #9, elev. 7,000 feet/2,134 meters). Seana rode through the night, eyes on the ubiquitous white line between road and shoulder. Time stations Tuba City and Kayenta fell next at mile markers 677 and 749. Desert gave way to scrubland.

Two Utah towns that could self-submit entries into the "best RAAM checkpoint names" contest came next: Mexican Hat and Montezuma Creek. In the unblemished red-rock stretches of scrub plateaus and semi-arid austerity, Seana lifted her eyes from the white line of the asphalt. The road was the only man-made element in the great expanse. But she was not alone.

Six or seven wild horses, no two the same color, ran free in the sagebrush scrub. "Paints, palominos, appaloosas," she remembers, unbound and unfettered. A pack at play. The crew members inside the van behind her were captivated by the untouched land of rock formations and background buttes adorned with such creatures running alongside their vehicle as in a game. The pack appeared to want the cyclist and van to keep up, but the racer was holding steady at fifteen miles per hour. She needed to not burn matches in a race *within* her race. When asked about why she would choose to ride her bike across this country, Seana can recall countless vistas and rocky bluffs and rangeland rainstorms as beautiful as those wild horses. "It's about going places that people don't go," she explains. Marathon swimmers and endurance climbers, ultra trail runners and long-distance hikers all describe some version of this gift. The unspoiled places cleverly mitigate, and offset, the pain spent to reach them. Especially vivid and enduring are the wild places one reaches under one's own power. For ultra athletes, reaching these unspoiled places never takes more than it gives.

As with many endurance undertakings, "under one's own power" does not necessarily mean without company or without some version of assistance. In other words, in Race Across America, crew matters.

In RAAM, Seana usually has thirteen to fourteen crew volunteers with her, divided into three groups of three to five members each who ride along the route in one of her team vehicles. The primary vehicle is a van that stays with Seana exclusively; getting gas is the one occasion they let Seana out of their sight. In fact, RAAM rules require a vehicle to stay directly behind the rider ("direct follow support") throughout the night. Because nighttime riding is the most challenging, the rotation of the crew is designed by Seana, the mathematician, so that the three strongest crew members—who all get along—are in the van at night. If the van ever needs gas (refueling only during the day), then direct follow support of Seana is done by an auxiliary vehicle. The aux car is largely used as a scout, doing reconnaissance and running errands for the team. The third and final vehicle is Seana's Ford Itasca RV; the crew vehicle for the crew. Just because Seana does not shower or eat food prepared in a kitchen during the race (most of her calories are liquid), it does not mean her crew can carry on in such fashion. In fact, *because* Seana does not sleep is precisely the reason her crew must. The RV serves to keep a rotation of her team semi-well-rested and semi-well-fed for their tough-as-nails roadie. They must think for the rider with the big smile and youthful bangs framing her face. They are her brain. As she is an expert in algebraic topology, this is a tall order.[23]

In 2019, Seana saw in the small mirror attached to her helmet that her RV behind her had a problem. The episode that followed explains much about crewing in Race Across America:

Seana (to the van, riding briefly alongside of her): "Hey, the RV has a front headlight out. Driver's side."

Van crew (feigning surprise): "Oh, no kidding? Great, Seana. Thanks so much. You are crushing. Keep it up."

Seana kept pedaling up Wolf Creek Pass, glad to be helpful. Before this exchange, somewhere between Durango (where Seana slept for two hours for the twenty-four-hour period) and Pagosa Springs, Colorado, the RV and a large elk had experienced an unfortunate collision.

The elk population in Colorado is the largest in the world. And the animals' frames are not small, either. Bulls can stand 5 or more feet at the shoulder and weigh more than a ton. Nose to tail, they regularly measure eight feet long. Include the neck, head, and antlers of a mature bull, and a measuring tape would stretch skyward to nine feet tall. Elk number in the hundreds of thousands in Colorado. It's estimated that in the stretch between

---

23 Algebraic topology studies how data gets represented as shapes. It's a form of highly abstract complex geometry. Finishing RAAM in less than a fortnight is confirmed to be easier than explaining algebraic invariants of spaces to (likely) non-mathematicians by a (conclusive) non-mathematician.

Durango and Pagosa Springs, where Seana's RV lost a side mirror and lights, 60% of car crashes involve wildlife collisions. (In good news, an $11.3 million migration overpass and underpass project for elk and other wildlife was completed in 2022 in the San Juan Basin area.) The Itasca's front door, bumper, fender, side mirror, and driver-side lights appeared to have experienced a few blows by both Muhammed Ali and Gordie Howe. Luckily, a professional driver—an actual semi trucker—was behind the wheel at the time of impact, as the vehicle was moving at the posted speed limit of sixty miles per hour.

This elk-RV-RAAM rider triad provides a random Polaroid picture from a day of RAAM. The natural world is robust in June in the expanse called North America; the areas around the RAAM race course are full of more critters, windstorms, squall raindrops, big game animals, and lightning bolts than humans. Often there are more insects on a RAAM van grill than residents in the closest town.

It also illustrates the stoic nature of RAAM participants, akin to lifelong mariners and old ranch managers. For example, when elk come out of nowhere and slam into your vehicle on the RAAM course, you don't wake the sleeping crew in the back of the RV by swerving or braking dangerously. Crews are mandatory at RAAM for safety reasons. Accident avoidance—for racer and vehicles alike—is a central focus during RAAM. So is sleep for the crew.

Also noteworthy, when a RAAM rider mentions that the crew RV headlamp is out, it is acceptable to act surprised, imply a bulb has burnt out, and reassure the rider that the crew will be replacing that bulb from their stash of car headlight bulbs in the stacks of labeled bins in three vehicles.

Finally, when a RAAM rider mentions the RV headlamp to the van team, the crew discloses absolutely no details about the temporary side-mirror replacement purchased at an auto parts store twenty miles ago, nor the Ford Itasca–specific side mirror ordered for pickup ahead along the route several hundred miles away. In crewing RAAM, as with many ultra endurance battles, the better part of valor is always, always discretion.

Following the big climb of Wolf Creek Pass (10,800 feet/3,293 meters) out of Pagosa Springs, Seana's saddle sore pain had reached levels of DEFCON 2. Saddle sores are the bane of cyclists everywhere and are quite common at distances well short of the RAAM 1,000-mile marker Seana had reached.

The term "saddle sores" can describe several unholy situations. Sometimes saddle soreness means deep sit-bones ache, as if one's tailbone area is bruised beyond recognition. Anyone who has ever fallen hard on ice or concrete can sympathize. Turns out there are small, fluid-filled sacs near each sit bone, brokering peace between the muscles, tendons, and pokey pelvis points of the region. Like every other part of a RAAM rider's body, this fluid-filled sac, or bursa, can become inflamed. Ask anyone who has had shoulder bursitis how this inflammation feels. Now watch their face as you ask them to imagine this same pain between the top of their hamstring tendon and their keister.

Sometimes that bruised feeling hits a different angle while in a more aero position, and the soreness lands squarely on the front pubic bone. Neither of these situations is pleasant with 2,000 more miles (3,219 kilometers) of cycling ahead.

The more common association of saddle soreness describes a multitude of godforsaken conditions of the flesh. Seams on shorts or seams on the specific cyclist padding (called "chamois"... rhymes with "Sammy") in bike shorts can inflict crippling harm to anyone from weekend warrior, to spin-class devotee, to RAAM qualifier. Sweat and its byproduct of salty crystals can pulverize the fragile skin of the human nether bits by chaffing. Female athletes are susceptible to unspeakable soft-tissue suffering to their undercarriage due to this abrasion. For men and women, pores and hair follicles in this vicinity are known to object to their work conditions and go on strike. The angry protests of furuncles (boils) and folliculitis (inflamed hair follicles) are aggravated by the pressure of sitting, friction (a.k.a. pedaling), and bacteria. Connect enough of these infuriated follicles in an unsightly collection under the skin, and soon you've got a carbuncle party.

Sometimes saddle sores are just a broad reddening of the skin (like a rash or erythema). But the initial rash, when compounded by blockage of the skin (occlusion) and complicated by sweat and bacteria, can turn from redness into the worst kind of abscesses in the worst possible of places. Before long, saddle sores can leave a cyclist begging and bargaining for a case of floppy neck muscles instead.

Seana had a front-row seat on the saddle-sore sufferbus. Her crew marked the spot on the road in duct tape near Alamosa, Colorado, where they made the decision to give Seana's saddle sores some specific attention. Per the thirty-six-page race rule book and the fifty-nine-page route book, RAAM regulations allow a rider to leave the course in this fashion, as long as the competitor reenters from the spot they exited. To a motel, her crew declared, she must go.

Like many endurance undertakings, RAAM is affectionately described by veterans as a long series of problems loosely related. The 2019 edition proved no different. This being RAAM, every motel in town was sold out.

The Rails and Ales festival in Alamosa was underway, with a massive block party in town and the Rio Grande Scenic Railroad providing rides up 9,500 feet (2,896 meters) in the Sangre de Cristo mountains for a high elevation festival with music, barbecue, forty-three craft breweries in a field...and no vacant hotel rooms anywhere nearby.

Seana and her crew had to drive 72 miles (116 kilometers) (one hour and fifteen minutes of extra driving) to Walsenburg, Colorado, to find a Best Western Rambler. The news after arriving in Walsenburg was not great either: Seana's female crew briefed her trusted crew captain, Stephen Peters, a cyclist in his early thirties from Sylacaga, Alabama. He's a lad with a taste for cross-country adventure and a capacity to stay preternaturally positive all the time. Given the state of the saddle sores described to him, Seana remembers Stephen breaking the news to her, "Seana, I don't think we are gonna be able to do this." By this, he meant, finish what they started. They both held eye contact as she cried.

The epitome of crew chief discipline and resilience, aware of his racer's needs and the implications of crew contagion, Stephen kept it together. The emotional regulation demanded of a leader in this situation can be one of the first casualties of sleep deprivation. "In front of Seana, there were no tears. But later on the phone, I cried to my mama," Stephen admitted, in the lyrical Talladega County accent (where the word "MAAHM-ma" is enunciated with sanctity). To participate in endurance events—as crew or athlete—is to be guaranteed such low points.

Seana, having won RAAM and DNF'd (Did Not Finish) a handful of times, admits she had to repress the urge to quit. But she did not react or overreact to the present state of affairs. A shower and sleep did her good, as did time out of the saddle. Stephen recommended Aquaphor, which he had packed for such a situation, while fellow ultra cyclist and friend Ellen Kirk fortuitously tracked down a new cream to try: Calmoseptine Diaper Rash Ointment. Adult diaper rash cream was never more extolled aloud among a group of gentlemen and ladies. The crew resupplied, regrouped, and held their collective breath.

Despite the atrocious sores, Seana didn't want to stop. "Okay, let's give it a go," she said, before driving backward—west—to the spot she had left the RAAM course between South Fork and Alamosa. It was the last shower and bed she thought she would see for a while.

While riding through Colorado, past La Veta (Time Station 19, mile 1,135; more than five days and three hours into the race), rider #161 stopped to assess her growing chamois discomfort, when out of nowhere a stranger appeared to two of the vehicles and their rider. The stranger, who owned the land abutting that stretch of state highway Colorado 12 offered them a guest house, a cabin just a little up the hill. Seana accepted. Racer #161 entered the cabin, cleaned her wounds, and proceeded to sleep for eight hours straight. The toilets and showers of the RAAM oasis were a gift to the Itasca and aux car crew. The beauty of the San Isabel National Forest all around them, next to a road in the Colorado Scenic and Historic Byways system, was overshadowed that day.

Deep down, Seana had been secretly resigned to the fact she would likely have to DNF the 2019 race. But then the beauty of the kindness of a stranger and the subsequent contagious rejuvenation of the crew that followed transcended the moment. People are good. You won't convince Seana Hogan otherwise. She got back on that Bianchi.

With fresh legs, Seana climbed up Cuchara Pass, pounding the pedals out of the saddle—this standing pedal stroke providing relief from sitting on the troublesome saddle. Through the descent to Trinidad (Time Station #20) she flew, and then she caught a tailwind in the eastern flats of Colorado. She might have blinked and missed her next check-in: the time station in Kim, Colorado (#21), has a population of sixty-three persons, give or take. With unobstructed views, 5,690 feet (1,734 meters) above sea level, this part of the ride often allows a view of more than one distinct weather pattern occurring on the plains. Instead of a quantity of census households, in every direction there are fields of swaying wheat and cattle ranches. The last stop in Colorado was hosted by Walsh (Time Station #22), a youngster of a town created by the Santa Fe Railroad in 1926.

Kansas continued the theme of flat fields of wheat, corn, soybeans, and sorghum through Ulysses, Montezuma, Greensburg, Pratt, Maize, and El Dorado (pronounced "El Dor-*raid*-o"). While the amount of land farmed around these towns throughout the sunflower state is roughly the same acreage as 1920, the number and average size of the farms tells a story. In 1920, there were 167,000 farms averaging 272 acres each. In 2019, there were only 58,500 farms averaging 781 acres each. Small family farms may someday go the way of Kansas bison, a statewide herd of hundreds of thousands eliminated entirely—because of their grazing—between 1871 and 1875.

On the way toward the eastern part of the state, racers pass the 100th Meridian (the 100th longitudinal line west of Greenwich, England), a north-south demarcation that served as a national boundary for more than one chapter in North American history: first as a border between the land holdings of Spain and France, then as a boundary of the Louisiana Purchase, and then as a border between the US and Mexico. It is now just an invisible climatic boundary, where land to the west runs arid and eastern land swings humid and moist. In practical terms, RAAM racers ride through wheat fields in the west, and around the 100th Meridian they begin to travel through fields of corn.[24]

Between Yates Center (Time Station #29, at mile 1,718) and Fort Scott (Time Station #30, at mile 1,778), Kansas, Seana listened to the same song on repeat for four hours and thirty minutes. A reminder that strength is not always measured with a leg press or in watts on a power meter. The song playing on loop was by the British band New Order, all rhythmic and electro in the 1980s' New Wave tradition. Its title? "Shellshock." Like an

---

24 A study from Columbia University's Columbia Climate School has reported that the warming of the climate appears to be moving the invisible vertical "wheat-corn" line further east, closer to the 98th Meridian.

The subject of the changing climate has concerning implications for a race course as long as RAAM. Per the documented rising average summertime temperatures across the United States, it appears possible that future RAAM participants will face a monumentally more difficult challenge than in previous eras. Future RAAM racers are not alone. It is worth noting, extreme weather events such as dangerous heat domes and skies choked with wildfire smoke are not compatible with long-distance sports over land or in water.

arrow hitting a bullseye, and a second arrow splitting the first, so perfect was this title for a midnight ride. Seana almost forgot that delicate parts of her anatomy were minced like ground beef.

Pushing through Weaubleau (Time Station #31, mile 1,844) and Camdenton (Time Station #32, mile 1,893), Missouri, the long, unsteep climb to Jefferson City wore on. "Every single RAAM, somewhere in Missouri or Oklahoma, I start thinking, 'What the heck are you doing?' and the urge to quit takes over every thought," Seana said. Sleeping only two to three hours per day plays these tricks. If pressed about how she handles the Missouri-to-Oklahoma moments, Seana explains how she cleverly distracts herself by solving complex math problems. As one does.

It's only reluctantly that the admission "my mind is pretty darn strong" leaves the mouth of the female transcontinental record holder (9 days, 4 hours, and 2 minutes, set at RAAM '95, still the record). She is shockingly, but not surprisingly, without ego. She is grateful specifically to every rider in the competition for helping her do her best. In RAAM, strong minds are even more important than strong necks. Try listening to one song on loop for one hour; now imagine three-and-a-half more hours of that same song. Now put yourself on a road bike at midnight. That's what a strong mind can do. And it's what RAAM's mileage calls upon entrants to do.

Pedaling toward an inevitable old red barn ahead is Seana's only assignment. Riding, county to next county, day to dusk, Milky Way night to the sanguine dawn. These are the small bites that long-distance cyclists must take if they hope to eat the whole beast. Maybe it's a bug, but likely it's a feature of the human species: no, you cannot race your bike across the United States, but you can ride from grain silo to grain silo.

The only way to make the process go faster is to go faster. But go too fast, push too much, and you burn matches you don't have for a mileage that totals over three thousand. Speed is a tightrope walk.

For twenty-seven years, no RAAM racer could go any faster than the beloved Pete Penseyres, who rode the 1986 course of 3,107 miles (5,000 kilometers) at a record pace. His record stood untouched year after year—despite stellar performances by greats like Americans Bob Fourney, Rob Kish, and Danny Chew; Austrian Wolfgang Fasching; and the Slovenian Jure Robič. Penseyres, who won RAAM twice, averaged 15.4 miles per hour for the route in 1986. It wasn't until 2013—when Austrian Christoph Strasser averaged 15.58 mph—that Pete Penseyres was not the first and last word of all the excellence encapsulated in RAAM. (Amongst women, the fastest speed recorded ever was 13.23 mph, by Seana Hogan in 1995.) For the experts, Pete's 1986 ride, in Avocet touring shoes with shoelaces and flat pedals with toe clips, with no cell phones or GPS, and with folded-up gas station maps for guidance, will forevermore be the most pure RAAM ride ever completed. Amen says the congregation in the cathedral called cycling's toughest event.

RAAM in the 1980s was not the beginning of this story. Transcontinental two-wheeled adventuring and the need for road maps in the United States predates RAAM by a century. In fact, it was cyclists in the 1880s and 1890s who pushed for reliable roads where previously just lay dirt. Before there was the Interstate Highway System (from the Federal Aid Highway Act of 1956) or the National Highway System (the first unified system in 1926), the loudest voices pushing for quality roads came from cyclists. Called "wheelmen," they reflected the deeply American independent spirit in the cities: à la "Why wait around for a horse-drawn streetcar, when I can go—with two wheels—on my own schedule via my own route?" Beyond the metropolises, most of the land of the forty-three states and the US territories in 1890 was not just outside of cities and towns. Most of the young country was outside, undeveloped and unpaved. Cities like New York, Philadelphia, and Chicago tallied populations of over one million residents in the nation's first census in 1890, but the country's vastness was not its pullulating population, but its *space*. And the land was ripe for exploration. The two-wheeled "feedless horses" were much lower maintenance than the equine standard of the day. What began as transportation in the late nineteenth century, before long became tied to ideas of personal liberty and trailblazing. Bikes galvanized the Good Roads Movement, uniting cyclists and farmers—like the ones in Kansas—for whom safe and direct roads meant timely goods to market, resulting in expansion and profits. In the 1880s and 1890s, cycling fever took hold in the U. S. of A.

Since time immemorial, wherever there's an adventurous heart combined with this fever, tomfoolery often follows. And *that* often involves a bet.

In 1896, the *San Francisco Chronicle* described one such example. The lads at two Brooklyn cycling clubs threw down a $1,000 wager (more than $36,000 in current value), on whether the Olympic Wheelman's teammate William England could ride from San Francisco to New York, "from ocean to ocean in forty days." England left Brooklyn in June—*The New York Times* reported—with a sendoff by the cycling club and about a hundred friends; riding from east to west to scope out the best route west to east, given the geographic hurdles and lack of decent roads. *The Brooklyn Daily Eagle* described his ride from east to west: "All the way to San Francisco he was buffeted by head winds and his progress was made slow by bad roads." With a quick turnaround time, his west-to-east venture eventually failed, for surely he felt the effects of the first 3,000–mile (4,828-kilometer) trip. (No word if the bet was collected from the Olympic Wheelman by the Battery A boys of the Fort Hamilton club.) Beyond William England, there were a multitude of transcontinental trips and attempts—more than fifty are documented—by men and women, soloists and tandems during the summer and early autumn months amid the cycling craze. Notable are the more than eighty magazines that came to print across North America during these years, such as: *The Pacific Cyclist*, a weekly out of San Francisco; two identically named *Southern Cycler's*—one published in Memphis, Tennessee, the other in Louisville, Kentucky; *The Wheelman's Record*, from Indianapolis; and *The Scorcher—A Hot Paper for Hot Cyclists*, indicating the amount of rowdy fun that has always been in the marrow of the cycling tradition.

Also, in that batch of periodicals, printed in Boston, shone *Wheelwoman*, with the subtitle: *Costumes, Wheels and Cycling News*. The mission statement of the magazine practically roared: "Devoted to the interests of women who ride the wheel and to the conversion of those who do not." The bicycle upended the previous social norm of chaperones for women outside their homes. Bicycles provided an excuses to ditch tight corsets and billowing floor-length skirts.

John F. Kennedy eschewing a hat at his 1961 inauguration altered the course of dress in the twentieth century just a fraction as much as female cyclists in the 1890–1900s.

Activist Susan B. Anthony, in an interview in 1896, captured the zeitgeist:

"I think/kilometer the bicycle] has done more to emancipate women than any one thing in the world. I rejoice every time I see a woman ride by on a bike. It gives her a feeling of self-reliance and independence the moment she takes her seat; and away she goes, the picture of untrammelled womanhood."

When Seana was young, it was a used bicycle that got her both to school and to after-school swim practice. It was a beat-up bicycle that delivered transportation, but it was a fraught home life that prepared her for the mile markers after. The math was simple: the amount of parental support was zero. Unlike math, her childhood featured no orderliness. RAAM is many things; sometimes it is a solution key. Spend enough time forged in the fire of unforgiving annealing, and you grow both softer and harder. The unpleasant bits from childhood, yesteryear's regrets, or elegiac laments burn off or get hammered away, stroke by stroke, feed zone to feed zone. For some ultra athletes, the ache of distance can mean recovery. Sometimes a form of treatment and recovery. Sometimes bad suffering can be replaced with the good kind of suffering to move past the past and be better for it. Research around the subject of grit in adults has found that childhood environments like Seana's can teach real-world adaptability and create an optimistic mindset. It's like the words from Texan musician and writer Kinky Friedman: "As my sister likes to say, a happy childhood is the worst possible preparation for life."

In a related truism, brought to us by the preeminent American female distance cyclist: the first chapter is not the story.

The vexing ache of the Missouri-through-Oklahoma hours eventually abated for racer #161. Her crew's surprise of matching adhesive costume mustaches in various neon colors helped, by giving her a moment of relieving laughter. A crew captain's work manifests in many ways.

Time stations like Number 34 in Washington, Missouri, served as anesthetic, too. The Revolution Cycles bike shop had pulled out all the stops: energetic mechanics, a gigantic potluck buffet, even a swimming pool for racers to submerge their scorched shanks. They fed and restored Seana's crew before and after her short stop at 11:10 p.m. local time. She gladly accepted the Coke they offered, then hopped right back on the Bianchi; a stop so short she never turned off her seat post's red taillight. It takes discipline to not stay longer at places like Revolution Cycles, where the slow cookers are warm and the coolers are full. Independent bike shops, especially family-run stores like Time Station #34, have been the quintessence of cycling since *The American Wheelman* was printed in St. Louis beginning in 1887 and *The Western Cyclist* began publication in 1895 in Omaha.

Between the Illinois-Indiana-Ohio mile markers, the anesthetic of surprise stick-on 'staches and neon goatees worn by the crew was no longer required. Somewhere between miles 2,116 (Greenville, Illinois) and 2,588 (Athens, Ohio), a kind of sustained two-wheeled teleportation or transmogrification occurred. At some point, Seana describes herself "as not even there." You're no longer riding, she explains, you are just a part of the bike. Time is suspended. It has to be. Platitudes like "take it a moment at a time" make Seana snort. During RAAM, she takes it hours at a time.

Reaching the eastern edge of the state cemented a stake in the ground for Seana. She was staking claim. She had made it to the Ohio River, the last of the four major river crossings of her voyage. The blue stretch before her was at least as beautiful as the precious Colorado, at least as substantial as the Missouri (America's longest river), and appeared as mighty as the Mississippi. The network arch bridge crossed seventy-six feet above the boundary between the Buckeye State and the Mountain State in the backdrop, with Blennerhassett Island mid-span. The four-mile-long island is the spot Vice President Aaron Burr fled from in 1806 after killing Alexander Hamilton in a duel the previous year. When Seana reached Time Station #45 at 2:41 a.m. (West Union, mile 2,673, day 11, hour 10, since her Oceanside departure), she knew it was time to tighten the chin strap and face the hills again. Sometimes in life and in RAAM, you just need to take your medicine. For endurance cycling fans worldwide following Seana's tracker, it was a climbing duel worthy of a Lin-Manuel Miranda score.

It helped that her crew captain riding in the van behind her was wearing a 1970s terry cloth headband with a faux mullet fringe attached along the nape; it was all party in the back. Facing rough climbs ahead, humor was the answer. "I may not be the best crew chief," said Stephen Peters, "but I am the most fun." Scientists have found at least sixty-five species of animals that use a vocal play signal equivalent to laughter. In humans, laughter diffuses tension and increases bonding between individuals. Seana refers to the young man with the mood-boosting laugh as her best friend. Take a peek at trail running groups, cycling clubs, or open-water swimming meetups; one of the lesser known benefits of endurance sports are the age-diverse friendships, built on laughter, that the outside world might be surprised to learn about. The combination of mentoring, crewing, pacing, the specificity of the niches, and the lifespan of long-distance sports for many athletes as adults fosters "age-gap friendships." This unsung benefit of long-distance endurance sports yields arguably one of life's sweetest pleasures for all involved.

What Party City fake mullet wigs provide in mirth, West Virginia provides in natural beauty. Almost heaven, John Denver called it in a song. There are fourteen states in the US that contain four syllables, but John Denver chose West Virginia for the first line of his 1971 gem about country roads. Unexpectedly hilly are the country roads there. To the uninitiated, it's not called the Mountain State for nothin'. US Highway 50 features a shocking number of switchback assents. Despite the previous twelve days, in 2019 Seana's legs never cracked in the Allegheny Mountains of the Appalachian range. Having reached Grafton, West Virginia, the hard way before, Seana faced the morning, vaguely remembering the tough miles ahead. To ride 2,719 miles (4,376 kilometers)—and to sign up to do this more than once—requires a certain kind of memory loss. Not dissimilar to the blurring of recollection that occurs when a woman who has birthed a baby opts to get pregnant again. Veterans of this event call it "RA-AMnesia."

In the remarkable way that many people have siblings born of the same mother, a second RAAM entry is a wonder. Like the rowdy words spoken in the throes of childbirth, riders like

Seana—and their saintly crews—avow year after year mid-course, verbatim: "I am never doing this fucking thing again." At least once. Truth be told, numerous times. Sometimes under their breath in an Itasca that still smells like RAAM 2015. Sometimes while sitting in the dirt, weeping. Sometimes back behind the van with a cigarette. Often this exact declaration is screamed into one of the pitch-black nights.

Providing context, Frank Strack explains: "There is no state in the United States with only good weather and flat roads. There are, however, a few with very *straight* roads, and some of those can be worse than the biggest of mountains. Heat, cold, rain, mountains, hurricanes, tornadoes. Honestly, I don't know why anyone would consider living in this place when you really break down the problem, because none of it is any good. To then decide you're going to ride your bike across it as fast as you can, repeatedly? I just don't know why in the world anyone would keep doing that."

He continues, "Except for the fact that I know exactly why: because when Seana is pedaling her bike, no matter the weather or the terrain, she is in control. She is in control of everything anyone could ever want to control. Her mind, and her body. And there is real, genuine beauty and freedom in that. The truth is, once she unlocked that power, I imagine it is very difficult going back and doing anything else."

After riding thousands of miles through stretches of the dark and The Dark Place, all at once, a race finish is revealed as possible. Hope slowly returns. Ever so slowly, the possibility of cessation of the discomfort begins to unfold. Then, poof, a finish line. Some celebrating, and a shit-ton of feel-good relief hormones are released to the sleep-deprived, and, voilà, a chronic case of RA-AMnesia sets in. For that which is hard to endure, once completed, is sweet to recall. Mathematicians and non-mathematicians begin calculating the many ways it can be done *better*, and *faster*, and *sweeter*. To the ounce, eleven-pound heads fill quickly with ideas to crack the RAAM code *next time*. And the planning for the next year, on cue, begins.

Seana rode the final miles through Maryland, to Pennsylvania (Rouzerville, Time Station #50, and Hanover #51), and up the final climb of the 2019 race to Mount Airy (Time Station #52, checkpoint 3 of 3), arriving at 4:03 p.m. In the past thirty-seven editions of the event, maladies for other racers before this spot have included, in the riders' own words: "nutrition problems," "swollen knees," "broken ribs/collar bone," "neck problems," "support vehicle problems," "loss of vision," and "leg mutiny." At this final checkpoint of the race, Seana had but one nut to crack—the traffic from Mount Airy to Annapolis would be more substantial than they had become accustomed to in their thirteen placid days of riding across America. But it was all over but for the shouting.

In the final miles, there's a Shell gas station that is the unofficial last stop for the racers to pee, change, and maybe clean up a bit before they ride to the finish line. It's the first glance in a mirror in a long time for many of the haggard competitors. To get to this point, beating cutoffs, means sacrificing all manner of vanity: Every minute spent grooming, glossing, or gussying up during RAAM is time not moving forward. During RAAM, Seana brushes her teeth on the bike. She reapplies sunscreen on the bike. Any food consumed is chewed on the bike. The sensory pleasures of a shower's hot water, of shaving, the flattery of cosmetics, the joy of freshly washed hair—are all sacrificed for the fortnight of RAAM. Champion endurance athletes—especially the women—often have this ability to compartmentalize vanity. They do not have the time to stare in mirrors. And thus, they must cast off expectations: delicate nails, shaped brows, deodorant, proper exfoliation, glossy hair smelling of green apples. Women cut from this cloth are climbers, runners, swimmers, sailors, cross-country skiers, alpinists—and cyclists. You'll know them by their no-nonsense pixie haircuts or their messy ponytail or their sea-salt curls. You'll know them by the chalk or dust or bike grease under their practical nails. You'll know them by their *dirt pants*—legs stained by the outdoors from the bottom of the hem of their shorts to the top of their precise sock line. They are not afraid of, in Seana's words, the likelihood of getting "pretty crusty" after 3,069 miles (4,939 kilometers) in 13 days, 4 hours, and 23 minutes. Dirt, dust, salt, and sand are the coins of the realm for these kings and queens with the weird tan lines.

Later that evening, on June 24, 2019, at 8:31 p.m., Seana Hogan crossed the timing mat at the finish of Race Across America. The RAAM spectators online following the thirty-eighth edition of the ultra-distance race lost their collective mind for the six-time winner. No group celebrated more than her crew. The jollity was that intoxicated fun, dizzying and unbridled. Like wild horses at play.

The cheering included Michael Shermer: "Seana is one of the most disciplined and dedicated athletes I have ever known," he said, "and I have known many of the greats." He ticks off a list that includes John Howard, Jonathan "Jacques" Boyer, Greg LeMond, Lance Armstrong, Lou Haldeman, and Pete Penseyres. "Even though I had competed in the race five times myself, I still marvel at Seana's stamina and strength of character." He watched her grow year after year, stronger from the suffering and travails of RAAM, creating physical and mental toughness, culminating with the way Seana threaded the needle again in 2019. "On top of this toughness, Seana has a sense of humor and is almost unfailingly upbeat both on and off the bike." Seana has been liked by RAAM folks as much as she has been admired.

The race organizers asked her crew if they thought Seana would want to receive the famed "Red Lantern" award for being the event's final finisher. The award is named for the red safety lantern hung from a train's caboose, the last tip of the tail at the end of a race field in cycling. But the award is no zonk, no teasing booby prize. The award symbolizes the courage it takes to finish a race that others would have abandoned. It honors the spirit of persistence that makes distance cycling meritorious. It showcases the elegance of the sport. A humble champion, Seana's face lit up, "Hell yeah, I'll take the award," she said. "That's the only thing I haven't won in this race." Her crew erupted in cheers. Seana Hogan, as ever, one of one.

In those final pedal strokes, Seana had become the first 60+ female finisher in the event's history, neck strong, head held high.

With this template, for as long as Race Across America exists, hardihood will never go the way of the Kansas bison.

The ultimate road bike pain cave starts under a truss that, in fairness, states clearly, "The World's Toughest Bicycle Race." Seana Hogan departed Oceanside in 2019, on the road to bonus backroads and extra gears she would find. These are backroads and gears that only RAAM can beget. *(photo by RAAM photographer Vic Armijo)*

CHAPTER SEVEN

UN-DOG RACING IN THE SEASON OF THE HARD WATER

John Stamstad

O my good friend, patience is bitter, but its fruit is sweet!
—*Jean-Jacques Rousseau*, Julie, or the New Heloise, *1761*

THE LOCALS WHO CREATED ALASKA'S MOST EPIC BIKE RACE—
Iditabike—knew how to speak plainly: "Cowards won't show and
the weak will die," goes the event tagline. There was no sense
in sugarcoating the mid-winter madness of mountain bike tires
on a loosely marked course in The Last Frontier. Event slogans
can aim to reduce bear bait; that's how they do it in Alaska. The
inaugural race in 1987 was held in February, so, in good news,
sleeping bears would not be included in the long list of potential
race hazards. But to take a bicycle into such conditions benumbed
all logic and reason.

The event of 130 miles (210 kilometers), or some distance
approximating this, began near Anchorage, across—what

else?—a frozen expanse called Big Lake. The first half of the out-and-back route was a portion of the famous dog-sled race held on the Iditarod Trail. "Iditarod," an Ingalik and Holikachuk word that means "distant place," was first the name of a 325-mile river, a tributary of the Innoko River. The word then became the name of a village-turned-town. Once, the town hummed with prosperity—and as many as ten thousand residents in 1911. In the tradition of the boom-and-bust gold fever of the west, the village is now a ghost town. In that spirit, any two-wheeled adventure in the Alaskan bush in mid-winter is likely to produce binary boom-or-bust outcomes for any soul brave enough to try.

News of this epic bike event reached Cincinnati, Ohio, via *VeloNews*, the go-to newsprint bike magazine of the 1970s and 1980s (and still today online). Iditabike sounded like madness to one Midwest kid who knew enough about snow—from growing up in Wisconsin—to know better. Riding bikes on snow? No one did that. It made as much sense as two bald guys fighting over a comb.

While in college, the strawberry-blonde kid, John Stamstad, had once pedaled from the Badger State to Colorado with a friend, covering more than 900 miles (1,448 kilometers) in eight days one summer. During his first winter trips to Colorado in the late 1980s, he was an early adopter of the first snowboards seen on the slopes around Frisco. But nowhere in Colorado had he seen anyone ride bikes in winter. The term "bikepacking" was not part of the common parlance, even among cyclists.[25] Whatever this survival test of a sport, John's curiosity outweighed what some would call common sense.

His first question: Why would a 130-mile (209-kilometer) bike route need a 75-hour race cutoff time?

In the run-up to the February 1992 Iditabike event, John Stamstad left Cincinnati for the Rocky Mountains of the Centennial State to prepare for his first visit to Alaska. What he lacked in cold weather ultra-cycling experience, extreme weather equipment, and local AK knowledge, he would make up for with curiosity. Empty of preconceptions, free of expectations, he would lead with wonder. Later, when it was all said and done, he would wonder why he thought Wisconsin, Ohio, and Colorado could be anything other than piss-poor simulations of cycling five degrees latitude south of the Arctic Circle. But to John, naturalist and biophile, The Last Frontier was a puzzle worth solving with his mind and his bike.

The race organizers of Iditabike arranged for southerners like John to board with host families near Anchorage upon arrival to the forty-ninth state. On a nervous night before the event, John

---

25 Cycling nomenclature can be a real mess. Bikepacking used to be called "bike touring" by some. "Gravel touring" or "adventure touring" also have entered the chat, in an attempt to delineate between the kind of bike used, the surface of the trail, and a bike's bag set-up. There are no agreed upon definitions here, but broadly speaking: bike touring connotes paved roads or bike paths on road bikes with racks and pannier bags. On the other end of the spectrum there is bikepacking, which occurs on unpaved roads (no pavement) on mountain bikes or gravel bikes and is without racks and side panniers, but instead with bags in the frame or close to the centerline of the bike. One of the most famous bikepacking events currently is the Tour Divide—the 2,700-mile (4,345-kilometer) event from Banff in the Canadian Rockies to the US-Mexico border. Its hours are as wild and unforgiving as anything on two wheels. It takes between two and eight weeks for someone tough enough to finish the distance. John Stamstad would later not shy away from this course, either.

was asleep on his host family's sofa in their living room when odd noises coaxed him to the room's picture window. A moose stared back at him through the casement, taller and broader than the length and width of the glass. In North America, second to bison, there are no larger mammals. It was the first moose John had ever seen. The animal's name comes from the Algonquian word *mooswa*, meaning "twig eater," because willow, balsam needles, birch bits, and the like are all that's available above the snow blanket in the die-back of the deep dark. To survive on withered bark, inhospitable needles, and desiccated twigs requires a digestive tract with the best qualities of a woodchipper. This explains how moose have successfully lived in the interior of Alaska for more than eleven thousand years. Archaeologists have found moose bones in a bluff-top camp in Alaska from 9,000 BC at the convergence of Shaw Creek and the Tatana River, all thanks to some highway construction in 1989. A University of Alaska Fairbanks scientist has found moose antlers in Alaska's North Slope dated to fourteen thousand years ago. Rare is a digestive tract in the animal kingdom this impressive. The moose staring at John did not have the large palmate, bowl-shaped antlers associated with male moose, but racks are shed in January. And as it was February, that moose staring at John—male or female—was likely hungry: in tough winters, moose often starve to death. Six months is a long time with a lack of fat reserves and not enough high caloric food. If you are in need of nutrient-dense fare in the crevasse of winter, almost anything is more helpful than woody browse. Winter kill, it's called. No matter your size, it's hard to keep up with the calories required of an Alaskan winter.

Food and calories were top of John's mind, too. He wasn't quite sure what foods would hold up to the extreme cold. He had heard rumors that the water bottles he usually carried on his bike frame would likely freeze. He wore a hydration pack on his back from a new company called CamelBak. Their patent, dated October 29, 1991, featured a silicone bite valve connected to a tube by which water in a hydration bladder could be consumed without any leaking, and completely hands free. And hydration is essential in the battles against hypothermia and frostbite. The lightweight backpack that held the bladder could also hold bike tools, food, and spare innertubes for his wheels, the last of which—little did he know—would later come in handy. By using his body heat, the bladder contents remained in liquid form and the food would not crack a molar (as a lifelong cyclist, John has learned this cracked-molar lesson with frozen items the hard way). He chose foods that would remain edible and tasty in the cold: sesame paste-based halvah, dense and rich, and satisfying chocolate-covered almonds and easy-to-source peanut M&M candies. The food was carefully tucked in his pack close to his 135-pound form. The first-place finisher of Iditabike in 1987 was on course for 33 hours and 50 minutes. Stay outdoors in the interior of Alaska for that long, and you'll be glad if it's only your water bottle that's frozen.

When John landed in Anchorage, no one could accuse him of being unprepared. Looking back, he recalled, "I definitely overpacked." But given the wide range of conditions and equipment, the first-timer was his characteristically careful self. Just off the tarmac, he surveyed his gear: one cardboard-boxed bike, a bivouac sack, a sleeping pad and sleeping bag, a stove and fuel, riding lights (with batteries the size of a stick of dynamite), all manner of bike repair curios, a first-aid kit, and the clothes and nutrition to keep him from most preventable discomfort. Hopefully.

In July of 1897, the day after the steamship *SS Portland*, full of two tons of gold from the Klondike River, arrived at Schwabacher's Wharf (now Pier 58) in Washington, *The Seattle Post-Intelligencer* ran the front-page headline: "Gold! Gold! Gold! Gold!" In large typeset, the subtitles read, "Sixty-Eight Rich Men on the Steamer Portland," "Stacks of Yellow Metal!" and "The Steamer Carries $700,000." Ads were quickly made overnight by Seattle outfitters: "If You Are Going To Alaska—By All Means Go Fully Prepared," read a full-page Cooper & Levy advertisement. The words from the First Avenue shop near Yesler Way applied to John Stamstad's maiden trip almost a century later: "You will find yourself hundreds of miles from civilization where it's utterly impossible to secure necessary articles." Men like Clinton C. Filson opened new storefronts in 1897 with the ubiquitous business shingle "Alaskan Outfitters." "Don't get excited and rush away early half prepared," read an outfitter's ad, strategically placed next to the "Gold! Gold! Gold! Gold!" headline on the front page of *The Seattle Post-Intelligencer*. The list of supplies provided at Yukon Supply Co. on First Avenue near Marion Avenue in 1898—"provisions, clothing, sleds, and bedding...needed for a safe and comfortable journey"—was not too dissimilar from the goods in the mismatched bags at John Stamstad's feet at Anchorage International Airport in 1992.

Like the prospectors who rushed to Alaska in the late nineteenth century, sleds were necessary for the first Iditabike participants. Entrants towed their required race gear behind them on homemade contraptions. A few cyclists tried to cram the required packing list of items into a wobbly four-bag set-up—imagine a duffel bag mounted vertically on the center of both wheels on both sides. This is harder to get evenly balanced than it looks. In deep drifts, the pannier side bags, which can extend past the wheel hub, can crush momentum due to poor clearance. Bag weight can also mangle bike handling. John, thrilled by the puzzle-solving challenge of this undertaking, tried combinations of packing and towing solutions, settling on a large pack in front of his handlebars and another extended above his back wheel attached to his seat post and saddle rails. Charlie Kelly, an entrant of the 1987 Iditabike race, and one of the first of the beloved Marin, California, Mount Tamalpais mountain bikers, described the California-Alaska nexus: "Once the technology expanded outside our limited Northern California climate, people dealt with things that we didn't have to," he says with a laugh, "And came up with solutions we didn't need." This whole undertaking was one big exhilarating game.

Those born and bred in Alaska, indigenous and non-indigenous Alaskans, seemingly have game-playing and sporting stories as part of their DNA. There are Native games and large youth competitions, such as the annual Junior Games (the JNYO, grades 1–6) and Native Youth Olympic Games (grades 7–12) in Anchorage. Fairbanks is the host of the four-day World Eskimo-

Indian Olympics, established in 1961. The WEIO organization and the Dena (or Athabascan) people host the Dena Games in March, and invite all people, regardless of ethnicity, to come and play their captivating traditional games, free of charge.

Native games range from throwing contests and kicking contests, to height-defying blanket tossing, and stick-pulling contests—mimicking the strength needed to grab a fish by the tail. Games are often for all ages; for example, seal-hopping contests. In this race, athletes hold a horizontal plank position (like a push-up) parallel to the floor, with flexed toes and flat hands (for children) or bare knuckles (for grown-ups). From this plank position, contestants cover the race distance in a horizontal hop. It is a test of core muscles, upper body strength, intense calisthenics, and some righteous knuckle pain for the adults. The combination of isometric (the plank) and concentric (the push-forward mini leap) exercise is taken from a real-world application; it is a motion utilized by seal hunters in the wild that their prey do not find alarming. Much to their detriment.

There are also imported games in Alaska—like the Midnight Sun game played since 1906 in Fairbanks. The traditional nine-inning baseball game begins at 10 p.m. and has never used artificial light, owing to being held on the summer solstice.[26]

But the most famous and beloved sport in Alaska, and the official state sport, is dog-sled racing.

---

26 When the path of the sun in the Northern Hemisphere is at its most northern point—usually June 20 or 21—a town like Fairbanks experiences what feels like twenty-four hours of straight daylight. Technically, the sun does set around 1 a.m. and rises before 3 a.m., but to the human eye it can feel like as many as seventy straight days of sunlight from mid-May through the end of July there. However, sports fans, here's the rub: the inverse is true in winter.

The Iditarod event is still the longest annual dog-sled race in the world. It commemorates the tradition of sledding with canines and toboggans, indigenous traditions of the Alaska Natives, and the timeless role of sleds in transportation and freight hauling around the forty-ninth state. Relative to its size, Alaska is a place with few roads and lots of jokes about small aircraft crashes (*"There are old pilots here, and bold pilots here, but there are no old, bold pilots in Alaska"*). Sleds, guided by some very good dogs, are as reliable a mode of transport and hauling, pound-for-pound, as any modern equivalent in a state where, as John Muir explained, "nothing in the far-famed Yosemite Valley...will compare with it in impressive, awe-inspiring grandeur."

The Iditarod event pays particular tribute to the notable valor of mushers and dogs in one specific case. In 1925, the icebound port city of Nome was on the verge of a diphtheria outbreak. Six children had already suffocated from the cruel upper-respiratory-tract illness created by the toxin-producing bacterium *Corynebacterium diphtheria*. A Nome doctor sent the following telegram via the Washington-Alaska Military Cable and Telegraph System on January 22:

"An epidemic of diphtheria is almost inevitable here STOP I am in urgent need of one million units of diphtheria antitoxin STOP Mail is only form of transportation STOP."

No boat or airplane could reach inaccessible Nome. Despite icebound conditions and the snarling impediments of the season and latitude, Alaskans galvanized to arrange a wild baton pass of life-saving serum via sleds. Connecting legs of a relay route from Nenana (the most northern reach of the railroad) to the Yukon, across the harrowing ice of Norton Sound and finally to Nome, the distance would require more than 150 dogs. A high-pressure system from the Arctic met the sled teams with winds measured at 65 mph (with gusts up to 80), and the temperatures registered between –40°F and –85°F (-40°C and -65°C). It required 127.5 uncertain hours and twenty sleds to deliver the serum in a Hail Mary plan to arrest the runaway diphtheria bacteria of Nome.

Just north of the Children's Zoo and east of the Willowdale Arch in Central Park in New York City stands a patinated statue of the dog named Balto, credited with leading the last fifty-five miles of the final leg into Nome. *The New York Times* called it a "New Honor in Dog History" when his statue was dedicated in December 1925. The plaque reads, "Dedicated to the indomitable spirit of the sled dogs that relayed antitoxin 600 miles over rough ice, across treacherous waters, through Arctic blizzards, from Nenana to the relief of stricken Nome, in the Winter of 1925." They were the dogs Jack London described in *The Call of the Wild*, the "strong of muscle...with warm, long hair"—working breeds, unassumingly compact, so as to not overheat like larger dogs. Reading between these lines of bronze, the statue really commemorates the many dogs who *died* during the journey for the "urgent need of one million units" for the people of Nome. This is the unwritten history about the dogs in those harnesses who perished from cold and exhaustion during those 127 hours.

As a kid raised on the stories of the polar explorers and doomed icebound ships, John had read all the tales of Arctic and Antarctic exploration and survival homesteading. The long-distance story from 1925 impressed on him early the dog power required to stay alive when darkness accounts for much more than half the day.

Statue or no statue, the dog lauded by *Alaskans* for the most difficult job and leading the hardest leg of that legendary journey was a Siberian Husky named Togo. The compact canine led from Nome to his sled's serum pick-up point, only to turn around and run the most dangerous portion of the route *again*. Across the forty-two-mile shortcut across Norton Sound, it was Togo who is credited for choosing the safest line; his sled driver and owner Leonhard Seppala was helplessly dozens of feet back (and oft blinded by the whiteout conditions), trusting the twelve-year-old husky to avoid cracking ice. It is estimated that Togo's line cut a day's worth of travel off the route. Togo led a total of 260 miles (418 kilometers) through the blizzard. The effort of the lead dog with ice-blue eyes was designated the "greatest mushing tale of them all" by a historian for the *Anchorage Daily News*. It's the kind of story that is too remote for journalists to be able to submit copy about and too great a distance for photographers to haul equipment. It's the kind of story you must see with your own eyes, but in the –85°F wind chill of the Arctic's high-pressure systems, it's too cold and windy a place for the blood vessels of the human retina.

In 1992, first-timer John Stamstad stood staring at the behemoth head of a moose with only double-paned glass between them. "How could anything be that large?" was his query to the lampblack night. The scale of nature in Alaska would continue to be like nothing he had ever seen or could have prepared for.

The weather leading up to the race had been mild by local standards; temperate for February. The morning of the race, the world outside the insulated glass revealed a cold dazzle of stars, as the sun would not rise until later, at 8:43 a.m. The clear sky was a sign. Alaska was a tough teacher to the willing. The race-day temperatures were forecast to be benign. This influenced what went into John's drop bags.

Briefly, drop bags are weatherproof bags transported by race organizers to designated checkpoints for athletes to resupply or add new or remove old, unnecessary gear. Ironman® 140.6 triathlon races (2.4-mile swim, 112-mile bike, and 26.2-mile run) allow racers five drop bags. Resupply items might be extra energy gels, new items might be a tube of sunscreen, and an example of removed items would be bike gloves as an athlete starts the run. In an extreme race, such as Hardrock 100 in Silverton, Colorado, where the average elevation is 11,186 feet (3,410 meters) and there are 66,394 feet (20,237 meters) of total elevation change in 102 miles, ultrarunners may have seven drop bags. In the Iditarod, mushers are allowed three drop bags at each of the twenty-three checkpoints—for a total of sixty-nine drop bags—and no drop bag may weigh more than sixty pounds. Feeding twelve to sixteen working dogs deems these amongst the hardest-core drop bags in the world. At John's first Iditabike, he delivered his three drop bags to volunteers the day before the race, based on a forecast that would prove wide of the mark.

John examined the eclectic group who gathered at the start around the modest Big Lake Lodge. "Maybe the motel had three rooms?" John offers by way of description. The diner attached to the motel was Northern perfection, described by the first-timer as "greasy spoon and real nice folks." It has been said that nobody is accidentally in Alaska. But compared with fancy Category-1 road racing in California or Florida or Arizona—or la-ti-dah Europe—the start line did look like a group of accidental cyclists.

A similar ragtag rally of bike riders were captured in early Betamax and VHS-tape footage from Marin County, California, more than a dozen years earlier. The forest renegades rode Frankenbikes in the hills around towns like Larkspur, Fairfax, and Mill Valley: old 1940s newspaper-boy frames beefed up and/or stripped down for riding off road. Sometimes the old cow horn-shaped handlebars were replaced by cross-braced BMX bars for strength, or extra gearing was added to make the ride back up Mount Tamalpais possible. The fun-lovin' counterculture of Klunkers (or Clunkers or Klunkerz) rode in worn denim; their steel-toed boots showed the wear of dragging their inside foot on downhill bends. The bravest daredevils went downhill much faster than one set of back brakes could stop them. The sideburns were rowdy and so were the cheering spectators at the hairpin turns of their Mt. Tam clandestine races. Never was free fun more fun.

A few of the original Klunkers crowd included guys like Joe Breeze, Otis Guy, Charlie Kelly, and Gary Fisher; the latter two worked with a road-bike frame maker named Tom Ritchey to build some of the first versions of the "ballooner" bikes with wider tires and gears (the first known bikes of this style were hand built by Joe and called "Breezers"). A kind of perpetual summer, it was the season when wheels turned, kegs were pushed uphill, weed was rolled by hand. Grainy late-1970s photos depict counterculture Nor-Cal wheelmen who spent far more time riding trails and enjoying the woods with their friends than visiting the barber shop or the tailor.

That rogue spirit shone bright in 1992 next to the Big Lake Motel. The mismatched Iditabike outerwear had that distinct second-hand-store quality, sharing connective tissue with the Nor-Cal hippies. (The Marin County Klunkers slogan about biking being better "with no cars, no concrete, and no cops," applied to the independent-minded Alaskan ethos, too.) The colors clashed and the insulated hiking boots appeared clunky and ill-fitting compared to the soigné gentlemen of road cycling. In the apotheosis of Alaskan fashion, closer inspection confirmed base layers were pilled, waterproofed items were unwashed, and occasional bits of duct tape were in use. The snow could not dampen the sussurating sound of insulated nylon and hardshell woven fabric wrapped around thirty-one cyclists trying to stay warm on a February morning.[27]

It wasn't only cyclists being noisy in nylon at the start line. The Iditabike event had evolved to "Iditasport" in 1991. The race organizers had successfully built an inter-sport lab of winter competition by allowing athletes to compete as snowshoers,

---

27 Cyclists pedaling around in backcountry outerwear before a race is a peculiar sight, but it creates an even stranger sound. The description of the soundtrack of Iditabike—the swish-swish-swishing of heavyweight outerwear for hundreds of miles of hiking and pedaling—is unintentionally provided by Bill Watterson, comic-strip illustrator. On November 16, 1986, Watterson published a comic in his "Calvin and Hobbes" series. The long first frame is empty except for the profile of young Calvin walking in profile toward the right. Behind him is Watterson's copy for the frame, "zip zop zip zop zip zop zip zop." This text follows the six-year-old across the entirety of the panel. In the next frame, the towhead Calvin turns and addresses the reader directly with a two-word explanation: "snow pants."

skiers, cyclists, runners, or triathletes (racing one third of the course in three of the activities). Athletes could pick their 200-kilometer equipment of choice that morning. "Choose your weapons!" was the refrain. The purists would not budge from their sport's gear, but some all-around outdoors people would let the course conditions determine their weapons of choice. John had no other equipment but his bike. Others were committed to their specialty due to their sport's obvious superiority over the others. And many had trained hard all year, not for themselves, but on behalf of bragging rights for their sport. Befitting that lower portion of the Chugach Mountains where the race began, ribbing snowshoers trash-talked skiers who trash-talked snow cyclists, back and forth, round and round. The 1991 race had been won on skis by Fairbanks' own Bob Baker in 28 hours and 33 minutes, throwing peat on the fire about who were the toughest athletes and what was the best equipment at Big Lake. Seventeen skiers, five triathletes, and four snowshoers came to play in 1992. Of course, Alaska does not hold the monopoly on this sort of banter and bloated challenges of skill. But in the callused hands of Alaskans, it's damned near an art form.

John had no dog in the locals' smack-talking fight and was not familiar enough with the route to know what the recent weather and season's snowfall to date would mean for the course. This suited him. John carried a "learn as you go" and "play like you're behind" approach like his portable alcohol stove and his lightweight sleeping bag, rolled tighter than a Marin county joint in his saddle pack.

With a name suggesting he was born for the job, race director Dan Bull kept the speechmaking to a minimum at the race start.

A mover by trade ("custom relocations") and legit Anchorage cyclist, Bull took over the Iditabike event the previous year, changing the name to Iditisport to include skiers and snowshoers. And in 1992, he invited runners. Bull, as engaging as he was good looking, could charm the snowy owls from the trees, if the Arctic tundra to the north weren't treeless. He would lead the event with rapscallion finesse and the heart of a scamp for ten righteous years. A one-time preacher, a talented day trader, Bull would later fake his own death in the Chugach Mountains. He has successfully disappeared since.

In the spirit of such individualism and buccaneer ethos, Bull started the race and John and the other entrants set off, not required to follow any marked route; they only needed to pass through mandatory checkpoints. John would confront Alaska in winter head on, without restrictions or race officials. Dependent solely on one, or so he thought.

The organizers were not in the business of putting people in danger, *per se*, but they were not there to apologize for Iditasport, either. Dan Bull didn't even want to offer anything other than product awards for the winners: "It seems that in an Arctic event with its inherent danger, promoting purses for which people will extend themselves is a liability we can't put up with," he said before the February 15 event. Thus, no cash, no race expo, no speakers blaring jock jam music to hype the event, and no merch tent. Hell, there weren't even reliable trail markers ahead. If you needed laminated arrows with distance updates and neon pink plastic tape tied to trees, this was not the race for you.

The clear skies overnight meant colder temperatures than they had seen in the week before the race. The temperate weather pattern was replaced by plummeting digits even the locals admitted were indeed cold. John considered the mid-weight riding gloves on his hands, the ones he had comfortably worn riding daily in the run-up to race, and he shook his head imperceptibly. "Gloves. I should have kept the gloves." His heavyweight hand gear—called "chopper gloves," which get their name from Northern wood choppers—were packed in a drop bag at a faraway checkpoint. Given the weather forecast ("Temps in the 20s!"), the novice guessed he would not need them until the night. He had guessed wrong.

John stayed with the lead pack of riders from the start-finish line headed toward the shore of Knik, another lake about eight miles away, and the first checkpoint. He had lead-pack leg power and a conditioned engine to match. While folks were water skiing and swimming in 2,500-acre Big Lake the previous summer, in his first non-road bike race, the nice Midwest guy had ridden 181 miles (292 kilometers) in a 24-hour race that began in Montezuma, Colorado, in a loop that included a checkpoint at 14,270 feet.

That February morning, John was big ringing it (pushing the hardest, fastest gear) on a frozen lake only 144 feet above sea level. The local thermometers registered –18°F (-28°C). Big Lake was completely frozen over. It was the kind of spot where snow-mobiles and full-sized trucks with extended-view side mirrors are randomly parked out on the lake. The wheels of those trucks are made of a hydrophilic rubber that remains softer, and thus more flexible, in cold temperatures. A dozen inches below those trucks' winter tires were burbot, Arctic char, and Sockeye salmon for ice-auger-toting fishermen arguably as sturdy as those fish. In a place called Anchorage's playground, John saw how seriously the locals play, even in the season of hard water.

How hard is the water? Neighbors plow a road on the ice of the lake. The Big Lake Ice Road runs east-west for more than six-and-a-half miles (ten kilometers). Not maintained by the county or state, the road is maintained by Big Lake's neighbors, using their own trucks and plows and fuel. And it's not just a trail for ATVs and snowmobiles: stacked lumber trailers, propane tankers, and concrete trucks with their massive revolving drums all use the Ice Road. That's how cold it gets in Alaska.

John felt the shattering temperatures in every bone in his two hands. He was facing an innominate foe: sweat vapor. In the early 1990s, cold-weather gear serviced alpine athletes and outdoors people, but forward-motion athlete gear for extreme climates had not yet been perfected. In below-zero temps, trapped water vapor—like the frozen swamp in John's gloves—freezes like the freshwater of Big Lake. Frozen sweat vapor can cause the water inside the cells of human skin to freeze in a matter of minutes at −18°F. The cold creep next moves—stinging, throbbing, numbing—into the underlying tissue, where the fluid freezes, without mercy, into ice crystals. Frostnip would have turned to extreme frostbite quickly on the Knik Arm of Cook Inlet that February, but John knew to keep windmilling his arms, driving blood into his hands using centrifugal force. He kept every finger moving as he pedaled. And he never squeezed his grips too tightly, when most racers would have been clutching that handlebar for dear life.

From Knik, John rode west toward the Susitna River, headed for the Big Susitna ("Big Su") checkpoint, where his chopper gloves waited. Susitna, a glacial river, flows from just north of Denali National Park. It heads at (originates from) Susitna Glacier, although more than a hundred glaciers flow into the upper forks of the river. Countless creeks, seasonal streams, unnamed tributaries, and anonymous rills feed her. With significant runs of King (or Chinook) and Coho salmon, rainbow trout, Arctic grayling, and Dolly Varden trout, the productive Susitna flows for more than 300 miles (483 kilometers), bejeweled with these spawning, migrating, and rearing fish, iridescent as hummingbirds, and just as busy.

In his frozen river riding in Alaska, John's trail had sections so thick with fish in the summer you could practically walk across the water on their backs. These Alaskan fish don't like water this cold. They adore it. They are disciples of it, swimming toward it with purpose. Cold water, which holds more oxygen, is critical to Alaskan fish during parts of their life cycles. (If one wanted to connect the relationship between Alaska's cold water and the fish of her ecosystems to the unequivocal evidence of the surface temperature increases in a warming world, this could be that intersection.) Without clean and very cold water, incubation and hatching are at risk for Alaska's fish.

While cold water is a requirement of these cold-blooded creatures, cold water trapped in clothing has the opposite effect on warm-blooded humans. John was cold and getting colder from the exertion of racing a bike overland toward an unseen checkpoint. Occasional pockets of really, really cold air could make a mere –18°F feel tolerable.

John swallowed the sting of the cold and gazed at the expanse of snow before him. To navigate the unfamiliar snow blanket, with hours of cycling—or worse—ahead, John's mind and physiology found equilibrium in endurance relativism. Endurance relativism is the framework where an endurance athlete's paradigm is relative only to some indeterminate set of hard-core data. It's a universal model where "X is Y in relation to Z."

For example, Rabbit Lake (X) was cold (Y), but it sure beat riding in Prospect Creek, Alaska (Z), where the low temperature was once recorded—not including windchill—at a Trans-Alaska Oil Pipeline camp at –80°F (-62°C).

John's bike (X) might have been traveling slowly (Y) on the trail due to the low tire pressure required while riding on snow, but John was miles in front of the fastest snowshoer (Z) on the racecourse.

John would later ride through the blackest night with his headlamp flashing fiery white-eye reflections locked on him from the woods (X), which was on the razor's edge of terrifying (Y), but was possibly better than hiking up fourteener Grays Peak alone, in the dark in Colorado, with a bike strapped to your back (Z) during the 24-hour Montezuma's Revenge race. John's a devout and practicing optimist; he chooses to see the CamelBak as half-full rather than as half-empty.

In other words, when testing the edges of endurance, everything is relative. Over the course of future decades of adventuring, this would remain a core tenet of John Stamstad. This trait, honed in Alaska, would prove even more dependable than the four-foot lath stakes that mark the 975-mile (1,569-kilometer) Iditarod route to Nome.

Rolling into Rabbit Lake checkpoint, before him stood a wall tent, the four-sided kind reminiscent of an African safari.

A volunteer offered water—snow boiled and cooled—which he gladly accepted to refill the bladder in his backpack. There were offers of food and warm Alaskan hospitality, but John knew better.

Racing in Alaska in February puts into sharp relief some truisms about stopping during endurance efforts. John had a firm ten-minute policy at checkpoints, aid tables, and nature's places of wonder. Ten minutes, firm, not a second longer was his limit. Ten minutes is enough time to take care of all matters outhouse and resupply. More than ten minutes in endurance distance delivers pivotal temperature change. In this case, frost on John would have condensed and melted, leaving him soaking wet. That moisture would indeed refreeze, for example, when back outside the wall tent of Rabbit Lake. Also, if you wait more than ten minutes, your muscles will tighten up. More than ten minutes creates inertia, with a multiplier effect. More than ten minutes actually damages your sense of time. More than ten minutes and unlimited snacks and caring volunteers and a warm fire can lure an athlete into comfort seeking—for which there is little place for enduring bodies going long. The lure of comfort seeking must be eschewed, the grizzled veterans warn. There is a reason that ultrarunners are known to give specific advice about dawdling at aid stations: "Beware of the chair," goes the saying.[28]

Back on the bike, pedaling toward Skwentna checkpoint, John felt a new kind of cold creep, the particular kind of cold delivered

---

28 The fourteen-time winner of the Western States Endurance Run, Ann Trason—of the "You-can-be-a-whiner-or-an-ultrarunner-but-you-can't-be-both" school of thought—famously wore a custom shirt specifically about dawdling at aid stations while she crewed the 100-mike (161-kilometer) race. It read, "You're not puking and nothing's broken...so get going!"

by winter afternoons. As the interior of the frontier turned away from the distant sun once and for all, John, not yet halfway on the course, would no longer be this warm again.

The inimical cold would next harm more than John's body. It started with that familiar sound—*zip, zop, zip, zop*—drowned out by a tragic *pssssssss!*-sound. The "dreaded hiss"—to use John's words—of a punctured tire is universally unwelcome, in any weather. But in temperatures around –20°F (-29°C), a flat tire is another thing altogether. Out of the saddle, gloves off, into his pack John excavated for a patch kit, a spare tube, levers to remove and replace the tire, and his pump to inflate the repaired or replaced tube. When, like John, you savor the pleasure of a beautiful sport, changing a flat tire is no big deal. It's a small price to pay to be a cyclist. "I love what I'm doing, or I wouldn't do it," John says with an easygoing smile, but with unblinking conviction in his eyes. The expression of someone who knows what it's like to ride with significant pain in his hands for more than an hour after fixing a flat in the ridiculous dark of early evening in Alaska in winter.

About the same time John regained feeling in his hands, it happened. A second flat, with the same tube-changing routine for the cyclist followed. Within the hour, an unthinkable third flat occurred—now with an added element of stress, as John installed his last spare innertube.

Back in the saddle, not more than a couple hours of riding a trail that was covered in wolf-paw prints, and again, *mush-THUMP, mush-THUMP, mush-THUMP*. A fourth flat tire. John had no choice but to ride a front flat for more hours than should be ever asked of a cyclist. The wolf prints averaged about 5 inches long and 4 inches wide.

"When racing and you flat, the response is, 'That's unfortunate.' And in the case of a second flat, you think, 'Oh, that's a case of bad luck, but these things happen.'" But four flats since 5:45 p.m. when the sun went down? John's mind went to work. All four compromised innertubes had the spot of inflation—the valve stem—shorn off. And the tires seemed loosy-goosy, as if they were suddenly a half size too big for the rims.

John later confirmed his hypothesis: The cold of the night on snow and ice had caused the metal of the wheel rims to constrict. This resulted in his tires coming loose on the rim. Tires migrating when a cyclist like John is pedaling hard, cause the tube to move with the slipping tire, while the inner-tube valve is firmly held in place by the eight-millimeter hole in the rim between two of the thirty-six spokes. In other words, the low tire-pressure required by snowy conditions and John's kilowatt output on the bike (he was in second place) were in stable equilibrium until *night* in this great Alaska experiment. Then the changing temperature shrank a rim, caused a tire to drift, and resulted with an innertube to decamp while its valve stayed in place. On four occasions he flatted in the monochrome of snow and nightfall in the remote terrain.

And then it happened: after being slowed for so long by the slackened front wheel, John was caught from behind. The current third-place rider, Carl Tobin, rode up to John and listened attentively like the thoughtful academic he was. But then an even bigger thing happened: the Fairbanks-based scientist, who also was a serious alpinist and survivor of a near-fatal avalanche, handed the novice his spare tube. Good sportsmanship of this caliber warranted more of a spotlight than John's two Nite Rider lamps could ever provide. No one else was there to see this good deed. But John never forgot Carl Tobin's generosity. It made even more of an impression on him than the cold. And the real temperature at that point was in the territory of −30°F (−34°C).

Carl's gift tube held for a couple of welcome hours. When it too became compromised due to the domino effect of cold on the metal rim leading to another sheared-off valve, John started to walk his bike. Ever the optimist, he regaled the ambulation, for cycling on metal pedals in sub-below temperatures makes one's feet desperate for circulatory relief. As in the morning, when John's hands pounded from the ache of mid-weight gloves in subzero temps, John got to work, wiggling digits, moving his ankles and wrists, remaining mindful not to squeeze the handlebars too tight or clench any parts of his feet. He shook his arms, he joggled his legs. He didn't make the rules, but he came to play the game. Challenge accepted, he said to the night.

He ultimately made it to the Skwentna checkpoint, where his salvation came in the form of glue. Turns out that the locals know to glue their tires to their rims—on the *cold* cold days—to avoid the tube-temperature torment endured by the freshman from Cincinnati. As experienced cold-weather cyclists know, Elmer's won't do. Glue can be the kind of tubular tire cement that road riders use with tubular—or sew-up—one-piece tires. The other kind of road tire in 1992 was a clincher tire, in which the tires clinch to the rim via a beaded edge with an innertube to hold the air—just like John's twenty-six-inch mountain bike wheels. Since 1999, mountain bikes have had a tubeless tire option—like automobiles—that creates an airtight seal using liquid sealant inside the tire and a "universal standard tubeless" system, for rim and wheel manufacturers to sing from the same songbook. Many gravel-bike cyclists enjoy tubeless wheels for grip and comfort and to ride without the fear of a pinch flat (a "snake bite" of the tube) when inflated at a low air pressure. Tubeless wheels can be run with or without an innertube, which (sans tube) saves weight or, in cases when a puncture sealant can't handle a puncture or fails, a tube can be installed, saving the day. (For the curious, sub-zero sealants for tubeless wheels are available in the marketplace, but none rated for the low temperatures John rode on February 15–16, 1992.)

John applied glue to one side of each rim; this held the tire in place, while keeping the other side available for the possibility of changing another godforsaken innertube in the dark.

In review, John unfurled some profanities during the night of five flats, but in his words, "Failure is an undervalued teacher." He turned the obstacles into challenges and proved to himself just how much he could take. In endurance adventures, mistakes teach more than triumphs. Mistakes deliver humility. On the far side, they imbue confidence. For years and years later, mountain bikers would tell the story of how John Stamstad faced down five flats at Iditasport. It was a saga passed around campfires and long rides and recounted at weekend bike festivals and countless pubs, as happens in legends in folklore. Passed down and around, the story of five flats was profound to off-road riders. It shifted collective tolerance and toughness. It felt like the "greatest mushing tale of them all" for a generation of mountain bikers.

In his book, *The Resiliency Advantage*, Dr. Al Siebert—an expert in the psychology of resilience—wrote, "Highly resilient people are flexible, adapt to new circumstances quickly, and thrive in constant change. Most importantly, they expect to bounce back and feel confident they will. They have a knack for creating good luck out of circumstances that many others see as bad luck."

In addition to glue, the Skwentna checkpoint held John's drop bag containing innertubes as well as much-needed calories. Riding on a flat or walking a bike takes much longer and more energy than one could ever plan. But he had made it to the halfway point. And even if the Skwentna checkpoint qualified as hell for the weather, it was heaven for the company.

Meeting the weary with an open door was Joe Delia, sixty-two, the postmaster of the Skwentna Post Office since 1948. A renowned woodsman and trapper, Joe offered his A-frame log cabin to the mushers, the travelers, and the Iditasport faithful—personnel, volunteers, and racers. Getting out of the elements, blunted by –30°F air for so long, John read the sign above his host's door before entering: "Be not forgetful to entertain strangers, for thereby some have entertained angels unaware." Even those unfamiliar with St. Paul's letters in the New Testament couldn't help but mouth an amen to the postmaster's hospitality.

Setting out for the next checkpoint thirty miles away, John adjusted his eyes to the dark. His water refilled, his innertube supply restocked, his relief renewed, he set his eyes on the trail. It was reassuring to follow the wolf prints, because they know the firmest track. "They don't want to sink into the snow, either," John thought. Luckily most wolves in the area that night were as shy as the young John Stamstad.

To his left, the skies glowed. John needed to keep his eyes on the paw prints, but in his peripheral vision, bands of charged particles were ringing into our planet's atmosphere, being deflected toward the poles, sky-battling Alaska's air molecules, and sprinkling solar particles over his ride. How do you pass the time alone during an ultra-cycling event near the North Pole? If you can bear the cold, and the night is clear, you can attend the greatest skywatching event available on this planet ...

John explains how he withstood riding the night of the five flats: "If you train hard and are intrinsically motivated, and deal with suffering by not feeling it as suffering at all, you can reach a level of fitness where your neurochemistry changes altogether."[29] Likewise, if you get past the fitness required to get to Joe Delia's cabin, you reach the point your system is flooded with dopamine, motivating you to perform harder and harder tasks.

If you can get past the cold, you can also have hours of *aurora borealis* all to yourself. And unforgiving blocks of time in the small hours will pass by with barely a notice.

Next, John was welcomed by the kind volunteers at Riversong Lodge on the banks of the Yentna River. With a rustic style and a staff able to put fishing clients on King salmon the way hotel concierges in cities arrange a car service for guests, the Lodge is more than a wall tent or a postmaster's house, but a proper retreat. Riversong Lodge, like a surprising number of places in the forty-ninth state, is accessible only by float plane. After a quick drop-bag

---

29 On intrinsic motivation, John's internal drive can be described as *autotelic*; that is, he enjoys his pursuits and his hobbies for their own sake. Like many endurance athletes who do immersive work with unwavering attention, autotelic types enjoy the exertion without seeking external rewards. This full immersion into the process driven by intrinsic purpose often delivers athletes, artists, musicians, scientists, and other experts into a state of flow. The psychologist Abraham Maslow described something similar with his term "peak experiences." In other words, John Stamstad's big mountain, backcountry play qualifies as "peak experience" squared.

resupply—in less than ten minutes—John returned to the course, the frozen Yentna River, the third quarter of the Iditasport '92 route. The Yentna river, where Alaska Department of Fish and Game track Coho, Pink, Sockeye, and King salmon, the river is an untouched place where these colored jewels push nutrients from the ocean back to the freshwater ribbon streams. The ribbons of this remote stretch host more fish than the land does people.

The vastness overhead was different from the night sky screens of Madison, Cincinnati, or even Frisco, Colorado, in the Rockies. The stars in the lower 48 seemed to lie flat, all length and breadth. But pedaling toward the coldest part of his ride, the black vault above John unveiled stars in three dimensions.

There were so many stars, the familiar constellations disappeared.

The *zip, zop, zip, zop* of pedaling toward the Susitna River over the Yentna and on to Big Lake provided the musical score for this show of special effects. The audience of apex predators with the silver mirror eyes in the riverbank bush did not appear impressed. The cumulative exposure to the elements and no sleep (X) were taxing (Y), but at least John made it to the shore of Big Lake near sunrise (Z).

He had eight more miles to go over ice, which were "up until that point, the longest eight miles of my whole life." But at least he survived a night where temperatures reached −40°F (−40°C), the Night of the Five Flats.

In twenty-four hours, John Stamstad finished the 1992 Iditasport race in third place, behind Rocky Reifenstuhl, a legendary outdoorsmen from Fairbanks, and, in second place, Carl Tobin, the noble sportsman who gave the youngster his spare tube, and sealed John's affection for Alaskan adventurers and their colossal playground.

Endurance athletes of the unforgiving hours know, and wish for those who long to be, this truth: the Alaskan sportsmanship lesson of 1992 ordains that one's fellow competitors—maybe even those deemed one's rivals—are not your enemies.

Despite fewer reserves than browse-searching moose in February, John navigated the Night of Five Flats in 1992, paid his dues, took careful notes, and registered the way Dan Bull, Joe Delia, and Carl Tobin stood nearly as tall as Denali at 20,310 feet (6,190 meters). The peak is the Alaska Range's crown jewel. Denali—her name was restored in August 2015 from "Mount McKinley" back to the original Koyukon Athabaskan name—rises an inch every fifty years, thanks to the nearby oceanic Pacific Plate sinking below the continental North American plate causing uplift in the 600-mile-long (966-kilometer-long) Alaskan Range. The 1992 deeds of Bull, Delia, and Tobin, like Denali, only grow with time.

From 1993 to 2000, John Stamstad toed the line at the event. This included the four later Februarys when the length of the race was doubled to 350 miles (560 kilometers), or to some approximate distance of unthinkable length, in the Iditasport Extreme.

Never one for a plaque and a statue, John rode as Togo the Siberian Husky ran: quietly, undersized for the breed standard, and always as if made for the moment. Justin Angle, the ultrarunner, cyclist, and product tester for Patagonia who is a multi-hyphenate professor, researcher, author, consultant, host of the smart podcast, *A New Angle*, and that rare athlete who could go long in wild places and keep up with both the intellectual rigor and pace of John Stamstad says: "John has a presence that is immediately disarming. They say, 'Don't meet your heroes,' but John defies that, for sure. He is welcoming, kind and generous. He has a wonderful way of being both a mentor and a partner at the same time." Ultrarunner Scott Jurek is another exceptional athlete who can properly grasp the outer edges of John's pluck and the bold endeavoring of John's pace: "Such a silent and unassuming legend, a giant then and now," Scott describes his mate with admiration.

Fearlessly out in front of the pack every time after 1992, John defined grit, resilience, and perseverance by breaking trail and setting track. It was the Iditasport racing equivalent of wearing the sled dog front harness when John led from the front from 1993–2000. It meant working with a professional back home to overcome shyness that could be debilitating at times. Some may say heavy is the back that wears the harness, but John knew Alaska would require more of him, and in turn shape him, from checkpoint to checkpoint. He summoned the courage to deal with the great unknowns of the great North, facing such suffering by not considering it suffering at all. John would set—and then break—the course records repeatedly, trying to make improvements every time, quick to laugh about the whimsy of Skwentna weather in February and the fickleness of the conditions of her trails. Such games are not for prizes, as such quests are never about competition; at thirty degrees below zero, drive and fulfillment are necessarily intrinsic. External motivations and extrinsic rewards cannot withstand even a few minutes of that shattering cold.

Years later, describing the longer iterations of this ride, race director Dan Bull said, "You can have your Eco Challenges and your Raid Gauloises, but there is no tougher race than this one."

"If you don't think so, come on up."

This era of ice biking, by using Alaskan Frankenbikes like the original Klunkers of Mount Tamalpais, would take the "ballooner" concept one step further, with a four-inch-wide tire on bikes now commonly called "fat bikes." John never rode a fat bike at Iditasport, but he did become a member of Marin County–based Team Ritchey in the mid-1990s (where he was described in the pro team materials as "ultra distance madman John Stamstad"). From 1993 to 2000, every time John toed the line at Iditasport, he solved that year's puzzle and crossed the finish line first.

In the end, riding a handmade Tom Ritchey frame from Knik to McGrath, Alaska (X), may be one of Alaska's toughest un-dog races (Y), but at least it was always winter, and John never needed to mountain-biker-shout, "Hey bear!" repeatedly while the wolves watched in amusement (Z) in the season, the immutable bike season, of the hard water.

The crowd cheered at the Iditasport 1992 finish line on Sunday morning, February 16, as first-timer John Stamstad improbably completed the course after the Night of Five Flats. With frozen hair and an iced beard, Stamstad finished in the dark, as sunrise wasn't until 8:41 a.m. that winter morning. *(photo by Tom Evans)*

CHAPTER EIGHT

THE ICE MILE: WHEN SWIMMING IS THE WARM PART

Melissa Kegler

Nothing is over until we decide it is.
Was it over when the Germans bombed Pearl Harbor?
—*John "Bluto" Blutarsky,* Animal House

AN ICE MILE IS A STANDARD BRITISH MILE SWIM (1.61 kilometers/1,760 yards) in water at or below 5°C, or 41°F. The sensation of those temperatures in Ice Mile water cannot be accurately replicated on land. Body heat is lost twenty-five times faster in 41°F water than the same temp on terra firma. Upon entry, Ice Mile water has teeth, but it's nothing compared to the predation that follows. The difference between the British mile and the longer nautical mile (1.852 kilometers/2025.37 yards) never mattered more than in an Ice Mile event.

The Ice Mile has a uniform. A swimmer may wear a standard bathing suit, a pair of goggles, earplugs, and one standard silicon or latex swim cap. No neoprene is permitted. A woman's suit may not go above her neckline; a man's jammers may not go below his knees. Cold-water greasing—the use of goop to protect skin receptors from the needle-like sensations of Ice Mile water—is not allowed. Anecdotally, some say 1 mm of lanolin, petroleum jelly, or thick diaper ointment can make Ice Mile water feel a degree, or maybe even two degrees warmer than the actual temperature. Some say balderdash to this insulative claim. Either way, greasing is not allowed, because in matters of planned hypothermia, every degree counts.

Grease is still employed in Ice Mile swimming, however. Like a cheese grater to the skin, chafing should be expected in open-water swimming. Anti-chafing goop is intended for locations like underarms, inner thighs, suit straps, shaving stubble, and the back, front, and sides of one's neck. Because skin rubs against skin, or fabric, or skin, fabric, AND sometimes salt water, Ice Mile swimming is that rare sport (like long-distance cycling) where diaper cream is a not-so-secret weapon.

Missing from an Ice Mile swim are neoprene, gloves, booties, or the possibility of snacks—feeds are not allowed in the Ice Mile, setting it apart from other open-water swimming events. This, and the other sixteen pages of rules and regulations, are issued by the International Ice Swimming Association which oversees, regulates, authorizes, catalogs, and formally authenticates Ice Mile swims. While Ice Mile swims are often unforgiving minutes rather than hours in time length—one of the fastest Ice Miles ever was delivered by a Polish college student who swam 1.0253 miles (1.65 kilometers) on March 12, 2023, in 19 minutes and 57 seconds in 39.83°F (4.35°C) water and 26.78°F (−2.9°C) wind chill.

Twenty minutes of swimming may not appear to be a stamina feat at first frozen-skin-blush, but *the preparation* involved in wearing a swimsuit in 27°F (-2.8°C) wind-chill weather before entering frozen water makes this sport an endurance event.

For American Melissa Kegler, her plan to swim 1.4 icy miles (2.2 kilometers) was a two-year undertaking. To an observer, the warmest part of the endeavor was while she was in the frozen water.

———

Melissa Kegler had completed an Ice Mile before—at elevation, in Colorado—in December 2020, so she was confident and excited to attempt to break the US Ice Mile distance record in 2022. Her two years of training funneled toward a 1.4-mile attempt in 39.2°F (4°C) water in her uniform of a pair of goggles, a swim cap, a pair of earplugs, and a blue and white bikini. With matching nail polish.

———

To the cold-water curious, Melissa swims in a bikini for a few reasons. After a stinging jellyfish entered her one-piece suit and had no way out, Melissa moved to a bikini, where no jellyfish would get trapped. She also found back-tied bikinis the fastest way to disrobe beneath a towel after a swim on her favorite freezing boardwalk of Alki Beach in West Seattle, Washington. Finally, in her cadre of body-positive mermen and mermaids, every female who swims has a bikini body: ectomorphs, endomorphs, mesomorphs. The tall and the short. The old and the young. The ghostly pale and the gorgeously melanated. Whether skin is smooth or dimpled or crepey or varicose or inked or scarred or stretched from the ninth month of pregnancy, bikinis are always appropriate. Bikinis are unapologetic. Bikinis have more fun than other swimming suits. Their parts are often sold separately for pragmatic custom sizing. For many open-water female swimmers, they come for the bikini practicality and stay for the two-piece wholesale joy and sororité.[30]

For modern female swimmers comfortable in bikinis or one-pieces—waiting for the rest of the world seeped in diet culture to keep up—a historical patron saint is Annette Kellerman. The Aussie swimmer was born in Sydney in 1886. Wearing a one-piece bathing costume, rather than the knee-length bathing dress of the era, Kellerman was arrested in 1907 on Boston's Revere Beach for indecent exposure. Indeed, the Costume Institute of The Metropolitan Museum of Art includes, in the Beachwear collection archives, a 1902 swim corset worn under those bathing dresses. Such were the expectations of women at the seaside at

---

30 Curiously, being comfortable in a bikini bathing suit—or in any swimsuit, for both men and women—often is a tangential benefit of open-water swimming. How? Anecdotally, the *awe* associated with swimming marathon distances or winter bathing or cold-water soaking, contributes to a transforming sense of wonder for the world and our bodies' abilities. The negativity associated with wearing a swim suit in public that many people experience is curiously eclipsed with a kind of ecstatic positive support uniquely provided by invigorating water. Actual buoyant support. Further support is provided by other stalwart swimmers, unvarnished plungers, and doughty dippers. The liberation from the self-inflicted insecurity can be quietly euphoric. Being around swimmers of all body types, experiencing wonder in water and the joy of community alters the brain, as awe increases feelings of wellness and connectedness. Scientists have found that awe also replaces feelings of inadequacy by turning off the part of the brain's cortex involved in self-perception. This default mode network (DMN) appears in MRI studies to be critically involved in self-rumination and appraisal of negative emotions. Awe creates a spirit of wonder and social optimism, which *shapes* our sense of self and shapes our connectivity to others. As a by-product, it also gets our mind off our *shape*.

the start of the twentieth century. Luckily, women swimmers led from the front for female athletes on land, and by August 1926, a twenty-year-old Gertrude Ederle became the first woman to swim the English Channel, breaking the men's record by two hours. In a two-piece bathing suit.

———————————

Whatever the coverage of one's swimsuit, male or female, icy cold water takes some getting used to. Getting used to swimming in cold water is cumulative. The more you do it, the easier it becomes to enter the water, and stay in—before hypothermia happens. The longest-distance ice swim ratified by the International Ice Swimming Association for a male is 6 kilometers (3.7 miles), swum by Krzysztof Gajewski in a lake at Czarna Góra Resort near Sienna, Poland, on April 19, 2023. Gajewski completed the swim in 1 hour, 46 minutes, and 16 seconds. The average water temperature during his swim was 4.84°C (40.7°F).

The frostiest part of Melissa's endeavor occurred in the autumn before her winter swim.

The governing body of the International Ice Swimming Association requires pre-participation medical forms signed by a doctor—like many events or high school sports. New health insurance through Melissa's work meant a new doctor to sign off on the boilerplate form.

Despite Melissa's perfect vitals, healthy blood work, and a sports CV several pages long, the new doctor standing in front of the swimmer refused to sign the standard forms. He could give her no medical reason why.

"By the Body Mass Index Chart, you are obese," he said curtly.

The BMI chart was introduced by a nineteenth-century Belgian mathematician, Lambert Adolphe Jacques Quetelet, around 1832. Mr. Quetelet was neither a doctor nor a sports medicine physician. The formula used to calculate BMI was never intended as a measure of health. BMI charts (or tables) are based on the nineteenth-century measurements of French and Scottish participants. All men. The calculation seeks a measure of body fat by dividing a person's weight by too much for a person of short stature, and by too little for people who are tall. Not only does the BMI chart have limitations as an indicator of body composition, the body-fat-mass numbers are misleading at best and, at worst, wildly irrelevant to health outcomes. The average Lao woman is 4 feet, 11 inches tall. The average height of Dutch women is more than 5 feet, 7 inches. Only weight and height determine one's BMI number. Life is nuanced, the BMI chart is not.

The doctor repeated to the swimmer of petite height: "I will not clear you for this swim, as you are obese." He said the words with the look of a big-box retail company executive intent on fighting any increase in the minimum wage. Melissa tried to explain that she had swum the previous July from Bremerton to Seattle and back—a 20.8-mile (33.5-kilometer) swim, in 10 hours and 35 minutes, in 58°F (14.4°C) water. She didn't mention that she was the first person in history to complete the swim.

Melissa explained she had been strong enough to complete the English Channel and Catalina Channel swims. She was healthy enough to not get sick after swimming in the oft-contaminated waters around the island of Manhattan for a total of 28.5 miles (45.9 kilometers). But the doctor—who had never seen her before—showed no interest in her Triple Crown of swimming or her strong vitals and healthy blood work. He said something about the numbers, suggesting she was at risk for a cardiac event. It is a pitiable authority who focuses on the pathologies of weight without considering the muscles that make athletes, athletes.

Her hands were trembling, her head was spinning. "The doctor had no medical reason to prevent me from swimming, so he just repeated the same words over and over," Melissa said. "The irony is, you never need to tell a woman she is obese more than once.

Trust me, she heard you the first time."

For love of the sport. For the thrill of the adventure. For the chance to race a car in a rally for eight days. Or run 100 miles (161 kilometers) in thirty hours. Or ride a bicycle from coast to coast, uninterrupted. Long-distance people don't expect any validation from strangers about their unusual hobbies, as often they look no different from the person next door. Successful long-distance athletes are like other amateur athletes—they often are just willing to plan more than the rest of us. They are seekers. Their sense of humor and their creativity also set them apart. They don't expect strangers to know about their hidden talents. But—like the doctor making assumptions about a thirty-nine-year-old record holder, based on some Body Mass Index Chart as an indicator of health—long-distance people don't expect strangers to impede their adventures because they don't look like athletes. Like twenty-one-year-old Terry Fox and his 143-day run across Canada in 1980. Or Rick and Dick Hoyt's thirty-two completions of the Boston Marathon. Or Sister Madonna Buder (known as "the Iron Nun"), who entered the convent in 1953 and has forty-five finishes of the 140.6-mile (226.3-kilometer) Ironman® Triathlon. Or the joy chaser Mirna Valerio, ultrarunner, epitome of a modern athlete, and role model. Endurance athletes come in many shapes and sizes.

Long-distance sports aren't a matter of life and death. However, if they reveal the way women's health has often been neglected by science, perhaps endurance sports are more important than they appear. In the matters of cultural conversation, long-distance sports are vitally important. Long-distance sports can reset assumptions about appearances.

Melissa didn't allow an outdated BMI chart and an outdated doctor to derail her two years of training for the 1.4-mile (2.3-kilometer) Ice Swim. She paid out of her own pocket to see her previous general practitioner and for all the tests to confirm what science and her swim résumé had verified: She was in excellent health. She was a phenomenal swimmer. She was a person who deserved to be judged not by her appearance (tan year-round), or her job (government compliance lead for Amazon Web Services), or by the presence of tattoos (many), or her accent (Michigander), or the size of her latissimus dorsi muscles (the real deal).[31]

---

31 Rather than discussing Body Mass Index tables, many in science and medicine are working toward proving the benefits of cold-water swimming. For example, studies show that those who swim in cold water regularly have higher levels of reduced glutathione, an antioxidant enzyme that protects against oxidative stress

Melissa's first successful Ice Mile swim in 2020 was hosted by marathon swimming's champion Sarah Thomas, of Colorado, at Denver's Wolcott Lake in December. The water was in the 40°F (4°C) range, what Melissa joked was "snowman status" cold. Following the swim, Sarah Thomas said, "Melissa is a phenomenal swimmer and has a really incredible cold-water tolerance, honed from years and years of cold acclimatization." After Melissa's first Ice Mile, she began a serious cold-specific training regimen for the 1.4-mile distance event in 2022, which would set a new American record. Weekly swims in Puget Sound and Lake Sammamish in Redmond, Washington, were complemented by soaks in a tub of ice and chilly water outside her home. There were also big hikes to glacial lakes across Western Washington to chase the bitterly cold, blue spaces where alpine water measures in the 30-to-low-40-degree range (−1.11°C to −4.44°C). These outings featured a tightly woven community of swimming friends. Most doctors likely wish their patients took such good care of their cardiovascular and respiratory systems, large muscle groups, and community-centric mental well-being.

On her personal board of directors were Puget Sound swimmers such as Guila Muir, the Seattle athlete who represented the United States in the 2020 Winter Swimming World Championships put on by the International Winter Swimming

---

and boosts mitochondrial health. As for the long laundry-list of health benefits avowed among winter swimmers, ice bathers, and cold plungers, some rewards are lab proven, but many are still anecdotal. Evidence-based science shows that cold-water swimming increases insulin sensitivity, which helps in the prevention of type 2 diabetes; decreases blood pressure; and stabilizes cortisol and serotonin—which aids in quality sleep. The noradrenalin rush, the anti-inflammatory effects, the increase in endorphin neurotransmitters—and even the fresh-baked goods and thermoses of warm drink—leave cold water swimmers some of the most energy-boosted, pain-free, and good-mood adventurers on this planet.

Association (IWSA) in Skellefteå, Sweden. Guila's 50-meter race was held in a pool cut from a frozen river, the coldest in Sweden. Massive chain saws formed the twenty-five-meter-long pool, sawing blocks of ice more than four feet deep. Guila took the age group gold medal for the 50m freestyle. The water was 28°F (-2.22°C).[32]

Another model swimmer based out of Alki Beach, enlarging the size of the world (and our imaginations), is the indefatigable Scott Lautman. At the January 2023 IWSA Championships in Bled, Slovenia, Scott broke the 70–74-year-old 50m Freestyle record (35 seconds flat) in the icy cold waters of Lake Bled. And at the International Ice Swimming Association in Samoëns, France, that year, Scott's 100m breaststroke broke the IISA 70–74-year-old category world record in Lac Aux Dames. But the swim that stands out as "most mind-bending" by the champion is a 1-kilometer swim in Lake Semyonovskoye, in 20°F (-7°C) wind chill and 32°F (0°C) water in 2019. His swim was electric; he won the 65–69-year-old IISA category, but that was not the point. To swim one thousand meters outdoors in March in

---

32 In a piece titled "The Extremely Cold Water Perception Scale," published by the World Open Water Swimming Association (WOWSA), cold water was put into seven categories. Twenty-eight-degree water falls into the "Severe Stage of Cold Water Swimming," defined by under 30.2°F (or sub-1.0°C). This temperature is described as "unfathomably cold and dangerously uncomfortable during the entire swim," and such a swim involves "highly acute and continued pain." Luckily, Guila is an experienced veteran swimmer, gifted coach, and an acclimatized cold-water athlete of the highest order.

As for the 28°F (-2°C) water Guila swam in, many factors contribute to when water freezes. And, spoiler alert, it's not always at 32°F even. For example, the freezing point of sea water is usually around 28.4°F (-2°C). In a river, such as in Skellefteå with ice 48 inches (1.2 meters) deep, the water below can be below the typical freezing point of fresh water. The movement of water, kinetic energy, keeps the liquid molecules from slowing down long enough to form ice.

Murmansk, Russia—the largest city north of the Arctic Circle—while a Russian violinist played on the frozen lake, THAT was the point. The once-in-a-lifetime swim in exhilarating Arctic ice was the glorious point.

Among such company, Alki Beach is an incubator. It just feels like a walk-in freezer.

But it wasn't all picturesque open-water swims with Guila and Scott and the Notorious Alki Swimmers at Alki Beach for Melissa in her two years of work. Training consistency meant hammering out mileage in chlorinated water, too. One training session in a twenty-five-yard pool—the traditional size of most high school and college pools—finished after fourteen thousand yards. To put the distance into perspective, that's more than 550 flip turns, broken into sets, without leaving the pool.

Back on the pool deck or shoreline, in proper endurance sport fashion, the Ice Mile required layers of preparation for Melissa. Organization of people and a safe and accessible location for the crew are absolutely critical in an event involving 39.2°F (4°C) water. In the case of her January 14, 2022, swim, Melissa arranged for four official event observers to take the test required for ratification of her swim. Two kayakers, one stand-up paddleboarder, and one fully neoprene-suited safety swimmer gave Melissa their undivided attention. Of note, each of the Seattleites who crewed the swim is an athlete of notable merit.[33]

---

33 Arguably, no swim crew was ever as talented as this crew: Jeff Crombie, safety swimmer; Kirby Drawbaugh, kayaker; Jerome Leslie, swim observer; Ofer Levy, stand-up paddleboarder; Glenn Lunev, kayaker; Alison Peterson, back-up observer; Sadie Schnitzler, stroke counter and video validation; Heidi Skrzypek, timekeeper; Stacey Sterling, stroke counter; Dr. William Washington, team doctor; and Rebecca Kegler, crew captain and observer. This is the actual definition of an A-team in open-water swimming.

The Ice Mile required one stroke counter, one timekeeper, one photo and video validation member, and a crew manager; roles that Melissa has filled on other swimmers' open-water swims. The final crew requirement was a medical doctor to oversee the swim and the rather prickly matter of the warm-up.

How cold was the water? "One week prior to Melissa's swim, the lake was frozen over," said Kirby Drawbaugh, an intrepid cold-water swim sage and one of her support kayakers. Her course was a self-designed 550-meter loop (601.49 yards) with ingress and egress provided by a wooden dock at the middle of the loop. The weathered wood and gray-scale sky suggested a Scandinavian postcard, where the traditions of *vinterbadning*, or *isbading* (both mean "winter swimming" in Danish and in Norwegian, respectively), have occurred for centuries—as cultural ritual, as movement, as social get-together, as personal rejuvenation. In places where the sky drops low in the winter, long on harsh darkness, swimming in cold water replaces the gloom and isolation of the season as it resets the brain. But first swimmers must enter the water.

Upon lowering herself into the lake that Friday morning, each droplet of the gelid water seemed to have serrated edges. In cold-water swimming, many have a "slow in, fast out" technique. Swimmers ease their way into the water, maybe standing in water to their calves, then their thighs, then their waists over the course of five to twenty minutes, depending on the conditions and the banter with fellow courageous swimmers. Melissa bit the bullet and eased herself from the dock into the water without milling about, without any banter. It hurt. That was left unsaid.

The next series of physiological events was an automatic response recognizable in diving birds such as penguins or marine mammals such as seals, called the "dive" or "diving response," or "diving bradycardia." When a mammal immerses its head in water less than 70°F (21°C), a set of physiological changes occurs automatically: one, apnea starts—which is a cessation of breathing, or holding one's breath. Two, bradycardia—slowing of the heart rate—begins, reducing the workload on the heart and limiting consumption of oxygen, given the apnea. This breathing and heart-rate response is the same physiological response experienced by (and connecting us to) otters, whales, dolphins, and other marine mammals. Finally, blood vessels constrict, redistributing blood to the vital organs. This vasoconstriction occurs to reduce the heat loss required to keep those organs healthy. The colder the water, the faster this three-step response. Melissa's training meant she recognized the feeling of this automatic response, and she remained calm when the protection of her core meant extreme cooling in her extremities, starting with rapid decreases in the temperatures of her hands and feet. Like the sting of standing barefoot in a snowbank with a snowball in each ungloved hand. While wearing a bikini.

She swam more slowly than was comfortable at the beginning to maintain an exacting stroke-per-minute pace. This silently communicated to her crew: "I am fine. My brain is still precisely counting strokes, my body can do this thing." Her crew paddleboarder, Ofer Levy, described Melissa's precision: "Her stroke count per minute was the same in the first five minutes of the swim as the last five minutes. She finished her swim at the time she told us she would at the pre-brief." Sometimes unforgiving spans are filled with song lyrics. Or rewinding and replaying of old memories. Or math problems. Or prayers to the Almighty from the recently religious. And sometimes the endurance athlete fills the unforgiving moments with numbers. Counting can be breath work, pacing of pedal strokes or footsteps, or a form of distraction. For Melissa, it had the rhythm of *one, two, three, breathe*. That Friday morning, counting meant tracking each time either arm entered the water, which silently spoke volumes across a silent winter lake.

Four laps in 39.2°F (4°C) water at fifty-four strokes per minute for more than fifty minutes whispered to the crew, "I am fine." But to the cold it shouted: "Not today, hypothermia, not today."

In her pre-race meeting with her team that morning she had needed to explain that hypothermia was coming. It was inevitable; a case of when, not if. But her body, her training, and her acclimatization made her equipped for what was ahead: hypothermia during the warming-up process.

Cold-water swimmers, elite and amateur alike, experience a phenomenon called "after-drop" following a cold swim. This is why "slow in" is followed by "fast out." Once a cold-water swimmer finishes their swim, the clock is running. The after-drop is coming with predacity. Simply put, this is the time when the cold blood in one's numb arms and legs begins to circulate with the warm blood surrounding the torso. Vasoconstriction switches to vasodilation. As the cold blood and the organ-protecting warm blood mix, a swimmer feels her coldest. The swimmer's internal temperature reaches the nadir of her swim *on land*. The coldest part of Melissa's swim was in the warm-up process afterward.

Elite swimmers like Melissa are physiologically trained to navigate the shuddering, teeth-clattering discomfort of the after-drop. They are prepared for its seemingly preternatural, unnerving, temporary effects. In Melissa's case in January, her rewarming strategy included a warm house not far from the lake dock. She had three female crew tasked with removing her two-piece bathing suit and then redressing her in dry clothes. The cold meant temporary loss of manual dexterity and tactile sensitivity, and a decrease in gross motor function. Once Melissa was dressed, fellow swimmer Dr. William Washington continued to monitor her various changes in heart rate as her body worked to rewarm. The cold of the after-drop caused dilation of her pupils and increase of pallor in her extremities, and an inability to speak that provided a stark contrast to the Midwestern gal's cheerful, chatty nature. She cannot remember the quaking that followed.

The jaw-clenching and thunderous shaking of the after-drop relented after forty-five minutes, just as Melissa had predicted to her team. She had succeeded in setting a new US record with precision. She had persevered after some misleading Body Mass Index rubbish-bin non-science and used the encounter as fuel. Melissa broke the US record that had remained untouched for more than a decade since Craig Lenning of Colorado swam 1.2 miles (2 kilometers) in Brainard Lake on July 10, 2011.

Perhaps the observation by Ovid applies here:

"Perfer et obdura, dolor hic tibi proderit olim."

To paraphrase: "Bear and endure hurtful words. Someday this pain will be useful to you."

From the psychology of resilience, Dr. Al Siebert, in his book *The Resiliency Advantage,* explained crossroads like the one Melissa faced: "You either cope or you crumble; you become better or bitter; you emerge stronger or weaker." Melissa's swim was the longest ratified ice swim by an American ever.

Joe Zemaitis, chairman of the International Ice Swimming Association's USA chapter and fellow ice swimmer, wrote, "We at IISA USA are impressed by the diligence and preparation of Melissa and her team as they worked to create a challenging but safe event. We congratulate Melissa as she raises the bar for what's possible in the ice."

The American Ice Mile crown unassumingly and quietly sat upon Melissa's head for six short weeks. The ink on her International Ice Swimming Association January 14th certificate had barely dried, when on February 26 another Washington female swimmer—Lisa Yamamoto, twenty-nine—swam a 1.61-Ice Mile (2.6 kilometers) at Fallen Leaf Lake in Camas, Washington.

But endurance athletes who adventure in nature, who deal in wonder, are not about records. To the uninformed, their adventures suggest that someone might have lost a bet. Like training in freezing conditions for two years in order to swim 51 minutes and 26 seconds in 39.2°F (4°C)water. Training for two years in freezing water just to lose the distance record before the end of the next month. Melissa laughs at the nonsensical sound of it. She just loves swimming in cold water. Moving among the bolts of silver smelt and sheets of sterling herring. Spying feathery sea pens attached to the soft sand floor of Puget Sound or watching the zig-zag stitch footwork of a dozen kinds of crabs of the Salish Sea. Cataloging the collage of nudibranchs, the soft-bodied neon pincushions of the oceans. Swimming with a new collection of seals every May through September, moored by sweet new pups each year as they experience apnea, bradycardia, and play, together. Melissa is a student of awe.

Between belly laughs, the swimmer immediately assured her swim friends that the ephemeral lost record was long-ago history, like an inaccurate World War II reference or an old BMI chart. Her two-year training for her next endurance event had already begun.

Lowering herself into 39.2°F water, Melissa Kegler authenticates her official "ice mermaid" status in the cold of Lake Desire, just outside of Seattle, Washington, January 14, 2022. *(photo by Dan McComb)*

CHAPTER NINE

PRECIOUS METTLE

Chris Jones

You are never more alive than when you're almost dead.
—*Tim O'Brien*, The Things They Carried

It was mid-August, but snow was falling on Hope Pass, Colorado. Chris Jones had been running for more than forty-five mountain miles (seventy-two kilometers). A summit climb and a quadricep-shredding descent down the backside of the Pass stood between Jones and his course's halfway point—a ghost town that didn't survive the silver crash of 1893. As shadows began to overtake the Rocky Mountains, Chris Jones, forty-five, added summer snowfall to the robust list of potential trouble ahead.

The list of things that can go wrong for a person dressed in shorts and a tank top grows exponentially 12,000 feet above sea level.

Weather be damned, Chris tried to focus on one thing: arriving at the turnaround point of his weekend's quest, the disarticulated skeleton of a town called Winfield. The task of running 100 miles (161 kilometers) requires breaking down the distance into digestible chunks. "Just get to the next aid station," ultrarunners say.

The snow fell as a reminder that things were not likely to get any easier that weekend. There are few absolute and eternal axioms in this world, but here was one: *a second fifty-mile run was never easier than the first.*

In the second fifty miles of a hundred-mile run, hot spots become blisters. Chafing suddenly occurs where before there was none. Teeth seemingly begin to sprout fuzz. Nausea can randomly smite the lower abdominals like a samurai's short sword in an act of *seppuku*. The mechanisms that govern muscle contraction and control are sent to the slaughterhouse. The second fifty is where toenails go to die.

To be clear, the *first* fifty miles Chris had already completed that August day weren't particularly easy either. He began his run toward Winfield from the highest-in-altitude incorporated city in all of North America.

Named for its former mining roots, Leadville, Colorado, sits at 10,152 feet (3,094 meters) above sea level. To contextualize the elevation of the place nicknamed "Cloud City," airplanes pressurize their cabins around 8,000 feet (2,438 meters).

Discomfort ruled the day from the start. Chris's alarm clock first sounded, depending on your perspective, in the late night or the very early morning at 2:30 a.m. Race volunteers began checking wristbands to the race corral thirty minutes later.

In military parlance, the to-do list that morning included all matters of "shit-shower-shave" (although the infantryman skipped the shave as he was not on duty or in uniform), as well as breakfast, gear assembly, and time to find parking near the race start.

The race corral marked the center of Leadville's National Landmark District, a downtown of old west architecture and Victorian-era buildings largely built between 1880 and the turn of the century. Not all that much had been updated since.

As runners finished their pre-race warm-ups, Jones joined the assembled mass at 3:45 a.m. under the scaffolding spanning the width of 6th Street. Pre-race speeches released additional roosts of nervous butterflies. A hush descended over the horde when an acapella version of the "Star-Spangled Banner," classic-soprano-clear, slow and euphonious, began. Runners rested their gaze on the American flag atop the left side of the scaffolding. The most choked-up amongst them stole glances upward at the inky night sky, to air-dry eyeballs furtively. A few knit gloves dabbed at faces during the last few lines of the anthem, not only due to the cold Colorado air. A member of the US Army infantry since 1990, Chris Jones understood.

Attention then turned to a five-foot-long digital clock that ticked down red numbers toward zero. At 4:00:00 a.m., a double-barreled shotgun blast rang out, followed by lots of pent up hootin' and hollerin'.

The race had begun.

One of ultrarunning's Grand Slam races, Leadville Trail 100 rests securely as one of the most prestigious and storied 100-mile running competitions in the United States. Like the Western

States Endurance Run, which put the 100-mile trail distance on the map in 1977, the number of participants seeking a bib for these premiere races grows exponentially each year. The numbers are staggering: UltraRunning Magazine recorded 14,148 ultra finishes in North America in the year 2000; in 2019, there were 129,656.

The Grand Slam of Ultrarunning requires finishing three of the following races: Western States 100, Leadville Trail 100, Old Dominion 100 or Vermont 100, and then running Wasatch Front 100...*all in the same summer*. Since its inception in 1986, the Grand Slam has been completed more than 420 times.

But Chris Jones had taken the Grand Slam to the next level: he had embarked on The Last Great Race.

The Last Great Race impossibly and rather subversively asks a runner to complete the following six races in one summer: Old Dominion 100, Vermont 100, Western States 100, Angeles Crest 100, Leadville 100, and, finally, Wasatch Front 100. The driving and travel time alone for the effort would amount to forty-five to fifty days for Chris. The Last Great Race has only been completed forty-five times since its inception in 1988.

Chris lives only eighty-five feet above sea level, so almost everything about Leadville 100 feels hard. Beginning with the entry process. The lotteries for Leadville, the Grand Slam, and Last Great Race events, and other grueling races like Hardrock 100 and Badwater 135, are all ridiculously, absurdly, discouragingly competitive. Chris wrote to a friend, "With four of the six races being lotteries, the hardest part was getting into AC100, WS100, LT100, and Wasatch100." The hardest part? Somehow mind-bendingly difficult events are being made harder by virtue of their preposterous popularity. When running up and over Hope Pass, not once, but twice, it was somewhat helpful for the lottery winners to remember they were considered the *lucky* ones.

And they *were* lucky. For lowlanders, reaching the top of Hope Pass at 12,600 feet (3,840 meters) can cause a clear-eyed runner to be overcome, half-drunk on endorphins and euphoria. Despite uncomfortably cold temperatures at the race start, the weather had been in the runners' favor all day. Blue skies stretched 360 degrees across the Sawatch Range, reaching toward the protected Collegiate Peaks, with nine mountain peaks over 14,000 feet (4,267 meters). The description "purple mountains' majesties" in "America the Beautiful" was written about the muted tint of peaks like these. Bright white snow decorated the parts of the Pass with northern or eastern exposures. Snowflakes fell at the peak. No one knows what Heaven looks like, but if it does exist, most ultrarunners would describe it like Hope Pass that August afternoon.

But maybe best of all, there were llamas. Creme and cocoa, black and tan. A sea of pert ears, haltered faces, and lengthy eyelashes. Upon cresting one of the last of the false summits of Hope Pass, Leadville 100 runners find themselves surrounded by dozens and dozens of llamas.

Hope Pass is such an inhospitable place for a runners' aid station that one of the only ways to cart supplies there is by llama. With their dense wool coats, the llamas don't mind camping out for thirty hours of snowfall, grazing leisurely atop the windswept pass.

But first, their backs bore stacks of firewood to keep a bonfire alight for more than twenty-four hours. They hauled first-aid and stock pots. Banquet tables and ten-gallon Gatorade coolers. Butane canisters and Coleman camp stoves. Awkwardly round watermelons and inconveniently bruisable bananas. Enough gallons of water for 604 registered runners—not just on the outbound trip, but the inbound trip, too. The llamas ferried the sleeping tents for more than fifty volunteers and massive, rectangular, event-sized tents for more than a hundred people. Leave-no-trace principles in place, about 3,000 pounds of gear was strapped to saddles and panniers cinched to llama backs above their sure-footed feet. And yes, llamas have feet; padded feet with two toes on each foot. Specifically, they do not have hooves. Their feet permit them ideal contact with the contours of the land for optimal hiking and hauling—from the Andes of South America to Hope Pass in Chaffee County, Colorado.[34]

Llamas don't require much water themselves, making them perfect companions in the mountains. Twice as big as alpacas, llamas can weigh up to 450 pounds but are surprisingly hard core. Elevation is their jam. They can run up to thirty-five miles per hour, which is about thirty-two miles an hour faster than most runners at the midpoint of the Race Across the Sky.

Matching the magical qualities of the two-toed, six-foot-tall mammals, the ten-toed humans there served the runners in every way, too. The locals understand. The locals know what almost dead in the pain cave feels like.

---

34 While technically Hope Pass resides in Chaffee County, the locals in Leadville and around Lake County claim it as theirs affectionately.

In its heyday in the 1880s, Leadville had been famously prosperous and the second-largest city in Colorado. The 1879 City Directory listed three daily newspapers, five theaters, six banks, seven watchmakers, ten boot-and-shoe shops, ten liquor dealers, eleven bakeries, eighteen blacksmiths, twenty-one restaurants, twenty-nine grocery stores,[35] thirty-four physicians, fifty-nine saloons, ample gambling houses, and an abundance of brothels. Not coincidentally, the town also had forty-eight lawyers.

"The city of Leadville is one of the marvels of the present age," the directory explained. "Two years ago it had no existence, while today it has its long streets and broad avenues many miles in extent, with large and handsome buildings on every side." It was suddenly a well-heeled town: "The numerous and well-stocked business houses, the many elegant and well-furnished private residences, the commodious hotels, theaters, churches and school, together with the broad and well graded streets, give the city a decidedly metropolitan air."

But boom towns often know busts as well. This part of Colorado is filled with such history. Forgotten places with names like St. Elmo, Vicksburg, Independence, and Winfield—places of abandoned buildings, closed US post offices, and deserted residences. Not so long ago, Leadville almost disappeared too.

Gold, silver, lead, zinc, and copper were all once mined there. In 1980, Leadville's Climax Mine was the largest underground mine in the world. But when Climax Mine halted production in

---

35 For some, the twenty-nine grocery stores in Leadville in 1879, and the thirteen butcher shops, seem the most improbable statistics. For quite a while, there has been only one full-sized national-chain grocery store in town, but it seems to work for the town's sturdy inhabitants.

1982, Leadville lost 3,200 jobs overnight. The peak population in 1882 of over 50,000 had dwindled to 3,879 in 1980. Without those mining jobs, it was nearly a foregone conclusion that the town would sputter and ultimately shutter.

A miner about to lose his job, Ken Chlouber, knew of a foot race in the Lake Tahoe area, run from Olympic Village to Auburn, California, called Western States. When contacted by an ultrarunner and race director named Jim Butera about hosting a 100-mile event locally, Chlouber suggested Leadville. Both men agreed Leadville had plenty of pristine land and back country views to enthrall such runners.

And Leadville's remote location meant any runner who wanted to challenge the terrain would need to sleep overnight. They would need hot coffee, a restaurant or two, and a hotel. Could a foot race save a town from the grave?

Leadville's quirky western frontier flavor and pickaxe past proved irresistible to runners. The first race had forty-four starters. The success of the run prompted Chlouber and his business partner, the graceful Merilee Maupin, to also create a mountain bike race to bring in another wave of overnight guests. Then came additional shorter races and training-camp weeks. Ken and Merilee's idea and execution were a defibrillator to the town's economy. There is still only one grocery store in Leadville, but now there are *two* exceptional bike shops.

The Leadville locals care for athletes at the aid stations of the Leadville Series races because they've *been there*. The highest checkpoint of the thirteen aid stations of the Leadville 100 run is called the Hopeless Aid Station for a reason. As the locals say, they know what it feels like to be shit out of luck in the middle of nowhere, somewhere between Fatigue City and Fuckthatville.

The sight of fluffy llamas at Hopeless Station is a great salve for the chewed-up and spit-out souls who left Leadville at 4:00 a.m. on foot. The novelty of llamas at mile forty-five on the outbound trip delivers bliss. The second sighting of them at mile fifty-five inbound confirms the completion of two climbs of the Pass. A bonus of the second glimpse of the llamas is the confirmation that the sight of the magical herd the first time wasn't imagined.

Hallucinations are a part of long, long ultra runs. While a 50-kilometer run (31 miles) can have a runner home by lunch, and 50-milers (80.4 kilometers) often allow runners to be home by dinner, running long, long-distances often involves running through the night to brunch the next day. But the goal posts of distance are moving: Among the field of those who "live long," 200-mile (322-kilometer) races are now a notable trend.

To run through the night, runners carry headlamps and/or waist belts with LED lights to illuminate their courses (older style incandescent bulbs are more fragile, less compact, and less efficient than light-emitting diode bulbs). Lightweight, inexpensive, often rechargeable, and completely hands-free, these lights, pound for pound, are some of the most valuable gear outdoor enthusiasts can carry.

But these lights cast some odd shadows. Shapes and movements are not always as they appear. Many lights come with multiple settings that provide degrees of *throw*—a longer beam for distance—and *flood*—a broad beam that lights up the area around a runner. A dimmer switch on a headlamp and a brighter chest or waist light can be used to minimize shadows and provide better depth perception. The following sounds preposterous. But those shadows can turn an eight-foot-tall withered tree stump into a Great Dane walking on two legs toward a runner at 3 a.m. faster than you can say, "Down, boy." The phosphorescence of decaying wood called "foxfire"—a luminescent oxidation from a strain of fungus that glows a bluish green—combined with the deep dark before the dawn can easily be mistaken for glowing monkey brains being eaten by a squatting goblin in a pointy hat. The phenomenal pro runner Courtney Dauwalter tells the story: "Running along these trails, it was getting kind of dark, and next to the trail a woman was churning butter." She laughs. "Like a colonial woman, was just standing there churning butter." More laughter, before clarifying: "It wasn't real. She wasn't there." Additional laughter. Courtney said her first two instances of these tricks of the mind—fatigued minds processing odd shapes and unnatural shadow movement—involved a pterodactyl and some giraffes.[36]

---

36 The immensely talented, champion of the people Courtney Dauwalter was a middle-school science teacher when she started running trails, and quickly made a massive impact in the world of ultrarunning. In 2016 she won Desert Solstice 24 Hour Run, Javelina Jundred 100K, Run Rabbit Run 100 Mile Run, Hideaway Hundred 50K, Continental Divide Trail Run 50K, FANS Ultra Races 24 Hours, Collegiate Peaks Trail Run 50 Miles, and others. She decided to try to run full-time as a professional before the beginning of the back-to-school fall season in 2017. She famously won Moab 240 in that autumn season outright in 2 days, 9 hours, and 59 minutes; beating the next finisher—male or female—by more than ten hours. In 2019, trail runners marveled as she won Big's Backyard Ultra, which is a "last person standing" format. She ran a 4.1-mile (6.6 kilometers) lap every hour for sixty-eight hours. A staggering 283.33 miles (456 kilometers) was the total distance. Since then, she is the only athlete in history to have won Western States Endurance Run, Hardrock 100, and Ultra Trail du

Headlamps and their shadows are only part of the problem. The other ingredient in the hallucination recipe is sleep deprivation.

By way of explanation, consider the 4 a.m. Saturday morning race start of the Leadville 100 run. Most runners do not report getting a good night's sleep before such an undertaking. A majority of entrants are sleeping in an unfamiliar room, on an unfamiliar bed, in an unfamiliar routine. For those sleeping at a higher elevation than they're used to, restful sleep can be elusive. And the omnipresent early alarm clock means few runners get enough hours of sleep before an ultra. Therefore, for a Saturday race, Thursday night is usually the last decent night of sleep. And many of these races do not end until *Sunday*. Tired eyes, exhausted brains, and headlamp shadows contribute to some trippy mind tricks and mild hallucinations for the sleep deprived running all night.

If the headlamps are ever shut off, many first-time ultra runners who go long, long in remote places like Leadville marvel at the river of stars overhead. The first sight of the Milky Way by grown adults evokes child-like wonder and the question, "How have I never seen this before?"

Mont-Blanc (UTMB) in the same year—2023. She set a new course record at WSER—15:29—in 2023. At Hardrock 100, she won the race in 2022, 2023, and 2024, each time setting a new course record in both directions, as the Hardrock course is run clockwise one year (such as in 2022), and counterclockwise the next (2023).
Courtney Dauwalter has resided in Leadville, Colorado, full time since 2020.

Less than one third of the American population live in a place where the Milky Way is visible. The act of stargazing—an act, like running distance—is as old as our species.

From amongst the cathedral peaks, one of Colorado's state songs, "Rocky Mountain High," by John Denver, describes "the shadow from the starlight (as) softer than a lullaby." High elevation, good air quality, and low population-density create a naturally dark night in places like Lake County that most Americans have never lived with. It's a little thing. But in the time since the first miner's tent was pitched in Leadville in 1859, many places around the world have lost the natural darkness that had been in place on Earth for millennia. So maybe it's not little at all.[37]

Chris Jones ran toward the 7:58 p.m sunset disappearing behind a hunk of mountain called the Sugarloaf. The stars burned bright in a benediction, but their electromagnetic spectrum and luminosity was no match for the Colorado forest. Groves of white-barked aspen below gave way to an impenetrable forest of lodgepole pine, spruce, and fir. Underfoot, the trail remained burly and technical; loose baby-head rocks and uneven roots in stony loam made no two steps the same. False summit after false summit did not relent until 11,156 feet (3,400 meters). Chris speed-hiked, hands on quads, through the 29%-grade bits. By midnight, Jonesy—his friends' affectionate term for him—had been running nonstop for twenty hours. And it felt as if he had

---

37 Worldwide, there is a movement to preserve the night sky for animals and insects that depend on dark skies for navigation and wellness. In a study using high-resolution satellite data, "World Atlas of Artificial Night Sky Brightness," scientists found that 99% of the United States and Europe live in light pollution. For more information on preserving the night sky, visit the nonprofit DarkSky International at darksky.org.

run a grand tour of the land he had been protecting for half his life: the south of Old Dominion 100 in Virginia June 3, Western States 100 in the Lake Tahoe area June 24–25, Vermont 100 representing New England July 15–16, and Angeles Crest 100 two weeks earlier in Los Angeles. He declared that this stretch of the Powerline Climb inbound made most mountain ultras and Hope Pass look silly easy.

"Powerline Inbound": The name sends a shudder through a segment of endurance athletes of the last thirty-plus years. No two words are more unforgiving.

But with his usual trail chattiness, Chris forged ahead. Such is his habit. Since his return from a difficult deployment in Iraq in 2009, running unexpectedly and fortuitously changed Chris Jones. The stories and mythology of war rarely address the chaos, intensity, and suffering endured in deployment. Or the chaos, intensity, and suffering of returning from war. But running pulled Chris back from the hell of irritability, the vex of ire. It seems impossible that the friendliest guy on the trail today[38] found himself getting in fights and caught up in a battle with anger as a result of the prolonged conflict called the Second Gulf War. A half-marathon followed by training for the Quad Dipsea in Marin County, California, rerouted Chris. Two out-and-back trips from Mill Valley to Stinson Beach

---

38 Two-time Western States 100 winner Hal Koerner, gifted professional runner, Rogue Valley Runners shopkeeper, and community-builder in Ashland, Oregon, described Chris as, "...Probably the nicest guy on the trails. Talk about somebody who exudes the spirit of this community and what we do: the love for the events; the camaraderie; the challenge; and everything else. That's you, my man." Hal, a talented and good-natured race director, presented Chris with a distinguished award in 2024 on the occasion of Jonesy's tenth completion of Hal's daunting Pine to Palm 100 mile event in the Siskiyou Mountains of southern Oregon.

totaling 28.4 miles (45.7 kilometers) on the legendary Dipsea Trail made an ultrarunner out of the man on November 27, 2010. Forged from the crucible of the Iraq War and reintegration emerged a runner dedicated to other runners in a particularly steadfast way. Fellow athletes, countless aid station volunteers, and race directing teams have been rewarded by being a part of the same mission—albeit unknowingly—as the runner with the hearty laugh, Chris Jones.

Military training translates to helpful intestinal fortitude on the trail in places like Sugarloaf. If made to find a complaint about the unforgiving miles of a Leadville 100 night, Chris reluctantly recalls the way the temperature dropped as zero three hundred hours grew darker in the forest. Before dawn he arrived at the perimeter of Turquoise Lake, named for nearby turquoise mines—the slightly scarred and dirt-dunked features synonymous with the place and the people of the Race Across the Sky. Chris was dirt-dunked like everybody else on and along the course. What they couldn't see and did not know on that early Sunday August 20 morning: This was Chris's fifth 100-mile race since June 3.

Whatever is happening in ultrarunning—despite the dark—is worth watching. In the year 2000 in North America, there were 218 ultra races; by 2019, there were 2,433.[39] And trail runners are only getting faster, like the 2017 first place finishers—gifted Devon Yanko, who crushed the course in 20:46:29, and the

---

39 With thanks to *Ultra Running Magazine* for their comprehensive statistics about the hypergrowth of the sport, including these stats about North America. There were 2,819 ultra races in 2023, and more than 35,688 first-time ultrarunners in North American races. Take a look at their latest stats on "Ultrarunning Finishes" in North America: https://ultrarunning.com/calendar/stats/ultrarunning-finishes.

always excellent Ian Sharman, who has won Leadville in 2013, 2015, 2016, and 2017 (in 17:34:51). And stringing together races to create new races—like the Last Great Race—suggests we have only scratched the surface of virtuoso performances in limitless combinations of unforgiving possibilities in this running category.

Chris Jones and 603 other starters found treasure in a dusty old town in a nearly forgotten place in 2017. Ultimately, 287 runners carried home a silver finisher's belt buckle for the effort, half dead but more alive than before.

Chris's idea might have been absurd and audacious, but it was not impossible. Before his next deployment—to the warfront in Afghanistan in the spring of 2018—the Army infantryman got into the half dozen Last Great Race events and finished all six 100 milers across the country he served for thirty-two years. To date, he is the only active service member of the military to have seen the country in such a way in one summer. Like the mountain clearer from the plain, America, The Beautiful, shimmered that summer of 2017, for and through a soldier sworn to her care.

It was a season of excavated mettle and medals.

Running 100 miles (161-kilometer) between 9,200 feet (2,804 meters) (near Twin Lakes) and 12,532 feet (3,819 meters) above sea level (Hope Pass) and finishing on a red carpet on Sixth Street may smell like hard work, but it looks like ultra glee. Chris Jones's smile in the final steps of the iconic Leadville 100 feels almost as wide as the distance run on the third weekend in August 2017. (*photo courtesy of Life Time/Leadville Race Series*)

CHAPTER TEN

FIRST ASHORE (FE)MALES

Tina Ament and Anne Thilges

It was her habit to build laughter out
of inadequate materials.
—*John Steinbeck*, The Grapes of Wrath, *1939*

IN THE LATE 1960S AND 1970S, WHEN ROBERT CRAIG "EVEL" Knievel started hauling himself into the air on a motorcycle in ramp-to-ramp jumps over buses and rattlesnakes and canyons dressed in red, white, and blue leathers, he captured the public's imagination with his high-horsepower bravery and toughness.

In 1974, with a five-foot crossbow hidden in an architect's blueprint tube smuggled into New York City's Twin Towers, a twenty-four-year-old man named Philippe Petit managed to lay a steel cable from the roof of the North Tower to that of the South Tower. He proceeded to give New Yorkers and the world a knee-knocker lesson in physical stamina and guts. The young man walked the one-inch-thick cable 110 floors above the World Trade Center Plaza for more than forty-five minutes without a net, 1,350 feet (411 meters) above the crowds gathered below. At the time, this was the pinnacle of derring-do of the era.

But it was a senior from California Polytechnic State University, San Luis Obispo, who completely dunked over Knievel and Petit in 1982. She captured the imagination of the public and redefined the image of bravado and courage, overshadowing the daredevils of the day. ABC's *Wide World of Sports* broadcast her performance in a segment about an athletic competition that combined an open-water swim with a transition to a significant bicycle ride, before the 591 competitors had to go run a full 26.2–mile (421.2-kilometer) marathon. The setting was none other than an archipelago paradise, fittingly on the youngest of Hawaii's islands. What viewers saw on their televisions on that Saturday afternoon, two weeks after the race, could qualify as the index case for a worldwide sports outbreak that would follow.

Viewers could practically smell the coconut fragrance of the day's last application of Hawaiian Tropic sunscreen. They could very nearly taste the Bonnie Bell Lip Smacker piña colada lip balm. Viewers could well-nigh feel the last sherbet sunbeams of the sunset on the west side of the Big Island. Twenty-three-year-old Julie Moss was running in the twilight of that sunset, on the nearly artificial-light-free streets of Kona. At 2,400 miles (3,862 kilometers) from the closest landmass, a particularly pitch-black night could descend on the place. The ginger-freckled Moss with the pale apricot hair led the women's race in this new-ish event called the Budweiser Light Ironman® World Triathlon (the next year it would shave weight to be called the Bud Light Ironman® World Triathlon). What the viewers did not know was there was more than the $85 entry fee on the line for

Moss; these hours would be the Queen Stage[40] of her senior-year kinesiology project, "Physiological and Training Considerations in Preparation of the World Ironman® Triathlon," required for her college graduation. Every ultra distance finish line is flush with such untold but compelling backstories. There is an expression that goes, "You saddle today and ride out tomorrow." In long-distance endeavors like an English Channel swim or Race Across America or the 140.6-mile (226.3-kilometer) triathlon, you saddle, you saddle, you saddle, and you saddle some more, before you ride tomorrow. In all that saddling, the most marvelous backstories are born.

The video footage about that day made by *Wide World of Sports* shows the Cal Poly student and her fellow competitors in clear Kailua Bay during the 2.4-mile-long (3.9-kilometer-long) clockwise swim loop in the first leg of this unusual event. The swim was the least problematic leg to the surfer-turned-lifeguard from Carlsbad, California. After her solid 71-minute swim in her red one-piece Speedo swimsuit, she cycled the tough 112-mile (180-kilometer) bike course in 5 hours, 53 minutes, and 39 seconds on her $295 Univega bike.[41] Much to her surprise, Moss overtook the top female on the next segment, leading the entire women's

---

40   "The Queen Stage" refers to the stage of a multiday bike race (called a cycling stage race) which is most difficult or demanding. Just as a Queen Stage is not usually the last stage in a stage race, Julie Moss needed to compete in the February 6, 1982, triathlon event, and then return to California to write the kinesiology paper for graduation.

41   Given the quality of the basic road-bikes of the era, including toe clips on the pedals, bike shoes with laces, no aerobars up front, and an un-aerodynamic skateboard helmet, metaphorically speaking, Moss rode her socks off in the biking portion of the race. In current dollars, adjusting for inflation, a $295 bike is the equivalent of a $963 bike today. Many of the wheelsets used by amateurs at the top races today cost at least this much, often two or three times that amount—just for two wheels. You don't need to buy a $6,000 to $10,000 tri-specific bike to race 140.6-mile events, but quite a few people do.

field through the run. The television audience watched as Moss—in the final stretch of a whole 26.2-mile marathon—willed herself through drop-dead fatigue along the final homestretch. Earlier in the changing tent, the front clasp of Moss's sports bra intended for the run had broken, and a volunteer kindly gave the co-ed the white non-sports bra off her back. As it was 1982, the sartorial choices leaned toward short Dolfin shorts and snapback trucker hats with foamy front panels. On both the men and women, hair was feathered. It was 6:30 p.m. Through the dimming light, viewers watched as with a quarter of a mile to go from the finish, Moss's legs gave out. The instrumental music of the television segment swelled.

At her recent average pace, the twenty-three-year-old was less than three minutes from the finish. Totally cracked, she nevertheless willed herself forward. The ill-fitting white bra straps kept slipping off her sparrow shoulders. With less than fifty feet to go, her legs buckled under her a second time. Beneath her trucker hat, her head swiveled, eyes ever so slightly unfocused. She wobbled toward the finishing tape. There was no inflatable arch or well-lit chute—but the red tape was within eyesight. Less than forty feet to go. The camera captured her limbs contorting and folding unnaturally, her disequilibrium in front of a nationwide audience. Thirty feet stood between agony and sweet relief.

Her attempts at an orthostatic vertical position revealed an athlete listing hard, shorts now soiled. The commentary provided by open-water swimmer and ABC commentator Diana Nyad said it all: "When you push beyond your physical threshold you may lose control of some voluntary muscles like your thighs. You may also lose some control of some involuntary muscles, like your bladder and your bowels. But she still didn't quit," Nyad narrated.

Less than twenty feet to go. Racer number 393 started crawling. The Kona crowd on Ali'i Drive knitted itself around her, willing her to find a few footsteps to finish this thing. The television audience held its breath as the college senior crawled, unrhythmically, fifteen excruciating feet on her hands and knees, head down, only paces from the finish line and victory. It was then, on the left side of the screen, that an unknowing Kathleen McCartney, bib number 290, sailed through the disarray surrounding the prostrate Moss. Up the right side of the course toward the red tape, the University of California Irvine student ran unawares. The upright McCartney, twenty-two, with an easy stride, bright eyes, and wide smile—about her assumed second-place finish—crossed the line at 11:09:40. Moss agonizingly clawed her way to the line at 11:10:09. And neither woman was seemingly appraised of the other. It became one of the most memorable scenes of the televised sports of the time and can be credited with introducing the mainstream world to the triathlon.

Journalist and host Jim McKay called it, "The greatest show of courage in the history of *Wide World of Sports*."

Televised sport had a new paradigm: surviving—on one's hands and knees—was winning. And for the first time, the "ball" sports or the Olympics or the men's Pro Leagues weren't the apogee of physical achievement. An imperceivable shift in space-time-sports continuum occurred. To the average spectator's eye, the Cal Poly student on ABC's broadcast left more on the course than 1982's stars Joe Montana, Moses Malone, and Wayne Gretzky combined. Anatomical firepower took a backseat to every(wo)man grit, resilience, and perseverance when combined with the X-factor of distance.

Travis Vogan, PhD, Director of American Studies at the University of Iowa, with a specialization in the nexus of sport, media, and US culture, and author of *ABC Sports: The Rise and Fall of Network Sports Television*, described the broadcast of the race: "The 1982 Kona finish line encapsulated the mission of *Wide World of Sports*, as the intro says, it captured the thrill of victory and the agony of defeat, and the human drama of athletic competition. The idea was to use sports as a starting point to tell dramatic stories, and Moss embodied the values that we attach to sport about not giving up, working hard, perseverance in the face of adversity— and that resonated with audiences." It was the era when viewers reacted by writing letters to the ABC mailroom. "This is how an instant became a part of sport lore, by exemplifying the myths we have about sporting competition," he explained.

Five hundred and thirty-seven people, including Julie Moss and Kathleen McCartney, finished the 1982 Kona race. No one had been spared the gritty distance or the temperatures hovering over 100°F (38°C) for most of the day. The apex of the athlete archetype became the girl next door. And we could be her.

———————

Anne Thilges, fair daughter of Rock Island, Illinois, grew up watching ABC's *Wide World of Sports* on Saturdays. When she and her family watched the replay of the February 6, 1982, Kona race, they, folks across the neighboring Quad Cities and around America made the segment a part of one of the highest rated *Wide World of Sports* episodes ever. Recall, or imagine, network television programming used to be a campfire event. Julie Moss's words to Diana Nyad in the finisher's tent reverberated across the nationwide watch party; her earnest voice met the moment: "This is the first time I've found something that I wanted so bad, I was willing to crawl on my hands and knees to get it."

Kristina "Tina" Ament remembers the first time that voice and the Moss-McCartney finish of 1982 played on her television. The events lived up to Jim McKay's promise of "Spanning the globe to bring you the constant variety of sport. In the thrill of victory... and the agony of defeat... the human drama of athletic competition." Jim Lampley, Arthur Ashe, Eric Heiden, and Diana Nyad's descriptions of the vivid challenges of triathlon depicted successes that could not be bought and sold; the journalists' words averred that the only price was dedication and drive. Tina Ament listened intently.

Atop *Billboard* magazine's Top Hot 100 list of songs for 1982 was Olivia Newton-John's "Physical." Number two? Survivor's "Eye of the Tiger." At the same time, a Japanese company named Sony added a radio feature to their new portable cassette player, the Walkman WM-F1. For the first time in the history of endurance sports, going-long training could include the endorphin boost that is music by high-octane musicians like AC/DC, Queen, and The Ramones. "Hey/ Ho/ Let's go!" said 1982.

Most people trace triathlon's origin story to the San Diego Track Club in southern California. The 1970s' jogging, running, and biking crazes burgeoned in "America's Finest City"—with its postcard weather and unimpeded access to training four seasons of the year. The growing marathon-racing community, alongside and within the San Diego Track Club, began to incorporate what is now called "cross training" into their marathon-fitness regimen. Big mileage days could be followed by recovery spins on skinny-framed ten-speed bikes. Non-impact swimming made perfect sense for running fanatics, too: San Diego's beaches were second to none. And any flight into Lindbergh Field in the 1970s revealed how omnipresent swimming pools were across the county. Blue stained glass in the Cathedral of the Endless Summer.

"San Diegans had a full calendar of swim, run and bike events in the 1970s, including weekday outings and multisport occasions," explains participant Judy Collins, who was in her early thirties at the time. "The San Diego Track Club (SDTC) had held two annual run-swim events by 1974," recalling the burgeoning multisport scene. Before long, the San Diego Track Club (with direction from Jack Johnstone and Don Shanahan) put together the area's first-ever swim-bike-run contest in 1974, consisting of ten segments. There was a 2.8-mile (4.5-kilometer) run, a bike of more than five miles (eight kilometers) and about five hundred yards of swimming in four to five run-swim segments, in-and-out of the Bay. To make a triathlete laugh on cue, the race entry fee for the event was $1.00. To make them laugh a second time, the event began at 5:45 p.m. "Of the forty-six people in the Mission Bay Triathlon on Wednesday, September 25, 1974," notes Judy Collins, "five were named Collins." Four came from the same family.

Naval officer John Collins, wife Judy, and their two children, Kristin, thirteen, and Michael, twelve, lived in a south-bay coastal peninsula town called Coronado, formerly home to a curious number of hog, dairy, and chicken ranches—and even an ostrich farm. It was also home to a very grand 399-room oceanfront hotel. Any account of the Collins's town ought to begin with its namesake grand dame, the Hotel del Coronado. Constructed in 1887, the white-wood Queen Anne Victorian-style seaside hotel featured a distinctive, red-tiled roof and an architectural beauty befitting the natural wonder of each evening's Pacific Ocean sunset. The hotel even predates any significant military presence on the peninsula—such as the Marine Corps' Camp Thomas (named for Rear Admiral Chauncey Thomas) from March to June 1911, the camp named for Rear Admiral Thomas Howard in 1914, or the flying school and Army airfield called Rockwell Field, used from 1912 to 1939. Whether standing in "The Del's" 120-foot-tall turret above the Ocean Ballroom, or standing at attention among rows of neat white-canvas tents along the Pacific in Marine, Army, or Navy uniforms, you could enjoy unobstructed views in those early days from the sandy isthmus. Due south lay the hills of Mexico. To the southwest, about ten miles offshore from Rosarito, Mexico, sat the four craggy Coronado Islands (once a place of actual pirates, then a rumrunning haven during the Depression, and eventually a protected wildlife refuge today). Looking across the bay toward San Diego's downtown, you could see signs of the city's prosperity and growth from whaling, farming, and fishing dotting the landscape, including the stately eleven-story US Grant Hotel, finished in 1910. To the east, from Coronado you could see unobstructed views of the pine-covered Laguna Mountains in Cleveland National Forest. By comparison, Coronado was as flat as a turbot and overrun with jackrabbits. The chatter from the scrub came from California quail;

the sounds from the sandy stretches were the calls of slender-billed snipes.

Livestock ranches and barley farms were relocated to make way for the first squadron of United States' Naval pilots in 1917. Eventually the ostriches and their descendants were relocated to the San Diego Zoo in Balboa Park. In similar fashion, the Marines (as part of the Department of the Navy) relocated to permanent barracks on the dedicated Marine Corps Base just north of Lindbergh Field in San Diego proper. The Army completed the transfer of its airfield and buildings on Coronado to the Navy by January 1939, following an executive order by President Franklin D. Roosevelt (although proof of the Army's presence there is the Army Air Corp insignia still visible in the carved window shutters of Building 505 near Flag Circle on one of the original gate buildings of Naval Air Station North Island). Charles Lindbergh preceded his historic New York to Paris flight of 33 hours and 30 minutes with a flight from Coronado to New York (with a stop in St. Louis) in 21 hours and 40 minutes, a new transcontinental record. It was Coronado where the single-seat monoplane, *The Spirit of St. Louis*, was built. The first Pacific submarines followed, and the northern area of the peninsula ("North Island") would become the largest Naval Air Station in the Pacific. Not only the designated "Birthplace of Naval Aviation," Coronado was the place where the art and science of aircraft carriers was perfected. By 1935, all four of the Navy's Pacific Fleet carriers called Coronado home port. During World War II, originally commissioned the "Amphibious Training Base," the future Naval Amphibious Base ("Amphib" or "NAB") was built from fill material dredged from the bay to create both deeper water for the big ships and more land for the NAB's needs—such as Naval Special Warfare Command and facilities for the United States Navy's Sea, Air, and Land Teams, commonly called Navy SEALs.

Along the bay side, there is a statue dedicated to the US Navy's first Underwater Demolition Teams (UDTs). Where underwater obstacles deterred amphibious landings for Allied Forces in World War II, these Navy combat swimmers faced heavily defended beaches with nothing more than a face mask, fins, swim booties, shorts, a slate board, a pencil to record intelligence, and a Ka-Bar Knife—thus, the moniker "The Naked Warrior" on the statue's bronze plaque. Members of these Underwater Demolition Teams, who specialized in precious infiltration, reconnoitering, and sabotage, were nicknamed "frogmen." The Naked Warrior statue is the sole statue in Coronado commemorating the predecessors of the US Navy SEALs and the future graduates of Basic Underwater/SEAL training called "BUD/S." The motto of the Naked Warriors was "First Ashore."

Geologically speaking, if Coronado can be seen from above as a small, two-bite "lollipop" lamb chop, it connects to the mainland by its long unadorned rib bone. The meat of the chop is the oval-shaped sum of North Island and the civilian town of Coronado.[42] The bone handle is a spit of land called the Silver Strand (usually

---

42 Long-distance swimmers take this oval-shaped route, from Glorietta Bay Park on the San Diego Bay side, counterclockwise around North Island, to the Pacific and down to Gator Beach for an 11.5-mile (18.5-kilometer) swim.

There also used to be a race called "Coronado Around the Island Swim" for solo swimmers and relay teams—which Kristin Collins Galbreaith solo raced in 1993 in the speedy time of 4:45:44 at age thirty-two.

While counterclockwise is the more typical route, some swimmers enjoy varying it, including a two-way swim, from bay-to-beach-to-bay, of just over 23 miles (37 kilometers). This route has been finished twice, by Abigail Fairman in December 2021, and Abigail Bergman in July 2022.

"The Strand"), named for its silvery shell bits. Seven miles (eleven kilometers) long, but only as wide as four-lane divided highway State Route 75 in the middle, it is fringed with Pacific sand on one side and San Diego Bay sand on the other. This island and spit of land connecting it to the mainland is called a "tombolo," but it bears little in common with the Italian word's definition of "pillow" or "cushion." This flat tombolo contains the midnight beaches, the salt water, the grating sand rasp, the exacting bay-training travail in the DNA of every man who ever earned the SEAL's Trident pin. Coronado and its tombolo were the incubator for what was to come to endurance sport.

Coronado in the 1970s possessed the small-town charm, tidy streets, and good schools of the solidly middle-class, picturesque towns of America. But it was quietly different. Charleston had seersucker, Cape Cod had Nantucket Reds, Key West sported tropical prints; Coronado had Navy Dress Whites. It was a place borne of the steady intrepidity of the Naval officers who lived there. And the unseen, but even steadier, Navy wives. Steady like the unbroken sound of ocean waves as one sleeps with the window open in a Craftsman bungalow near Ocean Boulevard.

Other waterfront towns had ticky-tacky boardwalks or day-drinking tiki bars spilling onto beach sand. Coronado in the 1970s did not hew to such a mold. It hosted Greatest Generation veterans, Navy men who led the Allies on the seas. In 1973, then-Commander John Collins (US Naval Academy class of 1959) was a marine engineer and submariner, which meant he had learned from the best, and served under and alongside a class of sailors who delivered hard-earned NATO peace and Pax Americana to the back half of the twentieth century. Once the conflict in

Vietnam was in the rear-view mirror, a new kind of leisure-hour prosperity would be ushered into the United States, and beyond—Great Britain, Australia, New Zealand, across Europe—and the 1970s running boom was proof. But Coronado's discipline and earnestness ran deep. As adults in 1973, John and Judy joined the Coronado rec-pool evening swims; their kids swam on base in the same pool used by the Navy SEALs. The masters swim coach there encouraged novices to build up their endurance by recreational running. The family of four with the surname Collins entered the ten-leg triathlon in Mission Bay in the fall of 1974 and then helped get Coronado's own race off the ground: the Coronado Optimist Club Triathlon (with organizers Stan Antrim and Bob Weaver) on July 27, 1975—which would become the longest continuously running triathlon in the world. The Collins family was not finished leaving their mark on the sport.

When John was transferred from Coronado to Honolulu, Hawaii, the Collins family joined the Waikiki Swim Club and the Mid-Pacific Road Runners Club. The local cyclists' island loop ride measured 115 miles (185 kilometers). It was John and Judy Collins who recognized what could be stitched together if they combined the existing events of the island: where the Waikiki Rough Water Swim (2.4 miles/3.9 kilometers) ended, the Around Oahu Bike Race (115 miles) could begin. Trim off the final three miles of the bike leg, and one was deposited at the start of the Honolulu Marathon (26.2 miles/42.4 kilometers). Bolt the three events together, and a righteous homegrown adventure was underway: "Swim 2.4 miles! Bike 112 miles (180 kilometers)! Run 26.2 miles! Brag for the rest of your life!" John and Judy extolled in the photocopied race materials. Judy explains that at the time, "Typical sports club events in California and Hawaii had no age or gender restrictions and no sign-up. The events were open to the public and low or no fee. Our Collins Iron Man followed the same model." The entry fee was $5.00. It was show and go.

The first iteration of long-distance triathlon's introduction to the world arrived when *Sports Illustrated* featured a ten-page feature about the race. The subtitle of the article did not mince words: to earn the title of "Iron Man," the intrepid souls "swam vigorously through rough seas, bicycled 112 miles and ran a marathon, all in a single day of agony." The number of entrants in the first two events was scant: There were fifteen starters and a dozen finishers in the Hawaiian Iron Man Triathlon of 1978 (those twelve men were inducted into the USA Triathlon Hall of Fame in 2023). In 1979, bad weather postponed the race a day and again only fifteen participants toed the line. But those seeking folly on such scale typically just figure out a way to the start line; excuse-making is not their sport.

To explain how homegrown and hard core the Collins's event was, a Marine stationed in Oahu named Dave Orlowski took a pair of scissors to some jeans the night before the inaugural event. After his hour-and-nine-minute swim, he pulled on the cutoff jeans over his striped brief-style swimsuit for the bike segment—on a borrowed Sears' Free Spirit bike. The denim jean shorts got the call on February 18, 1978, for the pockets they offered. As there were no aid stations or cached supplies along the course (in modern parlance, it was a "self-supported" event), participants were carrying cash in their pockets for a lifeline to candy bars and water in the tropical heat and humidity from convenience stores along the route. Son Michael Collins and friend Dan Richardson welcomed Orlowski to the finish line after 140.6 miles (226.2

kilometers) as 13 hours, 59 minutes, and 13 seconds elapsed on the official stopwatch. Michael and Dan were later relieved by John and Judy Collins when John finished the race after 17 hours. Judy describes the staff of the Hawaiian Iron Man®: "The Collins family, Pearl Harbor Shipyard colleagues, and Waikiki Swim Club swimmers and friends."

For the 1980 event, Judy and John had given permission to ABC to film the race, but then John received Navy orders. The Collins family would be transferred to Washington, DC. Luckily, the Waikiki Swim Club had pledged volunteers to support the person who would direct the 1980 event. On short notice on October 15, 1979, John and Judy Collins turned over the race to local gym owner Hank Grundman. Judy summarizes what happened next: "Hank's partner Valerie Silk would become the 1981 race director, move the race to Kona, and copyrighted the present one word name, 'Ironman®.'" Silk also hired a Honolulu graphics firm to design the recognizable "IM" logo, partnered with unheralded worker-bees like Earl Yamaguchi, maintained the integrity of the spirit of the contest, and help grow the nascent race to keep its head above water before it became profitable. Understandable growing pains mark the three years from when the Collins family moved to Washington, DC, until February 1982 and the Moss-McCartney finish. Valerie Silk—who would lead the event effort from 1980 until 1990, despite no sports management background or event-planning bona fides—described the Moss-McCartney effect in an interview in 2015: "The response to the (February 20th) show was so tremendous that ABC televised it again only two weeks after the first broadcast. Suddenly, I was being contacted by sports marketing agents who wanted to help me find sponsors...Interest in the Iron Man surged. For the first time, the number of requests for applications far exceeded the number we could accommodate on race day. Soon the Iron Man® lottery would be born." Silk honored the request by John Collins at the turnover of the race: "If there should ever be cut-off times," John said, "I want everyday athletes to always have a chance to be in an Iron Man®."

Emanating from San Diego's jubilance and germinated in quiet Coronado grit and discipline, the test called Iron Man mesmerized like a siren's song across the country and around the world. The *Sports Illustrated* and *Wide World of Sports* coverage was not contained to American shores. There were 537 finishers in February 1982. By 1985, there were 965 finishers from twenty-four countries.[43]

Tina Ament had never screamed at work before. Her office was a buttoned-up place, on a staid floor of a reserved Washington, DC, office of the US Department of Justice. Involuntarily, the assistant US attorney screamed. Sitting at her desk, the federal prosecutor had opened an email that announced: "Congratulations! You are going to Kona!"

For athletes who have put their names into race lotteries like those for the New York or Chicago marathons, Western States 100 (WSER), or Hardrock 100 trail runs, or biking events like the

---

43 The four members of the Collins family would all complete the distance: John in Honolulu at age forty-one in 1978; Michael in Honolulu in 1979 at age sixteen; Kristin in Kona at age twenty-eight in 1988, and the dazzling Judy on the original course in the 2003 "Ironman® Revisited" event at the age of sixty-four. One final word about the Navy-wife-who-could, Judy Collins is the first woman to swim island-to-island, from Lanai to Maui on Mother's Day 1977.

UNBOUND Gravel Race,[44] their endurance is first tested by the lottery process.

So titillating is the sensation of winning a lottery spot that the big race lotteries spur actual parties, gatherings of the exuberant as they watch the names being drawn. The big belt buckles, race hats, and sartorial choices like ten-year finisher jackets[45] at homegrown lottery parties reveal and underline a deep devotion to the endurance craft. It's an understated and humble coterie; such gear often doesn't mean much outside of these rather tight circles. Plenty of popular races could use a lottery system, as the events are in such demand: from the poetic Vermont 50 Mountain Bike Race in scenic Mount Ascutney, Vermont, an early-fall New England classic, to the damn-near maniacal Georgia Death Race (with a logo that reads "Run Cry Die"—and 16,000 feet/4,876 meters of both climbing and descent in "74-ish miles") more and more races sell out in a matter of minutes every year. The popularity of endurance races creates and fuels like an accelerant a marketplace of exclusivity, which of course serves to make these races even more popular.

Sometimes these processes are a matter of pure luck, like the randomness of Powerball numbers or the arbitrary six ping-pong balls that deliver Mega Millions. Often, the race lottery is more of a selection—based on a spectrum of factors including past

---

44 In UNBOUND, thrill-seeking gravel riders choose between a 25-mile, 50-, 100-, 200-, or the whopping 350-mile race through the Flint Hills of Kansas—if they are lucky enough to get in.

45 Race directors frequently acknowledge athletes who have completed ten finishes at an event with a custom sweatshirt or jacket or perhaps a big belt buckle for the veteran racer. These treasured items are admired and coveted by participants. More than one endurance athlete has set their sights on ten or twenty finishes on a specific course for these one-of-a-kind personalized outerwear pieces gifted by organizers.

performances, qualifying race history, and volunteer hours; also some folks being "grandfathered-in" after, say, seven, ten, or fifteen years. To more than one shut-out athlete, often these lottery processes can feel like smoky backroom deals, a fuzzy selection process made at the sole discretion of a few event organizers, insiders whose interpretations and decisions need not be transparent but are final and binding. For an athlete like Tina Ament to ever earn a spot to toe the line at the granddaddy of all 140.6 triathlons, she would need to "win" such a lottery.

Neuroscientists have identified at least six emotions our species convey in an intense vocal burst. For Tina's colleagues and the good girl-dog at her feet, her scream was a non-alert, non-alarm, rage-free, pain-free, grief-free, and fear-free scream. The scream conveyed extreme joy and a kind of intense pleasure associated with Beatlemania or a Taylor Swift concert. Tina's thrill was as clear as the Washington Monument on a bluebird day from any spot on the National Mall. For an athlete like Tina Ament, a triathlete who had completed multiple 140.6 races, winning a lottery spot to the Ironman® World Championship Race in Kona, Hawaii, felt like a once-in-a-lifetime stroke of good fortune. Tina is a stellar athlete: a five-time Boston Marathon qualifier and finisher of Race Across America (RAAM) with a relay team.[46] But the only way to Kona for Ament was through the lottery, per the original intention of John and Judy Collins for everyday athletes to have a chance to be in the race. Thus, from Fourth Street NW in DC in the US Attorney's Office came a big ol' scream.

---

46 More information about Tina's RAAM relay is found in The Athletes section under "Team Sea to See."

That's how popular the Collins family's event had become to multisport athletes around the world. John and Judy Collins's bolted-together, audacious three-sport-event had become a multi-million-dollar industry of aero bikes and specialty equipment: triathlon clothing and quick transition gear; gels in flasks and powders in straws from aerobar drink systems; destination races; camps as damn serious as Camp Thomas and Camp Howard; programs and coaching and lifestyle commandeering. And even the enterprise itself: Wanda Sports Group Company sold the largest triathlon group—Tampa, Florida–based Ironman® Group—to Advance Publications in August 2020 for, reportedly, $730 million. There are now 70.3 and 140.6 Ironman® races in more than fifty-plus countries worldwide, with about thirty-nine races where an athlete may qualify for the Ironman® World Championship. In the US, triathletes can earn a spot in such places as Madison, Wisconsin; Lake Placid, New York; and Chattanooga, Tennessee. Across international time zones, athletes qualified for Kona 2014 in 140.6 events across the planet: New Zealand, Denmark, Brazil, Wales, and a multitude of countries in between.

Spanning the globe, the end of every one of these races shares a tradition: those age groupers who finish in the top ten-or-so in their five-year category (e.g., "Male 18–24" or "Female 25–29") gather the day after the event in a quorum of shuffling vanquishers, often with the sunken cheeks or pronounced collarbones specific to dehydration and caloric deficit and often with a bit o' sunburn acquired in ten, eleven, or twelve hours the day before. In the 140.6 races, this "Ironman® World Championship Slot Allocation and Rolldown Ceremony" (informally, the "Roll Down Ceremony") occurs the morning after the races. No one knows with certainty how many spots their group has. This is because each race is allocated a certain number of Kona slots, allotted by that race's distribution of entrants. For example, if "Males 40–44" has the most entrants (it often does), the most Kona slots will go to the top men in this group (often five slots, but sometimes as many as eleven). Usually, somewhere between one and five finishers in each category are given a Kona golden ticket. In the old days, a quorum of the hopeful would gather the day after their race, unsure about the number of slots in their category and unsure about who would be in attendance. Race organizers would announce the category, and beginning with the first-place finisher, they would offer a Kona slot to that age grouper. If that age grouper had already earned a Kona slot from a previous race in the year, or if they declined to go to Kona, or if they were not present at the roll-down quorum, the next eligible finisher in that age group's name was called. Hope springs eternal, but the informality and deep roll down of the quorum seems less casual with every event. The roll down slots have grown fewer every year as Kona qualifying times get faster, as the top age groupers seem to grow more elite, as fewer slots become available, and as more qualifying races make slots more scarce. In every sense, there are no more cutoff jean shorts on 140.6 courses.

Tina described her reaction to getting the email notification that she had won a coveted spot at the Kona race. "I've never screamed at work before or since." To describe the weight of the occasion, the caliber of the Kona field, and the thrill of the moment, Tina's parents and her sister heard the news and set out to book flights and hotels for the race.

After her family, Tina's next call was to Anne Thilges. Delivering the big Kona news, the federal prosecutor in the Beltway asked the business strategy consultant in New York, "Will you race it with me?"

"You know I will," was the response. "It's a huge honor," Anne said. Tina could hear Anne's smile from Manhattan.

Anne Thilges knew her way around an Iron-distance triathlon course. She is no supernova flash in the pan: Her first marathon was in 1988, her first 140.6 race was in 1995, but she is now also running ultras and has finished such stage races as the six-day Trans Atlas Marathon. At last count Anne has completed north of forty 140.6-mile races. If the finish-line announcer Mike Reilly has called out the names of triathletes and the results of an event— the iconic, "Jane Smith, YOU ARE AN IRONMAN®!"—chances are Anne Thilges has raced that course. And she's probably finished top ten there. By way of example, after Tina called Anne with her Kona 2014 news, Anne qualified for Kona 2015 with a second-place finish at Ironman® Maryland.

What's behind such finishes deserves at least as much praise as the ability to peak on race day. For those unfamiliar with long triathlons, a top-ten finish at the 140.6-mile distance reflects an ungodly number of months of punishing alarm clocks and early morning swim workouts. Practice often begins with an intimidating list of figures and specifics on the pool whiteboard. The 140.6 faithful are met with thousands of meters of work broken up into separate sets (as if to fool you about their sum) with too-short rests between assignments. These practices are often done with a swim team of masters, one's triathlon club, or perhaps with your tri coach and her athletes. This means sharing your lane with a couple other swimmers, requiring you to swim the sets of yards or meters at the speed inked on the whiteboard. Subgroups of speed work, endurance work, and maybe open-water specific skills punctuate these thumpings. As if the burning in the lungs was not bad enough, the pool chemicals quickly secure ground in the sinus and then lay siege to every pore of the dermis. In the run-up to a 140.6 race, the skin's natural scent is replaced with an unmistakable chloramines fragrance. The scent—"Eau de Waterpark"—is not the worst part, truthfully. One's skin actually begins to hurt. Swimsuit fabric grows brittle quickly in the treated water. Goggles can't defend against the eye irritation during these amphibious training exercises. Swim gear will create an alarming amount of laundry, matched only by soaked-through bike kits and running clothes mistreated in ways not covered by the Hague or Geneva Conventions. Teeth are not spared: The jaw remains clenched from too many century rides on uncomfortably narrow road shoulders, and the teeth are gnashed from more frustrating flat tires than one lifetime needs. During the 140.6 training, as mileage increases, teeth are fuzzy most of the time. Saddle sores never get a chance to fully heal during a training cycle. It no longer makes sense to pay attention to one's hair in the run up to a 140.6 race. Swim double days, or a tempo workout at the track before work or school and riding at lunch or later that night, obliterate the chance for fancy civilian hair. For the podium people of 140.6 (and many of the mid-packers), most days are at least two-shower days. Triathlon training makes even bathing exhausting.

With Anne's bounty of Kona logistics and race experience, she was an invaluable resource to the first-timer in the District of

Columbia. No trip computer could calculate Tina's gratitude for the woman on the other end of the phone. Just as in their races together in Atlantic City and Florida, Anne was delighted to help Tina—in the way you can light another's candle from your taper's flame without any loss to your own.

Tina and Anne represent—fairly—the tendency toward overachievers in the sport. There is no shortage of finance and tech people like Anne and lawyers like Tina in the long-distance tri biosphere. Scientists, entrepreneurs, medical doctors, and professionals with fifty-hour work weeks do seem to fill the rosters. There may be a connection between advanced academic degrees and long-distance triathlons, but correlation and causation, tax brackets and masochism, the exceptionally bright and the blinder-wearing hyper-fixated types cannot be deduced or defined or reduced to stereotypes.[47]

What veteran triathletes seem to have in common is drive.

Tina had attended Yale University, graduating with magna cum laude honors and a degree in psychology. Yale President A. Bartlett Giamatti described her as "One of the cheeriest and most socially concerned undergraduates at Yale College. Beyond carrying a heavy load of courses—ones that varied in diversity

---

47 By way of explanation, just because training for an Ironman® may (for example) get you out of visiting your in-laws, this is probably not a direct reflection on how you feel about your mother-in-law. To be fair, or at least symmetric here, there are plenty of potential slights to go around. There is a popular 140.6 poster held on the side of the route that reads, "If this race were easy, it would be called your mom." Other legacy posters include: "If you're still married, you didn't train hard enough," "Pass the weak, hurdle the dead," "Not almost there," and the memorable sign held by an attractive woman with an amused smile: "I like your stamina. Call me." Banter, wisecracks, and double entendres perpetually help pass the grueling hours training for and completing a 140.6 event.

from computer science courses in artificial intelligence through psychology to Russian history and the Russian language—she has also found time to serve on a number of committees at Yale and to participate in many extracurricular events." Tina was accepted straight from New Haven to Stanford Law School. She has raced at the Head of the Charles Regatta (she rows port) and has belly laughed her way along Register's Annual Great Bicycle Ride Across Iowa (RAGBRAI). She grew up horseback riding and downhill skiing, but not in a silver-spoon-sort-of-way: She was an Army kid, born in Germany with addresses in Virginia, Colorado, Wyoming, California, Hawaii, and Michigan. After law school she clerked for a federal judge, G. Thomas Eisele of Arkansas, before entering private practice and then ultimately going to work as an assistant US attorney. As if a 2.4-mile swim before a 112-mile bike and a full 26.2-mile marathon is not difficult enough with her schedule, the eight-time Ironwoman Tina Ament is blind.

Tina was born with Leber's congenital amaurosis, a rare degenerative disease that causes acute vision loss. She and her sister, Dr. Suzanne Ament, a Russian history professor, have been blind since birth. As Suzanne reads and writes Russian fluently and is a sponsored dressage rider, Leber's congenital amaurosis is toward the bottom of the list of the noteworthy line items about the sisters Ament.

The reason Tina needed to win a lottery spot to race in Kona is that the two most common ways into the race were not possible for her at that point. A complication of blindness requires the cycling portion of the event to be done on a tandem bike, a bicycle-built-for-two. Depending on the course and the riders, a tandem bike could be an unfair advantage over solo age-group athletes, and therefore blind racers are in the para-athlete category, and thus cannot win an age group ticket to Kona. The other way racers earn a spot at Kona is to finish twelve full-distance Ironman®-branded triathlons, the first of which must be at least twelve years before applying for a Kona slot. (And this "Legacy Program" Kona qualifying is only available for those who have never participated in Kona before.) A shot at Kona is like chickenpox or viewing Halley's Comet; it most likely comes but once in a lifetime.

So, Tina, accepting the limitations of the situation, had applied for one of the five spots offered to para-athletes for the Kona Ironman® World Championship on October 11, 2014. The race that started it all.

To have an athlete like Anne as her guide ("She's phenomenal," Tina says) and her family on the course cheering ("For my parents and my sister to be there was really great," she said with deep affection), made for an occasion equal in indelibility for the fifty-two-year-old as it did for all who saw what she did that day.

The Kona championship includes a lot more than the race. Anne and Tina arrived a week early to experience the events leading up to the big event. There were daily swims to the coffee-bar boat located in the bay, where swimmers hold onto the boat with one hand and drink coffee drinks in the other, mid-swim. They also ran together in the famous Underpants Run, the hilarious 1- to 2-mile (1.6- to 3-kilometer) fundraiser run open to all, in which underwear of some ilk is the dress code. The runners and spectators plan outfits well in advance, to great effect.

Tina's presence, while always understated and poised, crackled with inspiration for the multitude of entrants pinning bibs that weekend. Stephen Black, the Global Operations Coordinator and Athlete Coordinator for Physically Challenged, Intellectual Disability and Handcycle Athletes of the Ironman® and Ironman® 70.3 World Championship events, said, "Meeting Tina at Kona was a highlight of my involvement in the sport and World Championship events. Unassuming, grateful for our assistance, but never wavering from the goal...finishing the Ironman® World Championship."

For the day of the race, Tina and Anne joined more than 2,200 athletes at the crowded start, surrounded by many of the world's best triathletes from sixty-eight countries. They endured the chop of that day's swim, with a bungee cord attached to their thighs as their method of communication. The conditions made for a gamey and slower swim than usual for them in 1 hour, 46 minutes, and 18 seconds. Luckily, Tina is a precisely straight swimmer, so in theory Anne only needs to tug on the bungee for the two turns of the 2.4-mile loop. For those not familiar with the chaos of a triathlon swim with more than two thousand people, especially in choppy water, the water is wildly altered by strenuous human action and is often described as the water of a washing machine. In addition to enduring the conditions, Anne is also in the business of sharp elbows and a willingness to play rough with any racer who tries to swim over her athlete.

When leading a case at trial, Ament has never had the luxury of referring to files or notes quickly by reading them: she must commit a case or an appeal to memory. In the same fashion, she left the Kailua Bay swim, climbing the stairs out of the water, stairs she had memorized over the days before. With Anne at her side, she hustled to the area where she picked up her gear bag, then entered the transition tent—both places she had also committed to memory. Inside the tent, with the help of a galaxy of female volunteers, Anne and Tina's swimskin suits were off quickly, and they were kitted out in bike apparel in five minutes and fifty-three seconds.[48] Helmet, glasses, chamois butter, sunscreen, check, check, check, check.

Next they ran to Tina's bike, the only bicycle built for two in the competition. With Anne as her captain, Tina could focus on her favorite thing: the joy she feels while riding a bicycle. She likes to joke that a tandem bicycle is not just a blockade to keep a guide dog from getting into the cat's litter box. A bicycle is untethered freedom, in every sense. Solo or tandem, cyclists, sighted and blind, understand.

The winds were dealing blows that day, the lava fields of the route hotter than usual. The duo's typical pace for the 112 miles is 6 hours; with headwinds and crosswinds hammering racers in both directions of the out-and-back course that day, the duo finished in 7:49:06. To T2, they hustled, warming up their legs for a new assignment, a marathon with a red leash attaching them together.

It takes vulnerability at least as deep as the Pacific Plate below the eight islands of Hawaii, to let yourself be at the mercy of a guide at an event like Kona. It was Julie Moss's vulnerability that made a *Wide World of Sports* segment filmed at these coordinates

---

48 The tent between the swim and the biking part of the race is called "Transition One," or "T1," by triathletes, while the transition between biking and the run is called "T2." For the visual, imagine a large tent for an outdoor wedding reception but with walls, cheap folding chairs or benches, and poor ventilation, creating a distinct olfactory experience. Athletes enter from one side, change, then exit out the other side for proper wet and sweaty traffic flow. T1 and T2 are afforded heavy canvas walls and a roof, as, inside these tents, athletes are all in a state of undress. There is usually a helpful place on which to place a towel and sit, but the frenetic energy, gear chaos, and amount of nudity inside the tents of serious 140.6 triathlons can be so overwhelming to first-timers that it bears a mention. Shorter triathlon races often do not feature these changing tents, since a typical tri-kit can be worn through all three not-too-long segments of the event.

thirty-two years earlier one of the most dramatic athletic moments ever captured for television viewers. Tina's brilliant mind, her drive, or her ability to fall down and get back up merit mention. When you're visually impaired, there is an unfair amount of bumping, falling, and tripping that you'll never hear Tina complain about.

But it's Tina's willingness to be vulnerable that most sets her apart. When someone performing an outdoor run, an open-water swim, and any bike ride ever is required to ask another human to please help, each moment of training outdoors feels like a gift. It is a gift Tina holds in both hands. When any chance to sport outside is a gift—not a chore—this reframing inundates the brain with feel-good neurotransmitters. The fresh air and sunlight of outdoor therapy have a compounding effect on the brain's pleasure and reward systems. Asking for help and receiving it from the vibrant athletes who captain Tina's bike or guide her runs or swims in training, floods her brain with the oxytocin rush of connection. In other words, five seconds of vulnerability—"Are you free for a run?"—creates a grande-extra-shot-no-foam-dopamine-serotonin-oxytocin decoction for Tina. Her joy, shining through a beatific smile, is then contagious with her benevolent training and racing partners. Workouts are associated with the best feelings. In a society fraught with issues of isolation and loneliness and feelings of unwellness, Tina's long-distance hobbies feel like the inverse of modern malaise or forlornness. Her vulnerability is instantly recognizable, like the distinct painted red roof of the ten-story turreted Hotel del Coronado. Like the tallest landmark on a clear day. Her vulnerability is no weakness. To orient oneself using the recognizable is the time-tested way of sailors and pilots, captains and commanders. The sighted would be wise to follow her example, as the ability to ask for help might be Tina's real superpower.

And one word about Anne Thilges and the iron people who guide: exhausting is their task. Their endurance begins with the abdomen and requires the intercostal muscles, diaphragm, tongue, lips, larynx, and all the laryngeal muscles. Guiding requires a staggering amount of ceaseless narration: describing movement directions at least once a minute, explaining the wild world around them to the athlete with the bib.

Usually in life, works, not words, are proof of love. In guiding a 140.6-mile course all day, it is both.

There are crowds to navigate, speed bumps to describe and road fissures to avoid, water bottles to acquire, and food to deliver. There are "I'm Sure This Seemed Like A Good Idea Six Months Ago" posters to read and relay comic relief. Porta-potties definitely need inspection before their athlete enters. There is no "M E" in "guide." Protecting an adult human, even if they aren't a federal prosecutor, is a heavy task. Stephen Black of Ironman® synthesized it clearly: "Anne Thilges epitomizes selflessness."

With immense respect for Sebastian Kienle of Germany and Mirinda Carfrae of Australia, who won the 2014 Kona race in 8:14 and 9:55, respectively, maybe the unheralded but most noteworthy moment of the 2014 event occurred when Anne and Tina racked her bike. With the possibility of a crash or catastrophic bike mechanical failure behind them, and with more than seven hours available to Tina to complete her run before the 17 hour race cutoff, a kind of vibration descended into the T2 tent.

It was the lesson of the Moss-McCartney finish. It's the refrain of every song in the 140.6 hymnal. It's the distinct opening notes borne of Coronado and arranged by the Collins family:

"You cannot lose if you don't quit."

Guided by Anne, after 140.6 miles, Tina Ament, number 152, age fifty-two, crossed the finish line of triathlon's biggest stage in 16 hours, 18 minutes, and 5 seconds, and became the first blind female finisher of Kona.

Just as in 1978 and 1982, yet more than ever, as in every test of the unforgiving hours, finishing was winning.

Professional photographer Shiggy Ichinomiya recorded the women of team 152 leaving the bike mount area after Transition One of Kona Ironman®, October 11, 2014. As their legs prepare to move as one for 112 miles, the photographer captured the way Tina is carefully listening as Anne is providing commentary for her racer. *(photo courtesy of Shiggy Ichinomiya)*

THE ATHLETES

Kristina "Tina" Ament ▪ Determined and brilliant in equal measure, triathletes-turned-ultra cyclists do not come more resilient than Tina. Those who have worked through the specific challenges of riding a tandem bike across any serious distance have a sense of Tina's patience with hard things. When asked about the grueling seven days of racing RAAM, the US District Attorney's unwavering voice declares, "It was the best week of my life." Never having asked a tandem captain to slow down, she is that adventurer comfortable at speeds of over 60 mph on descents. In 2023, Tina won the World 24-Hour Time Trial Championships on her tandem bike with captain Roberta Smith. Of note, her bikes are all named after Roman politicians.

Lynne Cox ▪ If you name a challenging swim, Lynne (inducted into the International Swimming Hall of Fame in 2000) has aced it: the first female to swim Cook Strait and the first person to swim the Strait of Magellan, the Bering Sea between Little Diomede in Alaska to Big Diomede (then a part of the Soviet Union), and the length of Lake Titicaca at 12,507 feet. Her swim CV cannot be topped for her pioneering and her number of swim ambassador pilgrimages. Dr. Oliver Sacks, a friend, said, "Lynne Cox writes about swimming the way Saint-Exupéry wrote about flying." Her books are a treasure to swimmers and non-swimmers alike.

Kelly Danielson ▪ If stuck on a deserted island with only one companion to bring along, Kelly is that person her friends, colleagues, and neighbors on Bainbridge Island, Washington, would choose. A doctor of occupational therapy, yoga instructor, triathlete, podium-tier swim-run racer (first place, California Swimrun, teamed with darling Rose Filer), Salish Sea skin swimmer, diver, trail runner, champion of female friendships, and mother of twins, Kelly has all the skill sets—and endurance stamina to match. In her example with Team *Sail Like A Girl* and beyond, Kelly reminds us to lead with the word "Yes!"

Kathleen Egan ▪ Photographed up against the northeastern face of Mount Rainier on our cover, Kathleen is like the terrain between the Winthrop and Emmons glaciers in the Sunrise area of the national park: exceptional and understated. Recent adventures include winning the Bigfoot 200 Endurance Run in 2022 and fearlessly running through the Sawatch Range of the Rockies to 13,150 feet and climbing 23,500 feet overall at High Lonesome 100 in 2024. With a gentle temperament and the curiosity of a real-deal trekker and world traveler, this epidemiology and infectious disease specialist shares a mantra heard often among the finest endurance athletes: "I will finish this thing because there's no way I'm starting this battle again."

Yuichiro Hidaka ▪ Where there are potato chips you will find Yuichiro. A disciple of the exotic potato chip flavor—Cuban Sandwich, Super Curry, Matcha and Sansho Pepper—the college athletic trainer and strength and conditioning specialist rides his bike long-distances and tackles terrible track interval workouts, all in the name of potato chips. At Wyoming's remote Bighorn Mountain Trail 100 in 2023, the 20,500 feet of ascent and 20,750-foot descent payoff may have included Mesquite-Smoked Bacon-flavored wavy cut chips. Photos seen after the 30-hour-and-20-minute finish depict Yuichiro nailing his signature celebratory jump at multiple locations in the Bighorn National Forest. Most ultrarunners cannot trust their legs with acrobatic jumping after even a few hours of trail running with Yuichiro's speed at such elevation.

Seana Hogan ▓ With the North American women's transcontinental record (9 days, 4 hours, 2 minutes), the fastest—male or female—Seattle to San Diego record (3 days, 16 hours, 5 minutes, breaking Michael Shermer's record), the fastest—male or female—San Francisco to Los Angeles record (19 hours, 11 minutes, again breaking Michael Shermer's record), the 24-hour track women's world record (445.78 miles) and the 12-hour track women's world record (244.16 miles), Seana is arguably the first and last word in endurance cycling of this era. "RAAM (the 3,000-mile Race Across America) is analogous to life," says Seana, because "you go through hard times." She takes a pause to make the point, and continues, "But *that* is where the magic happens."

Chris Jones ▓ At trail runs, road marathons and the big ultras, everyone knows Chris. Via his example, extroverts will be glad to learn that they can be *long*, long-distance athletes too. He is renowned for spreading conviviality, eager to celebrate running friendships and outstanding finishes by fellow participants.

On his UltraSignup page, Chris has more than 240 races completed—from the furnace depths of Badwater 135 in Death Valley, California, to the Bear 100 in Utah, to the tropical heat of Hurt100 in Hawaii. Due to his thirty-two years in the Army, for more than one "A" race on that list, Chris trained exclusively on a treadmill while deployed, due to safety concerns. His advice for specific unforgiving moments of ultraracing, said with a wry smile: always bring more baby wipes than you think you'll need.

Melissa Kegler ■ The channel, marathon, and ice swimmer self-identifies as one of the official seal whisperers of Puget Sound. Besides athletic ability and endurance strength, Melissa has the temperament and organization (she adores doing her taxes) to create and perfect an event like her 2022 Ice Mile distance record swim. In addition to her swims, the Triple Crown finisher is quick to crew, to coach, to mentor, or to serve on panels and boards for open-water and marathon swimming. A favorite non-guilty pleasure is collecting cute bikini separates and coordinating matching goggles, caps, and swim nails for swims where the air temps are often in the 30s°F (54s°C). Foolish would be the person who underestimates Melissa Kegler.

Rob Krar ■ Named "Trailblazer of the Year" by *Canadian Running Magazine* in 2014 and "Ultrarunner of the Year" by *Trail Runner Magazine* in 2015 and 2016, in addition to Western States victories in 2014 and 2015, Krar won Leadville 100 in 2015 and 2018. Considered one of the best ultrarunners of this era, in 2024 Krar showed his versatility with a smokin' fast 7:29:12 finish of the Leadville 100 mountain bike race. Krar offers running camps in the trail running eden of Flagstaff, Arizona, and his ultra beard game is as strong as ever. Rob is proof that nice guys do finish first.

Scott Lautman ▦ Crazy fast in the pool with pages of US Masters swim records, Scott has also dominated at distance in open water, too. He has crossed the Strait of Gibraltar, the Catalina Channel, the English Channel, the Strait of Magellan, and around Manhattan in the Manhattan Island Marathon Swim. Greater yet are Scott's contributions in noteworthy swim support, elite coaching, and the personal crew connections he has gifted swimmers here and around the world. Scott's broad shoulders and distinct V-shaped torso are necessary to contain his enormous, amicable athlete's heart.

Dave McGillivray ▦ With the life motto, "It's my game, my rules," Dave has run the Boston Double many times. He has never missed a Boston Marathon in fifty-two years. Each year on his birthday, Dave runs his age in miles—a tradition he began at the age of twelve. He was also the kind of kid who graduated valedictorian of both high school and college. He has run 168+ full marathons, finished nine 140.6-mile Kona races, and raised hundreds of thousands of dollars for charity through his inspirational athletic fundraising. He once ran from Medford, Oregon, to Medford, Massachusetts (3,452 miles), for the Jimmy Fund and the Dana-Farber Cancer Institute. His salt-of-the-earth energy is contagious and his can-do spirit remains unwavering.

Guila Muir ▦ A gifted swim coach and swim-event coordinator for Say YES! To Life Swims, Guila calls herself an "adult onset" swimmer, taking her very first swim lesson at age forty-six. For her sixtieth birthday in 2015, Guila completed the 11-mile

Portland Bridge Swim. Her "Swimmers Over 60" Facebook page has more than 6,800 members, from Finland to New Zealand. In August 2024, Guila helped organize a history-making 10.5-mile relay swim around Blake Island in Puget Sound—average water temperature 56°F (13°C)—with a team of five generations of female open-water swimmers. Guila's gold medal at the Winter Swimming Championships in Skellefteå, Sweden, in 2020 is a reminder about courage at every age. Guila's swim expertise reveals the long game axiom captured in the unattributed wisdom, "The best time to plant a tree was twenty years ago. The second best time is now."

Pete Penseyres A member of the Ultracycling Hall of Fame since 2003, Pete won RAAM in 1984 and 1986, and his tandem transcontinental record with Lon Haldeman in 1987 stood for eighteen years. In 1993 Pete was the US Masters Road Cycling Champion. Famous for his dedicated bike commuting to work, the mechanical engineer might be the most overqualified League of American Bicyclists Certified Instructor by a factor of ten. As likeable as he is humble and tough, Pete's world record of 3,107 miles in 1986 RAAM of 8 days, 9 hours, and 47 minutes is the solo male ride that people still talk about—three and a half decades later. A gentleman and known cycling royalty, in San Diego he is referred to as "the master—(pause)—the legend."

Van Phan To date, Van has completed twelve 200-mile runs, like Bigfoot 200 at Mount St. Helens, Washington, and Moab 240 in Utah. Van (rhymes with gone!) was the first Pacific Northwest runner to run one hundred 100+ mile races, male or female. For a Van adventure in

2024, there was this faux ad to describe a weekend with Van: "Adventurers wanted for hazardous journey. Low wages, blistering heat, long hours of complete darkness. Safe return doubtful. Limited honor and recognition in unlikely event of success." She is the conduit of, and inspiration for, innumerable runs, races, and trail habits by those who have borne witness to her distance. It is a short list, the number of female runners who have run more ultras than Van Phan. Though she may be small, Van is mighty in all the important ways.

John Stamstad ■ Poor conditions on big mountains over serious distances ultimately bring most people to failure, but those who have cycled, adventured, and trail run with John can attest to his untouchable endurance, stamina, and mindset: "The harder it is, the more exciting it is," John says. Driven by expeditions rather than competitions, he still finished first at Iditasport (130-or-so-miles) 1993 through 1996 and at Iditasport Extreme (the 350-mile version) from 1997 through 2000. He was the first winner of the Leadville 100 MTB in 1994 and pioneered the first unsupported 2,500-mile Great Divide MTB ride in 1999, before beginning to tackle ultras—like his 200-mile unsupported run of the John Muir Trail in 2005. John is as insightful as ever, with a citrus wit and distinguished intellectual mind. And he remains tougher than nails.

Gunhild Swanson ■ A runner since 1978, a marathoner since 1980 (with a personal record of 2:56), and an ultrarunner since Le Grizz Ultramarathon and Relay 50-miler in Montana in 1987, no one loves the trails more than Gunhild. Gifted with positivity and surrounded by a pack of tremendous trail-running and hiking girlfriends, to date Gunhild has run more than sixty-seven ultras—from Rocky Racoon 100 miler to Lean Horse Ultra 100 miler to her 171-mile run at A Race for the Ages in 2023 at age seventy-nine, to her Hamster Endurance Run stellar finish of 93.6 miles in August 2024 at the age of eighty. In perhaps the most humble ultrarunning moment ever, Gunhild worried that the post-race hype of her June 2015 finish at Western States 100 might somehow overshadow the elite finishes of the professionals Rob Krar and the sublime Magdalena Boulet (19:05). Of course, the glow of Gunhild's red lantern was just a different and more nuanced wavelength of light. The five finest seconds still burn bright.

Glenn Tachiyama ■ Our esteemed cover photographer and talented trail and road runner (with a 2:38 marathon personal record), Glenn started toting a camera to the trails around Seattle in the 1990s. He would go on to become the premier ultrarunning photographer in the Pacific Northwest and beyond, hiking deep into the backcountry to photograph athletes in the most spectacular unblemished places. With quiet principle and polish, Glenn has always treated the last runner as the first, honoring the work of the mid-packers and the back-of-the-packers with distinction and respect. Glenn was known for staying in the remote places over hours—the unforgiving sort—in every kind of untamed weather, until each runner was captured by his cameras for a cherished 1/1000th of a second. Over fifteen years, Glenn donated his photos to create trail-running calendars for the Washington Trail Association. His work raised more than $250,000 for the Association.

Team Hugh Jass ▇ The quality of their riding far surpassed the story of their one pair of team shorts. There were never any better: Mike "Crapentar" Carpenter, Matt Franco, Thomas Jenkins, Jamie Keehner, Christopher Lenth, Joel Maynard, Pat Miller, Tim Richardson, Don Schepler, Erik Stenburg and Jeremy Wimpey. Grass-roots cycling reached maximum exultation in the hands of Team Hugh Jass. Did they win? Hearts and minds. All of them.

Team *Sail Like A Girl* ▇ The unfragile and full-of-fun all-female team who took the top spot at Race to Alaska in 2018. The team, in alphabetical order: Morgana Buell (with more than twenty five years of sailing experience), Kelly Danielson, Allison Ekberg Dvaladze, Aimee Fulwell, Jeanne Goussev (more than twenty years experience), Kate Hearsey (twenty years experience), Haley Lhamon (forty-one years of experience), and Anna Stevens (more than six years of sailing experience). These eight women raced the first tough leg of the adventure, from Port Townsend, Washington, to Victoria, British Columbia, together—with seven sailors continuing the rest of the distance to Ketchikan, Alaska. During the pandemic, *Sail Like A Girl* became a 501(c)4 nonprofit to bring more females along in the sport of sailing and "to inspire women to push limits, challenge assumptions and, through teamwork, make the impossible, possible." The work continues.

Team Sea to See ▇ With the tagline "9 Days, 3,000 miles, 1 vision," this squad entered the four-person team category of Race Across America in 2018. Tina Ament, Daniel Berlin, Jack Chen, and Kyle Coon alternated pedaling in the stoker position. They were assisted by four sighted captains up front on their tandem bikes—Caroline Gaynor, Pamela Ferguson, Chris Howard, and Charles Scott, as well as fourteen dedicated crew members. Their stellar time for the 3,069.8-mile ride was seven days, 15 hours, and 3 minutes. Team Sea to See is the first four-bike team of tandems with four blind stokers to complete RAAM.

Anne Thilges ■ The epitome of an endurance athlete, Anne has competed at the elite level, with a remarkable 40+ 140.6-mile triathlons and too many ultra-distance events to list. She lives by the saying "Finish what you start." In guiding long-distance runners and triathletes, she has helped her teammates achieve their goals and, along the way, inspired thousands of racers and spectators by her selfless example. With an unfailing smile, she explains that each accomplishment is a stepping stone to the next higher, bigger, better goal.

Sarah Thomas ■ The most exhilarating ultra-distance swimmer of the modern age, Sarah was the first person—male or female—to swim a current-neutral 100 miles. That record, set in Lake Champlain in 2017, was 104.3 miles in 67 hours and 16 minutes. From joining the swim team at the University of Connecticut as a walk-on in the autumn of 2004, to her induction into the International Marathon Swimming Hall of Fame in 2018, Sarah has quietly redefined long-distance in water with her imagination and graceful endurance.

Román Urbina ■ The first Latin American inducted into the Mountain Bike Hall of Fame, Román shone as a world class athlete before he deliberately turned the endurance spotlight on his country, the outdoor adventuring paradise which is Costa Rica. In 1982, Román intrepidly swam 25 pioneering kilometers (15.5 miles) across the Gulf of Nicoya (Golfo de Nicoya) in Costa Rica in a mere 4 hours, 24 minutes. He swims, surfs, skateboards, dirt bikes, triathlon races, and race directs in the same way he rides a mountain bike: with a confident smile and ever-thoughtful and clear-throated, "Pura vida" at the ready. From Román, the expression pura vida encapsulates the composure and the character of endurance excellence that has been his athletic lodestar for more than four decades: "Pure life," "Feeling full of life," or the contagious, "This is living!"

Gordon Wadsworth The Single Speed World Champion and eight-time US National Champion in cross-country and marathon mountain biking, "Quadsworth" is the humble hero that cycling needs. Profoundly gifted on two wheels going long, and affable beyond words, Gordon wins most for love of the sport. On every ride, at the biggest events, no one is ever having more fun than Gordon Wadsworth.

RECOMMENDED READING

ON RUNNING

Hal Koerner's Field Guide to Ultrarunning: Training for an Ultramarathon, from 50K to 100 Miles and Beyond, by Hal Koerner

Eat & Run: My Unlikely Journey to Ultramarathon Greatness, by Scott Jurek

What I Talk About When I Talk About Running: A Memoir, by Haruki Murakami

And Then the Vulture Eats You: True Tales About Ultramarathons and Those Who Run Them (John L. Parker Jr., editor)

ON CYCLING

The Rules: The Way of the Cycling Disciple (Frank Strack, editor)

The Hardmen: Legends and Lessons from the Cycling Gods (Frank Strack, editor)

The Rider, by Tim Krabbé

Fat Tire Flyer: Repack and the Birth of Mountain Biking, by Charlie Kelly

ON SWIMMING

Swimming to Antarctica: Tales of a Long-Distance Swimmer, by Lynne Cox

Winter Swimming: The Nordic Way Towards a Healthier and Happier Life, by Dr. Susanna Søberg

Salt on Your Tongue: Women and the Sea, by Charlotte Runcie

At the Pond: Swimming at the Hampstead Ladies' Pond, by Margaret Drabble, Esther Freud, and Sophie Mackintosh

Waterlog: A Swimmer's Journey Through Britain, by Roger Deakin

ON SPORT

Better Faster Farther: How Running Changed Everything We Know About Women, by Maggie Mertens

Crawl of Fame: Julie Moss and the Fifteen Feet that Created an Ironman Triathlon Legend, by Julie Moss

Grit, Guts & Determination: My Tale of a Cowboy, a Hundred Miles of Dirt and a Town so Magical They Had to Save It, by Cole Chlouber

ON THE NATURAL WORLD

Coming into the Country, by John McPhee

Landmarks, by Robert Macfarlane

The Language of Trees: A Rewilding of Literature and Landscape, by Katie Holten

My First Summer in the Sierra, by John Muir

Travels in Alaska, by John Muir

Into the Thaw, by Jon Waterman

WITHIN THE ATHLETE

Awe: The New Science of Everyday Wonder and How It Can Transform Your Life, by Dacher Keltner

The Power of Awe: Overcome Burnout & Anxiety, Ease Chronic Pain, Find Clarity & Purpose—in Less than 1 Minute per Day, by Jake Eagle and Michael Amster

Deep Survival: Who Lives, Who Dies, and Why, by Laurence Gonzalez

NOTES

CHAPTER ONE

Andy Jones-Wilkins, "Unforgettable Moments in Ultrarunning: Gunhild Swanson and the 2015 Western States 100," For the Call of the Beyond. https://www.irunfar.com/unforgettable-moments -in-ultrarunning-gunhild-swanson-and-the-2015-western -states-100.

Ultrarunning statistics: "The State of Ultrarunning 2020" study, by RunRepeat.com and the International Association of Ultrarunners, posted March 26, 2024, by Paul Ronto. https://runrepeat.com/state-of-ultra-running.

Hubert Howe Bancroft, *The History of California*, Vol. VI 1848–1859, San Francisco: The History Company, 1888, page 62.

UTMB: Europe's 106-mile "Superbowl" of trail running: https://montblanc.utmb.world/races/utmb.

Western States Endurance Run: https://www.wser.org

The Tevis Cup: https://teviscup.org.

Javelina Jundred Run, Swanson's qualifying race: https://aravaiparunning.com/network/javelinajundred.

John Muir's address at the Meeting of the Sierra Club held on November 23, 1895: https://vault.sierraclub.org/john_muir _exhibit/writings/nat_parks_forests_1896.aspx.

State of California, Department of Parks and Recreation, "Building, Structure and Object Record": https://demo2.parks.ca.gov /pages/1067/files/mountain%20quarries%20railroad%20 bridge%20chl%20draft.pdf.

Mountain Quarries Bridge National Register of Historic Places Registration Form, https://npgallery.nps.gov/NRHP/GetAsset /NRHP/04000014_text.

Interview with Ina Robinson in Gold Country Media. Michael Kirby, "Ina Robinson lived Auburn history but stays grounded in today," September 3, 2009. https://goldcountrymedia.com/news/6840 /ina-robinson-lived-auburn-history-but-stays-grounded-in -today.

"Wendell Robie: The Man Who Started It All" by Gus Thomson. Gold Country Media, August 3, 2006. https://goldcountrymedia.com /news/104321/wendell-robie-the-man-who-started-it-all.

Ina Robbins Robinson's obituary, published by the *Auburn Journal* on May 20, 2018: https://www.legacy.com/us/obituaries/auburn journal/name/ina-robinson-obituary?id=9660795.

Mountain Quarries "No Hands" Bridge National Register of Historic Places registration form: https://npgallery.nps.gov/NRHP/Get Asset/NRHP/04000014_text.

Bob Dylan, "The Times They Are a Changin'," Columbia Records, 1964.

Vimeo video of the last .3 miles of Gunhild's finish: https://vimeo .com/132290019.

YouTube video of last 30 yards: https://youtu.be/QqKinAETu8E.

CHAPTER TWO

James Boswell. *The Journal of a Tour to the Hebrides with Samuel Johnson* (5th edition). London:/kilometer C. Baldwin, printer], 1807, page 124.

Robert Burton. *The Anatomy of Melancholy*. New York: A.C. Armstrong and Son, 1885. Part 1, Section 1, Subsection V, page 191.

Race to Alaska: *r2ak.com*

Richards, George Henry. *The Private Journal of Captain G.H. Richards: The Vancouver Island Survey (1860–1861)*, edited by Linda Dorricott and Deidre Cullon. Vancouver, BC: Ronsdale Press, 2012.

CHAPTER THREE

World record coffee bean price (as of 2018): https://www.news.co.cr /costa-rican-coffee-breaks-record-in-auction-of-high-quality -bean/74391/#:~:text=%E2%80%9CWith%20a%20lot%20 of%20529.11,2017%20by%20Brazil%20at%20%24130.20.

Mountain Bike Action, "La Ruta de Los Conquistadores is the World's Toughest Race," 2008. https://mbaction.com/la-ruta-de-los -conquistadores-is-the-worlds-toughest-race.

New York Times, December 8, 2016: "Conquering River, Jungle and the World's Toughest Bike Race." https://www.nytimes.com /2016/12/08/sports/la-ruta-de-los-conquistadores-costa-rica -cycling.html.

Mountain Biking Hall of Fame recognition of Román Urbina: https:// mmbhof.org/roman-urbina.

The story of the cyclist who got lost in La Ruta: https://ticotimes.net /2015/11/24/colorado-cyclist-ruta-de-los-conquistadores-costa -rica.

A video about La Ruta: https://youtu.be/4SGxMIIZUjI?si=Jk _U9DDsSW6OlLPX.

On beer drinking in bike races: https://www.academia.edu/7065151 /Beer_breaks_during_the_Tour_de_France._Some_observations _on_beer_and_cycling_in_the_early_1900s.

For a brief history of Costa Rica, see *CR Handbook* by Christopher Baker: http://philip.greenspun.com/cr/moon/history.

CHAPTER FOUR

Quote from Michael Read, MBE: "The Knack: How to Swim the Channel," interview of Read by Fiona McClymont, *The Independent*, February 6, 1999.

Earl Gustkey, "Prep Soph Eyes English Channel," *Los Angeles Times*, July 13, 1972, page 24.

Earl Gustkey, "US Girl In English Channel Swim," *Corpus Christi Times*, July 20, 1972, page 46.

Lynne Cox, *Swimming to Antarctica: Tales of a Long-Distance Swimmer*. New York: Harcourt Books, 2004.

"Men's Underground Quarters," The Fan Bay Shelter: Imperial War Museum, London: https://www.iwm.org.uk/collections/item /object/11414.

"Fan Bay Deep Shelter," Kent Archaeology Society, October 6, 2014: https://kenthistoricdefences.wordpress.com/2014/10/06/fan -bay-deep-shelter.

Antoine Saint-Exupéry, *The Little Prince*, translated by Irene Testot-Ferry. Ware, UK: Wordsworth Editions, 2018.

"American Girl Sets Out for Channel Bid," *Huddersfield Daily Examiner*, West Yorkshire, July 20, 1972, page 13.

"Lynne Smashes the Channel Time," *The Daily Mirror*, London, July 21, 1972, page 2.

"Lynne Beats Them All," *Evening Post*, Bristol, July 21, 1972, page 28.

"Lynne's Channel record," *Western Daily Press*, July 21, 1972, page 1.

Estelle Cox's obituary: *The Orange County Register*, following her death on June 26, 2012, published on July 8, 2012.

CHAPTER FIVE

Madness, "It Must Be Love." Lyrics by Labi Siffre. Recorded in 1981.

Boston Athletic Association, "Past Results, Champions and the History of the Greatest Race on Earth!" at https://www.baa.org /races/boston-marathon/results.

Adharanand Finn, *The Way of the Runner: A Journey Into the Fabled World of Japanese Running.* New York: Pegasus Books, 2016.

Journal of Trauma and Acute Care Surgery, "Boston Marathon Bombings: an After-Action Review," September 2014, pages 501–503.

Journal of Trauma and Acute Care Surgery, "Tourniquet Use at the Boston Marathon Bombing," March 2015, pages 594–599.

Haruki Murakami, *Things I Talk About When I Talk About Running* (translated from the Japanese by Philip Gabriel). New York: Knopf, 2008, page 10.

The Metropolitan Museum, "The Ancient Olympics and Other Olympic Games," by Alexis Belis. https://www.metmuseum.org /perspectives/articles/2021/7/ancient-greek-olympic-games, July 23, 2021.

CHAPTER SIX

World Ultra Cycling Association, "A Pain in the Neck," by Walter Libby, LMT, and Sue Morris, LMT, about Shermer's Neck: https:// archive.ph/20130412024227; http://www.ultracycling.com/old /training/neck_pain.html.

Road Bike Action Magazine, "Michael Shermer: The Man of Many Miles," by Zap. https://roadbikeaction.com/michael-shermer-the -man-of-many-miles.

Lakartidningen, "Shermer's Neck: Rare Injury in Long-Distance Cycle Races" (original in Swedish), by Bo Berglund and Lukas Berglund. 2015. https://pubmed.ncbi.nlm.nih.gov/26671432.

"Everything You Always Wanted to Know About How to Do RAAM," by UltraMarathon Cycling Association, edited by Michael Shermer. https://www.raceacrossamerica.org/resources/historic/EverythingByShermer.pdf.

Rocky Mountain Elk Foundation, "Highway 160 Wildlife Crossing—Restoring Elk Country": https://www.rockymountainelk foundation.org/elk-network/highway-160-wildlife-crossing-colorado.

John Frank Dawson, *Place Names in Colorado: Why 700 Communities Were So Named, 150 of Spanish or Indian Origin.* Denver, CO: Golden Bell Press, 1976, page 51.

RAAM rules book: https://www.raamrace.org/_files/ugd/49fb96_7e5bf578c3e54c8fbdde99aad67fb66e.pdf.

RAAM route book: https://raceacrossamerica.org/userfiles/file/2020/RAAM2020/RAAM2020%20Directions%20(preliminary).pdf.

Kansas farming: "Kansas Farm Facts," 2000 US Department of Agriculture. From the Kansas Statistical Abstract, September 2022, page 34. https://ksdata.ku.edu/ksdata/ksah/KSA57.pdf.

The end of the Kansas Bison Herd. Bison History Timeline: https://allaboutbison.com/bison-in-history/bison-timeline.

"England's Long Ride—To Ride to San Francisco and Back Within Four Months," *The New York Times*, June 5, 1896, page 6.

England arrives in San Francisco: "San Francisco at Last," *Brooklyn Daily Eagle Press*, September 8, 1896, page 10.

"Tourist England Arrives—Across the Continent in Forty Days," *San Francisco Chronicle*, September 3, 1896, page 13.

Gary Hoover, "The American Bicycle Industry: A Short History." American History Business Center, August 21, 2021. https://americanbusinesshistory.org/the-american-bicycle-industry-a-short-history.

Bicycling magazines from the nineteenth century: John L. Weiss, "American and Canadian 19th Century Cycling Periodicals."

https://www.crazyguyonabike.com/doc/page/?o=3d2&page
_id=613073&v=1zp&src=page_prev.

"Champion of Her Sex," an interview with Susan B. Anthony, by
Nellie Bly, *The New York World*, February 2, 1896, page 10.

Grit from childhood: Bruce J. Ellis, JeanMarie Bianchi, and William
E. Frankenhuis, "Beyond Risk and Protective Factors: An
Adaptation-Based Approach to Resilience." *Perspectives on
Psychological Science*, Vol. 12, Issue 4, July 2017: https://journals
.sagepub.com/doi/full/10.1177/1745691617693054?trk=article-ssr
-frontend-pulse_little-text-block.

Angela Duckworth, *Grit: The Power of Passion and Perseverance*. New
York: Scribner, 2016.

Kinky Friedman's quote about happy childhoods: Joe Nick Patoski,
"Kinky Friedman Introduces Gold Star Kids to the Land That
Shaped Him," *Texas Highways*, May 2022. https://texashighways
.com/culture/people/kinky-friedman-introduces-gold-star-kids
-to-the-land-that-shaped-him.

100th Meridian and more arid soil eastward: Kevin Krajick, "The
100th Meridian, Where the Great Plains Begin, May Be Shifting,"
State of the Planet, Columbia Climate School, April 11, 2018.
https://news.climate.columbia.edu/2018/04/11/the-100th
-meridian-where-the-great-plains-used-to-begin-now-moving
-east.

S. L. Winkler and G. A. Bryant, "Play Vocalization and Human
Laughter: A Comparative Review," *Bioacoustics*, 30 (5), 499–526.
https://www.tandfonline.com/doi/full/10.1080/09524622.2021
.1905065.

"Take Me Home, Country Roads," sung by John Denver; written by
Bill Danoff, Taffy Nivert, and John Denver. Released by RCA on
April 12, 1971.

RAAM information: www.raceacrossamerica.org.

CHAPTER SEVEN

Jean-Jacques Rousseau, *Julie, or the New Heloise*, Letter XLVI. Hanover, New Hampshire: Dartmouth College Press, 1997.

Moose bones: *Foragers of the Terminal Pleistocene in North America,* edited by Renne B. Walker and Boyce N. Driskell, University of Nebraska Press, 2007.

14,000-year-old moose antlers: Found by Pam Groves, of University of Alaska Fairbanks: Ned Rozell, "Ancient Moose Antlers Hint of Early Arrival," Geophysical Institute, December 1, 2022, University of Alaska Fairbanks. https://www.gi.alaska.edu/alaska -science-forum/ancient-moose-antlers-hint-early-arrival.

Dena (Athabascan) games: https://www.weio.org/about-3.

Native Youth Olympic Games (NYO): https://nyogames.com /about-nyo.

World Eskimo-Indian Olympics (WEIO): https://www.weio.org /games.

Fairbanks Midnight Sun Baseball Game: https://alaskasportshall.org /inductee/midnight-sun-baseball-game.

John Muir on Alaska: John Muir, *Letters from Alaska*. Madison, WI: University of Wisconsin Press, 1993, page 87. Originally printed in the *San Francisco Daily Evening Bulletin*, October 16, 1880, page 4.

The 1925 serum run that saved Nome: "The 1925 Serum Run to Nome," http://alaskaweb.org/disease/1925serumrun.htm.

Balto's statue, in bronze—East Drive at 67th Street, Central Park, New York, cared for by the Central Park Conservancy, and deemed by the organization "arguably the most popular statue in the Park." https://www.centralparknyc.org/articles/balto.

Statue unveiling: *The New York Times*, "His Effigy Unveiled, Balto Is Unmoved." December 16, 1925, page 20.

Jack London, *The Call of the Wild*. New York: Grosset & Dunlap, 1903, page 16.

Science magazine, "Earliest Evidence for Dog Breeding Found on Remote Siberian Island—Inhabitants of Zhukov appear to have bred sled dogs as early as 9,000 years ago," May 26, 2017.

David Reamer, "Togo Was the Real Hero Dog of the Serum Run; It's About Time He Got His Due," *Anchorage Daily News*, March 1, 2020.

Klunking or clunking: "Evening Magazine," KPIX San Francisco, CBS, segment by Steve Fox, reporter. Piece courtesy of Paul Colardo, Evening Magazine cameraman and producer, in the William French Archive. Date: 1979.

Calvin and Hobbes, by Bill Watterson—"Zip zop zip zop...Snow pants" —November 16, 1986, the comic appears in *Something Under the Bed is Drooling* (1988), *The Essential Calvin and Hobbes* (1988), and *The Complete Calvin and Hobbes* (2005).

Quote by Dan Bull: by John Clark, "Forney, Reifenstuhl Favored in Iditabike," *VeloNews*, February 10, 1992, page 15.

"Glaciers and Climate of the Upper Susitna Basin, Alaska," A. Bliss., P. Hock et al. *Earth System Science Data*, February 18, 2020. https://essd.copernicus.org/articles/12/403/2020/#Ch1.F1.

The 1964 Wilderness Act: https://wilderness.net/learn-about -wilderness/key-laws/wilderness-act/default.php.

Al Siebert, PhD, *The Resiliency Advantage*. San Francisco: Berrett-Koehler Publishers, 2005.

"The Vanishing World of Trapper Joe Delia," *Time*, July 27, 1970.

Alicia Agos, "Iditasport Athletes Hit the Frozen Trail to Skewenta," *Anchorage Daily News*, February 16, 1992, page E 4.

Dan Bull on the hardest race: "13 Test Iditarod—Without Dogs," *Argus-Leader*, Sioux Falls, South Dakota, March 19, 2000, page 39.

Abraham Maslow, *Religions, Values and Peak-Experiences*. Victoria, BC: Rare Treasures, 1964.

On the changing conditions of Alaska, roughly between the time of the first Iditabike and today, from the perspective of a former park ranger: *Into the Thaw*, by Jon Waterman, Patagonia Works, 2024.

CHAPTER EIGHT

On awe: Ryota Takano and Michio Nomura, "Neural Representations of Awe: Distinguishing Common and Distinct Neural Mechanisms," *Emotion*, June 2022; 22(4): 669–677. doi: 10.1037/emo0000771. Epub 2020 Jun 4. PMID: 32496077. https://pubmed.ncbi.nlm.nih.gov/32496077.

Awe changing our body perceptions: Michiel van Elk, Annika Karinen, Eva Specker et al. "'Standing in Awe': The Effects of Awe on Body Perception and the Relation with Absorption,"*Collabra*, March 23, 2016: https://online.ucpress.edu/collabra/article/2/1/4/112683/Standing-in-Awe-The-Effects-of-Awe-on-Body.

Jake Eagle and Michael Amster, *The Power of Awe*. New York: Hachette Book Group, 2023.

Dacher Keltner, *Awe, The New Science of Everyday Wonder and How It Can Transform Your Life*. New York: Penguin Press, 2022.

"The Extremely Cold Water Perception Scale" created by Jim Barber and Bryan Boggs for World Open Water Swimming Association: https://www.openwaterswimming.com/the-extremely-cold-water-perception-scale.

Steven Munatones, reporting on the "Cold Water Perception Scale for Open Water Swimming" for World Open Water Swimming Association: https://www.openwaterswimming.com/cold-water-perception-scale-for-open.

Guinness World Book of Records, "Largest Ice Swimming Competition": https://www.guinnessworldrecords.com/world-records/736089-largest-ice-swimming-competition.

On hypothermia: John A. Downing, "Hypothermia: Understanding and Prevention," Minnesota Sea Grant: https://seagrant.umn.edu/programs/recreation-and-water-safety-program/hypothermia.

International Ice Swimming Association: https://internationalice swimming.com.

International Winter Swimming Association: https://iwsa.world

Al Siebert, PhD, *The Resiliency Advantage.* San Francisco: Berrett-Koehler Publishers, Inc. 2005.

Dr. Susanna Søberg, *Winter Swimming: The Nordic Way Towards a Happier and Healthier Life*, London: MacLehose Press, 2022. First published in Copenhagen, Denmark in 2019 as *Hop i havet - Vinterbadning gør dig sund og glad*. Translated into English by Elizabeth DeNoma, 2022.

CHAPTER NINE

On the Grand Stam of Ultrarunning and the Last Great Race stats: http://www.run100s.com/slammers.htm.

Marge Hickman and Steve Siguaw, *Leadville Trail 100—History of the Leadville Trail 100 Mile Running Race.* Independently published, 2019.

Cole Choulber, *Grits, Guts, and Determination—My Tale of a Cowboy, a Hundred Miles of Dirt and a Town so Magical They Had to Save It*, Independently published, June 2024.

Christopher McDougall, *Born to Run.* New York: Vintage Books, 2009.

1879 Leadville City Directory, Denver: Daily Times Steam Printing House and Book Manufactory, 1879. Available through Lake County Library System at https://lakecountypubliclibrary.org/localhistory/citydirectories.

Courtney Dauwalter on tricks of the minds or hallucinations on the trails, interview on YouTube: "Courtney Dauwalter Ultra Runner | Talks First Hallucinations in Ultra Race": https://youtu.be/imivD -wnmDs.

Courtney Dauwalter interview, *Out and Back* podcast, November 12, 2020. Interviewed by Andrew "Shanty" Baldwin and Abby Levene: https://podcasts.apple.com/us/podcast/out-and-back/id1511167286?i=1000498300503.

John Denver, "Rocky Mountain High," released in 1972, RCA Victor.

"The new world atlas of artificial night sky brightness," *Science Advances*, by Fabio Falchi, et al., June 10, 2016. https://www.science.org/doi/10.1126/sciadv.1600377.

Information about night sky health for ecosystems, human health, and a planet temperatures: DarkSky International https://darksky.org

Ultrarunning races figures, as gathered by *Ultra Running Magazine*: https://ultrarunning.com/calendar/stats/ultrarunning-finishes.

CHAPTER TEN

John Steinbeck, *The Grapes of Wrath*, Penguin Books, 2001.

On Philippe Petit: https://www.nytimes.com/1974/08/08/archives/stuntman-eluding-guards-walks-a-tightrope-between-trade-center.html.

ABC's "*Wide World of Sports*," 1982 Hawaiian Ironman World Championship.

Triathlete magazine, "Julie Moss Takes Us Inside Her Most Intimate Kona Moments," https://www.triathlete.com/culture/julie-moss-takes-us-inside-her-most-intimate-kona-moments.

YogiTriathlete podcast, November 2018, podcast no. 130 hosted by Jess and BJ Gumkowski: https://podcasts.apple.com/us/podcast/yogitriathlete-podcast/id1112164042?i=1000664151301.

Julie Moss, *Crawl of Fame: Julie Moss and the Fifteen Feet that Created an Ironman Triathlon Legend*. New York: Pegasus Books, 2018.

The Ramones, "Blitzkrieg Bop," released in 1976. It begins, "Hey ho, let's go!" repeated four times.

Interview with Judy and John Collins: Ramona, "The Ironman Story: An Interview with Judy and John Collins," Always Happy

Travels, April 5, 2014: https://alwayshappytravels.wordpress.com/2014/04/05/the-ironman-story-an-interview-with-judy-and-john-collins/https://alwayshappytravels.wordpress.com/2014/04/05/the-ironman-story-an-interview-with-judy-and-john-collins.

Capi Lynn, "Collins Family, Ironman's 'first family' to participate in Salem triathlon event," *Salem Statesman Journal*, July 24, 2021: https://www.statesmanjournal.com/story/news/2021/07/24/oregon-salem-ironman-first-family-john-judy-collins-founders-participate-triathlon/8060758002.

Timothy Carlson, "Longest Running Triathlons," Slowtwitch, April 28, 2016. https://www.slowtwitch.com/Features/Longest_Running_Triathlons__5740.html.

On Coronado and the Navy and Marines: A Brief History Of The Marine Corps Base and Recruit Depot San Diego, California 1914–1962, Marine Corps Historical Reference Series: https://www.usmcu.edu/Portals/218/A%20Brief%20History%20Of%20The%20Marine%20Corps%20Base%20And%20Recruit%20Depot%20San%20Diego%2C%20California%201914%20-%201962.pdf.

Elretta Sudsbury, *Jackrabbits To Jets: The History of North Island*. San Diego: Neyenesch Printers, 1967.

The Around Coronado Swims, verified and cataloged by Marathon Swimmers Federation (Marathonswimmers.org) https://longswims.com/events/around-coronado-island.

Coronado two-way swims: in 2021 by Abigail Fairman and Abigail Bergman in 2022: https://longswims.com/events/around-coronado-island/#two-way.

Barry McDermott, "Ironman—To earn that title, Tom Warren victoriously swam 2.4 miles through rough seas, bicycled 112 miles, and all/kilometer sic] ran a marathon, all in a single day of agony," *Sports Illustrated*, May 14, 1979: https://vault.si.com/vault/1979/05/14/ironman-to-earn-that-title-tom-warren

-victoriously-swam-24-miles-through-rough-seas-bicycled-112
-miles-and-ran-a-marathon-all-in-a-single-day-of-agony.

USA Triathlon Hall of Fame: https://www.usatriathlon.org/multisport
/hall-of-fame.

Scott Tinley, "A Silk Purse: How a Long, Tall, Blonde Quite
Accidentally Invented Modern Endurance Sports" (interview with
Valerie Silk), on Tri-History.com, September 1, 2015: https://tri
-history.com/features/silk-purse-how-long-tall-blonde-quite
-accidentally-invented-modern-endurance-sports.

On screams: Sascha Frühholz, Joris Dietziker, Matthias Staib,
and Wiebke Trost, "Neurocognitive Processing Efficiency for
Discriminating Human Non-Alarm Rather Than Alarm Scream
Calls," *PLOS Biology*, April 13, 2021. https://journals.plos.org
/plosbiology/article?id=10.1371/journal.pbio.3000751.

James V. Healion, "Blind Student Earns 'Spunk,'" *The Latrobe Bulletin*,
June 23, 1984.

Karin Hägglund, Göran Kennta, Richard Thelwell, and Christopher
R. D. Wagstaff, "Is There an Upside of Vulnerability in Sport? A
Mindfulness Approach Applied in the Pursuit of Psychological
Strength," *Journal of Sport Psychology in Action*, Vol. 10, Issue 4.
February 1, 2019.

Raymond Britt, "Ironman Kona 2014 Results Analysis: Overall, by
Splits, by Age Group, by Country, and More," RunTriMedia:
https://www.runtri.com/2014/10/ironman-kona-2014-results
-analysis.html?m=.1.

ACKNOWLEDGMENTS
& SLOW TWITCH MISCELLANEA

THANKS TO BACON. AND THERMOSES OF ENGLISH BREAKFAST tea. And ginger molasses cookies. And good coffee at zero-dark-thirty.

But mostly bacon. Ultrarunners travel silly distances to reach aid stations with an entire bacon theme. Cold-water swimmers swim toward it: bits of it folded into dough with grated cheddar for savory scones to share after the after-drop. I have watched cyclists climb to 12,537 feet between Wheeler Peak and Mt. Gawdammit for strips of it. Large parts of this book can be explained by bacon.

To the aid-station bacon pilgrims, the swim-feed pioneers, and the long-distance mavens in these chapters who generously shared their stories—my profound thanks. Your kindness to me, to the last athlete, exceeded your seismic talent, work ethic, and stamina. Thank you, Tina Ament, Lynne Cox, Kelly Danielson, Kathleen Egan, Yuichiro Hidaka, Seana Hogan, Chris Jones, Melissa Kegler, Rob Krar, Scott Lautman, Dave McGillivray, Guila Muir, Pete Penseyres, Van Phan, John Stamstad, Gunhild Swanson,

Glenn Tachiyama, Anne Thilges, Sarah Thomas, Román Urbina, and Gordon Wadsworth.

Thank you for the example in your healthy respect for the outdoors, curiosity, beginner's mindset, responsible planning, adaptability, teammate collaboration, focus for puzzle solving, conservationism and stewardship for the land and water, wonder and awe seeking, youthful enthusiasm, tenacity after middle age, and good humor in every stage of life.

And with so much appreciation, the volume of gratefulness could fill the packs of a herd of llamas:

To the experts who offered their immeasurable help—Tim Twietmeyer, Chris and Turlan Morlan, Andy Jones-Wilkins, Bryon Powell, Jeanne Goussev, Kate Hearsey, Sandy Lam, Jake Beattie, Anika Colvin, Australia's finest Chloë McCardel, Martin and Mary Ederle Ward, Tim Dahlberg, Gavin Mortimer, Glenn Stout, Tim Richardson, Bryan Moody, Mike McCormack, Richard Crowell, Reverend Nancy Taylor, Michael Shermer, Stephen Peters, Frank Strack, Vic Armijo, Charlie Kelly, Justin Angle, Scott Jurek, Joe Zemaitis, Susie Nolan, Dan McComb, Cole Chlouber, Merilee Maupin, Hal Koerner, Amanda Kussin, Julie Moss, Travis Vogan, Stephen Black, Emily Alvendia, Shiggy Ichinomiya, Kristin Collins Galbreaith, the marvelous Judy Collins, James Spackman, kind Andrea Evans, and Anchorage's finest, Tom Evans.

To the publisher and editor who believed, Brian McLendon. Warmest regards for the staff of VeloPress and Ulysses Press whose contributions helped make this book better, especially Keith Riegert, Kierra Sondereker, Renee Rutledge, Yesenia Garcia, Paulina Maurovich, Damon Meibers, and the especially generous and thoughtful Claire Chun. Special thanks to the dedicated Christopher Bernard, gifted guardian of the Oxford comma. Special high fives to these mega talented women: Kim Gray, Wendy Sheanin, Heather Curran, Stephanie O'Shea, Jill Lichtenstadter, and Kristen Klemens of Simon & Schuster. Also, for James Faccinto at Full Complement Communications, three cheers!

To a parliament of professors who provided the tools—especially Christina Thompson, Elizabeth McKetta, Brian Pietras, and the most superlative Sallie Sharp. In much earlier days I was educated by nuns—who either upheld the value of good humor or unintentionally reinforced my stubborn streak. Either way, I am now immensely grateful to this group of women. And to my peers from those charmed days, Pilots and Saintsmen, our early adventures laid a cornerstone. Way to keep it classy, San Diego. Thank you for so many years of friendship. Congratulations— time has proven that you were correct: 1980s music is the best.

On the subject of the best: To the finest writers' group I could have ever wished for—Eric Rasmussen, Jacob Sweet, Alex Rhoades.

On the topic of locations: The first chapters of *The Unforgiving Hours* took shape in Seattle, Washington, on the unceded, traditional land of the Duwamish People, both past and present. From the First Nations people, to the Indigenous peoples of Alaska, to Native Hawaiians, the many Indigenous tribes of Costa Rica, and the more than 330 tribal entities of the "Lower 48," may this work honor with gratitude the lands described here and serve to recognize all sovereign Indigenous people with ancestral ties to the water and terrain described in "The Unforgiving Hours."

Acknowledgments

To my teammates—To the Notorious Alki Swimmers, the 24-Hour teams of New England, San Diego, Hammerstein, and the Old Pueblo, the runners of Team Diablo, Team McGivern, Team Hogan, Teams Warburg, Astor, and Currier, Team Stender, Team Harrington, originally a gift from Dublin, to Team McMahon, friends since always, to my extended family borne of the Vermont 50, New England's finest, to the substance and style of Team Alex and Rebecca Yaggy, to the multi sport champs of Team Zoot, the five-star mechanics of Ride Roslyn Bikes, Bob Faulkner and the good folks at Swiftwater Fitness, Vanderkittens worldwide, and most of all, to the members of Lil Mountain Lodge: with you, experiences will always be better than material possessions. Even better than all-XTR, Di2 electronic shifting on a carbon frame with RockShox Flight Attendant and Danny MacAskill's favorite wheel set. THAT'S how good you are.

And special recognition for my bonus teammates, USNA Class of 1968 and the Seawolves of HAL-3, thank you for your example and support. I won't give up the ship.

To my forever girl gang—Melissa Waters, Michelle Kerby, Susan Petronio, Gina Mundaca, Shauna McGlynn, Michelle Chu, Amy Richter, Debbie McGinley, Marney Ellis, Skye Parrott, Martha McConnaughey, Kelly Pollard, Kristin Mott, Angie Thompson, Claire Nicklas, Annette Baker, Karin Guild, Rhonda Glass, and Naomi Mason. And distinct and deserving thanks to Kathrine Switzer and Rosy Spraker for your fearless girl gang example and athletic inspiration. "To sororité!" remains my refrain.

To the lads—R. J. Fleischmann, Jeff Leenhouts, Sherman Chu, Kevin Sawchuk, Randy Perkins, Joe Chick, Corey Waggoner, August "the IT department" Hall, Mike Kerby, Sean Durkin,

Evan Potter, Felipe Fozzatti, and Bob Kimber. This list of names is righteous proof that you can't keep a good man down. Thank you for the pacing goodness and training greatness, my dudes.

To the world's premier siblings, who have refilled water bottles, leapfrogged along courses, walked the dog, humored the cat, hosted river trips, and read first drafts—love times infinity to Kevin, Allie, Sarah, and Nate.

Finally, to my unmatched official crew and rad family—Paul, Ella, and Honor, all outstanding athletes in their different fields. My love and gratitude across deserts, through jungles, at 3 a.m., and switchback after switchback. What was hard to endure remains sweet to recall. And that's why our roadtrips and adventures will remain legendary. I love you to Canada and back. The really long way!

As you can tell by the dancing in the kitchen, that sanctuary of tea mugs and crispy bacon, these have always been the good ol' days.

Speaking of old, when asked by a lifelong friend about the time it took to write *The Unforgiving Hours*, the honest answer was "Thirty years, give or take," with an embarrassing laugh. The venues, the undertakings, and the distances herein move at a different pace. It's a speed that other tortoise-types can appreciate: book readers, artists, plant people, yarn crafters, woodworkers, anglers, and slow food adherents. In addition to slow twitch pacing, these niche specialties of going long are like many worthwhile endeavors—puppies, piñatas, childbirth—wonderful, but pretty messy. Perhaps this is why endurance athletes are often meticulous about one or more elements of their craft: race plans, training logs, specific hydration and nutrition, their equipment, the best people. Especially the best people.

The many decades of racing with, observing, crewing, and now interviewing the endurance athletes here have included an important test of time for these stories. Time has proven that these distances in such competent hands—while slow going and messy—were not daft, that the dedicated did not have a disordered relationship with risk-taking, and that despite deleterious comments and occasional derision, these XXXL-length athletes made meaningful, quiet contributions to their fields. The admiration in those fields for these athletes and their crews and their friendships is as epic as anything I have heard, read, or seen on this earthly plane or in the night sky. In the end, to crew or be crewed in an intense long-distance adventure is to know one of life's purest honors. These champions and their crews have played the long game in a way that we can learn from their planning, training, team building and ninth inning performances in this classic ballpark where, of course, Mother Nature bats last and Father Time remains undefeated. Their modesty reminds me of the expression of unknown origin: "Be humble for you are made of dirt. Be noble for you are made of stars."

Long-distance, like an informal thirty year study of endurance odysseys, will always be an exercise in postponed pleasure. In a world with a scary short attention span, long-distance has more merit than ever. For those accustomed to next-day e-commerce parcels and food delivery dashing of fifteen minutes or less, going long works the core muscle called forbearance. The strength to be able to delay gratification like the athletes of these ten chapters is to have a key on the carabiner of life. A key to portals like patient self-reliance and self-soothing when the tides rise and the conditions of non-sport life become a gripping spectacle.

One brief comment about sports journalism: The long history of massive rides or channel swims or gargantuan point-to-point pioneering predates glorious Gertrude Ederle, the 1880–1900s bicycle craze, or the creation of the marathon for the first modern Olympic Games in 1896. However, unlike these previous golden ages of long-distance, not only are the specialty print outlets ("The Scorcher —A Hot Paper for Hot Cyclists" c. 1898) that used to cover non-pro sports leagues withering, local and medium market US newspapers appear to be in freefall. For example, gone is the blanket of coverage Lynne Cox received across North America in 1972, before and after her attempt to cross the English Channel. Quality reporting about endurance athletes with Lynne's level of talent and the long-distance category are absent from the sports desks of those newspapers fighting for their lives.

I happen to believe in the value of the endurance archive. I am enamored by amateur sport. The wide open places are perennially providing endorphins and "outdoorphins" to long-distance adventurers, racers, finishers, and red lanterns. These arenas will surely continue to be a place for many former members of the ball sports and the team sports that do not offer outlets to adults after Division One college-level play. Because play matters, my plan is to continue to record and catalog these tales of distance and long efforts. If you can, support a local or legacy newspaper or nonprofit news organization in your area with a subscription in the name of supporting good journalism, which includes quality sports writing, which is a way to support these athletes.

Acknowledgments

For those worried about newspapers, the state of publishing, the health of independent bookstores and family-owned businesses like local bike shops (or the kaleidoscope of other issues that might give rise to "despairing thinking"—in the words of the insightful pacer Turlan Morlan), I recommend the perfect observation of the iconic 1967 Boston Marathon champion Kathrine Switzer, "If you are losing faith in human nature, go out and watch a marathon."

Watching amateur sport offers deliverables to those of us bearing stress and woe. There is merit in the mirth of cheering at No Hands Bridge or through Twin Lakes. Watching athletes move through aid stations can skate you off the puck of worry and ennui. There is brightness in watching a swim tracker all weekend. There is giddy hope in checking updates from the Barkley Marathons for 59 hours and 58 minutes to follow Jasmin Paris' first female finish on the Frozen Head State Park course. The prosocial behavior of applauding the kiddos who run the ten kilometer November Turkey Trot event in our hometowns—long, long-distance when you are in elementary school—never takes more than it returns.

On cheering, a final plaudit here for unseen routines. A tip of the hat to the athletes who rise before dawn to return at dusk (or later). A salute for they who dress for weather that resembles retribution or maybe a dare. Applause for the athlete who does not back out of the long run meet-up (or long ride, swim, sail, hike, climb, or ski meet-up). And cheers to those who quietly keep going, with one eye trained on rattlesnakes, or lion's mane jellyfish, or that one aggressive owl, or the insects that don't bite, but seemingly put their cigarettes out on you. A standing ovation to the unseen ham radio operators, the Search and Rescue teams, and event volunteers, who bring their own equipment, buy their own gas, and volunteer in service of others. To all those of the unseen routine, you who "force your heart and nerve and sinew to serve your turn long after they are gone," you are a triumph for our species over the dark seduction of instant gratification and constant comfort. To all those striking out to attempt the inestimable filling of the unforgiving minutes and hours, my rallying cry remains "Teeth to the wind!"

Finally, the exogenous benefits of growing our grit, resilience, and perseverance bears fruit in our navigation of the daily world back on shore, back in offices, back in the world of the hard pants, no longer going commando. These exogenous gifts remain when the backcountry is replaced with appointments at a Level I Pediatric Trauma Center. When a Casualty Assistance Officer rings your doorbell. When one of your favorite humans describes her condition as *inoperable*. When your twenty-four-hour cycling relay team wants to compete in only one pair of shorts.

Or any of the life scenarios, both serious and silly, timeless like the trails and the tides, depicted by Kipling in "If—" more than a century ago.

Fun was never better than when Team Hugh Jass filled unforgiving hours of one-speed fixie bikes and shared shorts with sartorial splendor. Bike race spectators laughed until they wheezed. *(photo credit to magnificent Bryan Moody, with special costume and design credit to the sublime Reece Carter)*

ABOUT THE AUTHOR

Shannon Hogan is a former pro mountain biker, ultrarunner, and open-water swimmer based in the Cascade Mountains of Washington state. She is the first female finisher of *La Ruta de Los Conquistadores* mountain bike race in Costa Rica. She holds the women's course record for the Pigtails Challenge 100K run and has successfully navigated multiple ridiculous-distance ultraruns, including a buckle-finish at Leadville Trail 100 and a sub-24-hour finish at the Javelina Jundred 100-mile (161-kilometer) run. Hogan has crewed every kind of endurance race on land and sea, including over eight hours of kayak support for an English Channel–qualifying swim. The mother of two graceful girls raised on the trail, Hogan has completed the Escape from Alcatraz swim, is a five-time finisher of the Ironman 140.6-mile (226.3-kilometer) triathlon, and is a seven-time finisher of the Leadville Trail 100 bike race. A devotee of salt water, she swims year-round in Puget Sound without a wetsuit as a proud member of the Notorious Alki Swimmers. After ten consecutive Boston Marathon finishes, the merciless hills of Newton still leave her cracked. Lately her favorite recurring adventure is the Breck Epic, a six-day mountain bike stage race in Breckenridge,

Colorado, once described as "Part chess match. Part recovery contest. Part DISCO INFERNO." She is old enough to know better, but young enough to do these things anyway. Hogan has written about cycling for *The Colorado Sun*, running for *Ultra Running Magazine*, and open-water swimming for *The Seattle Times*.

photo courtesy of Ella Warburg